Journal of the Early Book Society

for the study of manuscripts and printing history

Edited by Martha W. Driver
Volume 5, 2002

ISBN: 0-944473-60-1 (pbk: alk.ppr.)
ISSN: 1525-6790

Member

Council of Editors of Learned Journals

The *Journal of the Early Book Society* is published annually. JEBS invites longer articles on manuscripts and/or printed books produced between 1350 and 1550. Special consideration will be given to essays exploring the period of transition from manuscript to print. Articles should not exceed 8000 words or thirty typed pages. Authors are asked to follow *The Chicago Manual of Style*. A Works Cited list at the end of the text should include city, publisher, and date. Manuscripts are to be sent, in triplicate, along with an abstract of up to 150 words, to Martha Driver, Early Book Society, Department of English, Pace University, 41 Park Row, New York, New York 10038. Only materials accompanied by a self-addressed, stamped envelope (or international reply coupon) will be returned. Members of the Early Book Society who are recent authors may send review books for consideration to Susan Powell, Reviews Editor, Department of Modern Languages, University of Salford, Salford M5 4WT, England. Brief notes on recent discoveries, highlighting little-known or recently uncovered texts and/or images, may be sent (after 7/02) to Linne R. Mooney, Department of English, University of Maine, Orono, Maine 04469. Subscription information may be obtained from Martha Driver or from Pace University Press.

Those interested in joining the Early Book Society or with editorial inquiries may contact Martha Driver by post or e-mail (MDriver@Pace.edu). For ordering information, call Pace University Press at 212-346-1405 or visit http://www.pace.edu/press. Institutions and libraries may purchase copies directly from Ingram Library Services (1-800-937-5300).

The editor wishes to thank Gill Kent, as well as Kerry Morris and Mark Hussey of Pace University Press for their help and advice on this issue.

Journal of the Early Book Society

For the Study of Manuscript and Printing History

Editor:
Martha W. Driver, *Pace University*

Associate Editors:
Linne Mooney, *University of Maine, Orono*
Sue Powell, *University of Salford*

Editorial Board
Beatrice H. Beech, *Western Michigan University*
Norman F. Blake, *University of Sheffield*
Julia Boffey, *University of London, Queen Mary and Westfield College*
James Carley, *York University*
Joyce Coleman, *University of North Dakota*
Mary Erler, *Fordham University*
Vincent Gillespie, *Saint Anne's College, Oxford University*
Avril K. Henry, *University of Exeter*
Stanley S. Hussey, *Lancaster University*
Daniel W. Mosser, *Virginia Polytechnic Instititute and State University*
Ann Eljenholm Nichols, *Winona State University*
Joanne S. Norman, *Bishop's University*
Judy Oliver, *Colgate University*
Michael Orr, *Lawrence University*
Myra D. Orth, *independent scholar*
Steven Partridge, *University of British Columbia*
Derek Pearsall, *Harvard University*
Robert Raymo, *New York University*
Pamela Sheingorn, *Baruch College and*
   The City University of New York Graduate School and University Center
Toshiyuki Takamiya, *Keio University*
John Thompson, *Queen's University, Belfast*
Ronald Waldron, *King's College, University of London*

Contents

Descriptive Reviews
Susan Powell, Review Editor

Notes on Libraries and Collections

About the Authors

Sharing Chaucer's Authority in Prefaces to Chaucer's Works from William Caxton to William Thynne

ROBERT COSTOMIRIS

Early printing history indicates a consistently strong market for Chaucer's works, especially *The Canterbury Tales*, which was printed six times by four different printers between 1477 and 1532. But apparently even Chaucer's works, and perhaps especially costly folio-sized volumes such as *The Canterbury Tales*, required additional incentives to promote sales.[1] Examples of these incentives may be found in the printers' prefaces to *The Canterbury Tales*, which were regularly included beginning in 1483. While the hyperbole of the prefaces compromises their worth as accurate statements of printers' and editors' motivations, the prefaces repay close attention by revealing the growth and transformation of Chaucer's authority in the first sixty years of printing his work in England.

William Caxton was the first English printer of Chaucer. In the 1470s he printed *The Canterbury Tales* (STC 508 2, 1477), *Anelida and Arcite* (STC 5090, 1477?), the *Parliament of Fowls* (STC 50911 477?) and Chaucer's translation of Boethius's *Consolation of Philosophy* (STC 3199, 1478?). In the 1480s he printed *The Canterbury Tales* (STC 5083, 1483), the *House of Fame* (STC 5087, 1483), and *Troilus and Criseyde* (STC 5094, 1483).[2] *The Canterbury Tales* is the only work by Chaucer that Caxton printed twice. The first edition had no preface or title page and looked very much like an unadorned manuscript; the poem simply begins on the recto of one of the first leaves. In 1483, however, when Caxton printed *The Canterbury Tales* again, he included a preface which subsequently served as the template for prefaces to editions of *The Canterbury Tales* until the publication of Thynne's edition in 1532.

The prolixity of Caxton's preface can obscure what it actually says about Chaucer and about Caxton's motives for printing Chaucer's work. The first part of the preface is general and encomiastic, linking Chaucer with other writers who have preserved wisdom and learning in texts. Caxton praises Chaucer especially for single-handedly making "faire our englisshe," in effect isolating Chaucer's achievement as better than anything before or since. The second part of the preface continues to praise *The Canterbury Tales* for their generic and nearly encyclopedic goodness until, well after the preface's mid-point, Caxton reveals his reasons for reprinting the *Tales*. Initially, Caxton defended his first edition by stating that he had "dylygently ouersen and duly examyned [the *Tales*] to thende that it be made acordynge vnto his [i.e., Chaucer's] owen makyng."[3] Caxton then recounts the famous story of how the exemplar for his first edition, which he "supposed to ben veray true & correcte," turned out to be "incorrecte," lacking some things, including others, and in general "not accordyng in many places vnto the book that Gefferey chaucer had made." He was alerted to this problem by a buyer of the first edition, who said that "he knewe a book whych hys fader had and moche louyd / that was very trewe / and accordynge vnto hys owen first book by hym made." Caxton borrowed this manuscript and printed his second edition in order to correct his errors and "to satyssfye thauctour." Quite simply, the buyer convinced Caxton that the new text was more authentic than the text Caxton had used for his first edition of *The Canterbury Tales*.[4]

Caxton's desire to satisfy Chaucer grows naturally from the preface's enthusiastic praise of Chaucer. Praising Chaucer was not a novel nor a unique stance for Caxton; he wrote similarly of Chaucer in the epilogues to the *Boece* and to the *House of Fame*, wherein he respectively praised Chaucer as the "fader and first foundeur and enbelissher of ornate eloquence in our Englissh" and as an author who "excellyth . . . alle other wryters in our Englyssh. . ."[5] But, compared to these other comments about Chaucer, the 1483 preface extends and complicates Caxton's usual agenda by interposing Caxton as the arbiter of Chaucer's correct text.[6] In announcing this role, Caxton made public and explicit what, in a manuscript culture, had been unique and private, that is, that the person who transmits and presents a text can play an important role in the composition of the text and can become, in a sense, a work's second author.[7]

Caxton's awareness of his role as second author is evident in the benediction at the end of the preface, where he urges readers to "remember the sowle of the sayd Gefferey chaucer first auctour / and maker of thys book." Certainly, the epithet "first auctour" is intended to echo the beginning of the preface, where Caxton singled out Chaucer as the founding father of English poetry, the first English author to take something crude and make it fine. But in the context of reprinting *The Canterbury Tales*, Caxton's role as arbiter and purveyor of Chaucer's text also let him literally play the role of second author, as is evident in several notable Chaucerian echoes. For example, when Caxton writes that he will print "many a noble hystorye / of euery estate and degre / first rehyrcynge the condicione / and tharraye of eche of them as properly as possible is to be sayd," he is surely mimicking the close of the first part of the *General Prologue*, where Chaucer writes:

> Me thynketh it acordaunt to resoun
> To telle yow al the *condicioun*
> Of *ech of hem*, so as it semed me,
> And whiche they weren, and of what *degree*,
> And eek in what *array* that they were inne. (I (A) 37-41, my italics)[8]

Similarly, when Caxton mentions the agreement he reached with the buyer who supplied the text for his second edition of *The Canterbury Tales*, he writes, "And thus we fyll at accord," a faint but clear echo of the end of the *General Prologue*, where the narrator describes how the pilgrims "been acorded to his |Harry Bailly's| juggement"(I (A) 818). Finally, Caxton's request that the reader remember the soul of Chaucer and profit from the "good and vertuous tales" is remarkably like the *Retraction* to *The Canterbury Tales*, which asks "that ye preye for me that Crist have mercy on me and foryeve me my giltes" (X (I) 1084) and then lists the virtuous works which are profitable and renounces the sinful works. By appropriating Chaucer's language and rhetorical posture, Caxton begins to share Chaucer's authority and thereby reinforces the sense that he knows which text of *The Canterbury Tales* best reflects Chaucer's intent. The preface to the second edition reveals that Caxton had moved beyond simply attempting to duplicate Chaucer's manuscript in printed form: Caxton had become the work's second author.

Second authorship involved more than imitating Chaucer, and other elements of the preface show that Caxton was alive to the practical aspects of prefatory authorship. Prefaces are by nature intermediary texts by which the writer hopes to shape the audience's response to the text which follows. Having printed what he considered an incorrect first edition, Caxton sought to capture his audience's good will by reminding his readers of Chaucer's excellence and utility as a founder and preserver of the best of English literature. By this reasoning, it is in the readers' best interests to have Caxton's new edition, since reading the corrected Chaucer will have a greater salutary effect than reading the incorrect version. While Caxton established a renewed need for this edition of *The Canterbury Tales*, he also avoided blame for printing an incorrect text by shifting responsibility for the errors to the faulty text itself; Caxton argued that he was true to the text but that the text was not true to Chaucer. But Caxton also covered his own tracks and preserved his immunity by attributing the discovery of the correct text to the buyer.

Presumably, had the new text proven "incorrecte," Caxton would have had a ready-made reason to print another edition and preserve his integrity yet again. Finally, Caxton's request for "thayde of almygthy god. . . whom [he] humbly besece[d] to gyve [him] grace and ayde" (a traditional element of prefaces) not only echoes Chaucer's similar request in the *Retraction*, it also makes clear his dependence on the greatest authority of all, the first "first author."[9]

The preface Caxton wrote to the 1483 edition of *The Canterbury Tales* endured in the subsequent editions printed by Richard Pynson and Wynkyn de Worde. Although one expects de Worde, Caxton's assistant and heir, to be the first to reprint Chaucer upon Caxton's death, it was Pynson, a relative newcomer to the London printing trade, who continued the tradition (STC 5084, 1492?).[10] Although Pynson concluded his preface with the words "By Richard Pynson" and thereby seemed to declare his own authorial role, he actually adopted most of Caxton's preface *verbatim* and emphasized Caxton's role as intermediary while deleting Caxton's explanation of the discovery of the new manuscript exemplar for the 1483 edition. After alerting readers to the encyclopedic goodness of the *Tales*, Pynson refers to his exemplar as a

> boke diligently ouirsen & duely examined by the politike reason
> and ouirsight. of my worshipful master William Caxton accordinge
> to the entent and effecte of the seid Geffrey Chaucer and by a copy
> of the seid master Caxton.

Pynson's emphasis on Caxton's "politike reason" and his description of him as his "worshipful master" show the importance of Caxton's judgment in Pynson's eyes and the degree to which Pynson endorsed the idea that Caxton was able to produce the text Chaucer intended. In effect, Pynson justified his first edition of the *Tales* by invoking Caxton's authority, thereby reinforcing the sense that Caxton's second version of the *Tales* was authoritative. By praising the printer in the same breath with which he praised Chaucer, Pynson enshrined Caxton in his role as second author and, more generally, confirmed the printer's role as arbiter of authorial intent.

Wynkyn de Worde's 1498 preface (STC 5085) is remarkable for its faithfulness to Caxton's: except for the omission of a few words and differences in spelling, the text of his preface is identical to Caxton's until the end, where, in larger type than the text of the preface itself, de Worde printed "By Wylliam Caxton / His soule in heuen won." By reproducing nearly exactly what Caxton wrote and accentuating Caxton's role, de Worde essentially followed Pynson's lead. It seems from his preface that de Worde was bent on reproducing the 1483 Caxton edition exactly and wished to diminish any sense that his edition was different from Caxton's. He might have had good reason for this. First, some aspects of de Worde's text of *The Canterbury Tales* are *not* faithful to Caxton. Most obviously, de Worde did not adopt the tale order of Caxton's second edition, but instead chose an order similar to Ellesmere except for the placement of the *Second Nun's Tale* and the *Canon's Yeoman's Tale*. On a more minute scale, the *Tale of Sir Thopas*, which de Worde set up in such a way as to indicate the tercets in each stanza, shows that de Worde followed a manuscript exemplar, not Caxton's second edition.[11] Similarly, the marginalia of the *Parson's Tale* printed by de Worde show the influence of at least one manuscript, since no printed edition had such marginalia before de Worde.[12] Nevertheless, despite the significant changes he introduced to Caxton's text, de Worde did not reveal them to prospective buyers, presumably because he wished to capitalize on Caxton's reputation. For de Worde, the importance of Caxton's role in producing *The Canterbury Tales* apparently outweighed a desire to indicate to his readers any deficiencies in Caxton's text, even though he went to the trouble of printing the *Tales* in a way that he evidently thought more accurately reflected Chaucer's intent. De Worde's preface ignored a legitimate appeal to newness and correctness that it might have used to advertise the 1498 edition, and instead emphasized Caxton's authority. Thus, by 1498, at least in de Worde's eyes, Caxton's authority and reputation carried as much weight as Chaucer's.[13]

By the time Pynson published his second edition in 1526 (STC 5086), he was near the end of his career and had been the King's printer for many years. Clearly, in the thirty-four years since he had last published Chaucer, Pynson's status had improved, a fact that is evident at the beginning of the preface which confidently advertises itself as "The proheme of the printer." The text of the preface, which for the most part repeats the text of the 1492 edition, also shows signs of Pynson's increased authority. For example, where the 1492 preface emphasized Pynson's subjection to Caxton, the 1526 expresses its reliance on Caxton in more muted tones. Pynson writes in 1526 that Chaucer's book has been:

> dyligently and trewly corrected / by a copy of Willyam Caxtons imprintyng / acording to the true makinge of the sayd Geffray Chaucer / as herafter shall folowe all alonge by the helpe of almighty god: to whom I humbly beseche / that I maye it so atchyue and accomplyshe / that it be to his laude / honour & glory: and that all ye that shall in this boke rede or here / wyll of your charyte amonge your dedes of mercy / remember the soule of the sayd Geffrey Chaucer / fyrste auctour and maker of this boke.

Gone is the "politicke reason" and "worshipfull master" of the 1492 edition in favor of a more direct assessment the text's genesis.[14] Nevertheless, it is striking that even with the passing of so many years and the grander three-part design of the 1526 edition, Pynson remained remarkably faithful to his first preface which was, in turn, very close to Caxton's 1483 preface. In itself this seems like a missed opportunity for Pynson who might have championed his 1526 publication as a new chapter in the history of printing Chaucer's works. Instead, Pynson's preface is evidence of the lingering authority of William Caxton.[15]

The printing of Chaucer's works changed significantly in 1532 with the publication of William Thynne's edition (STC 5068). While Pynson's 1526 edition began a trend toward printing collections of Chaucer's works, Thynne pushed this idea to a new extreme, producing a single folio volume of 383 leaves containing over forty-three different works, all attributed to Chaucer. This comprehensive edition afforded the opportunity for a new and expanded preface, and Thynne did not miss the chance to lavish attention on it.[16]

Unlike Caxton's and other printers' prefaces to single works by Chaucer, Thynne's preface is much longer and more elaborately presented. The title-page border is not cobbled together in the manner of Pynson's 1526 title page, but is a handsome woodcut in the school of Holbein or perhaps by Holbein himself.[17] The table of contents is divided into two parts: the first lists all the major works of the collection in the order of their appearance; the second provides a more detailed list giving folio numbers and subheadings to mark divisions within the most important works.[18] Given the scope of the collection, this is a welcome device, but it was probably included to add to the grandeur of the edition and increase the buyer's sense that Thynne's edition was the definitive collection of Chaucer's works. The introductory matter concludes with three moral poems that flesh out the recto and verso sides of the first gathering's last leaf, and again contribute to the sense of the edition's completeness and suggest that one is getting good value for money.

The content of Thynne's preface is a combination of traditional and new elements. In Thynne's preface one finds the expected praise of Chaucer, yet it is reduced in proportion to the overall length of the preface and buried in a long and rambling account of the development of letters from the Phoenicians to the sixteenth century. An abbreviated excerpt reveals the tenor of this praise:

> . . . Geffray Chaucer / in whose workes is so manyfest comprobacion of his excellent lernyng in all kyndes of doctrynes and sciences / suche frutefulnesse in wordes / wel accordynge to the mater and-purpose / so swete and plesaunt sentences / suche perfectyon in metre / the composycion so adapted / suche fresshnesse of inuen-cion . . . that it is moche to be marueyled / howe in his tyme / whan doutlesse all good letters were layde a slepe throughout the worlde . . . suche an excellent poete in our tonge / shulde as it were (nature repugnyng) spryng and a ryse.   For though it had ben in Demosthenes or Homerus tymes / whan all lernyng and excellency

> of sciences florisshed amonges the Grekes / or in the season that
> Cicero prince of eloquence amonges latyns lyued / yet had it ben a
> thyng right rare & straunge and worthy perpetuall laude / that any
> clerke by lernyng or wytte coulde than haue framed a tonge before
> so rude and imperfite / to suche a swete ornature and composy-
> cion. (fol. Aii v)

Thynne echoes Caxton's claim that Chaucer rescued English letters from their
crude state, but his praise makes Caxton's hyperbole seem modest by comparing Chaucer favorably to Greek and Latin poets. In fact, Chaucer's
achievement comes off as greater since he had to overcome the obstacle of a
debased language.   Despite this hyperbole, an outstanding feature of
Thynne's preface is how much less of it is devoted to praising Chaucer when
compared to Caxton's preface. Instead, Thynne's praise of Chaucer shares the
spotlight with two new concerns: the adulation of the dedicatee, Henry VIII,
and   William Thynne's self-praise.   In sum, Thynne's preface breaks the
Caxton template by widening the authorial net to include the King as well as
Chaucer and his editor.

Although Thynne was not a printer or bookseller, his prefatorial role
as a purveyor of Chaucer's works is similar to Caxton's in the way that Thynne
emphasizes his role as the arbiter of Chaucer's correct text. Thynne notes in
his address to Henry:

> I haue of a longe season moch vsed and rede and visyte the same
> [works of Chaucer]: and as bokes of dyuers imprintes came vnto my
> handes / I easely and without grete study / might and haue depre-
> hended in them many errours / falsyties / and deprauacions /
> whiche euydently appered by the contrarietees and alteracions
> founde by collacion of the one with the other. (fol. Aii v)

Thynne's explanation suggests that he did not simply swap one text for
another, as Caxton's preface implies Caxton did; but Thynne's preface adopts
an authorial stance similar to Caxton's by claiming that Thynne detected and
expunged the errors that had crept into Chaucer's works and thereby reestab-
lished the text as Chaucer (the first author) intended.

Thynne's self-promotion, which goes beyond that of earlier editors
and printers, is most likely the result of his close association to Henry VIII, to
whom he dedicated the 1532 edition. Dedications usually express either
gratitude for something already done or gratitude in anticipation of something hoped for. Two aspects of Thynne's preface suggest that he is seeking
Henry's patronage. First, like Caxton, Thynne stresses the extent of his own
efforts in producing the edition. After noting how he discovered errors in earlier printed editions, Thynne writes:

> I was moued and styred to make dilygent sertch / where I might
> fynde or recouer any trewe copies or exemplaries of the sayd
> bookes / whervnto in processe of tyme / nat without coste and
> payne I attayned / and nat onely vnto such as seme to be very trewe
> copies of those workes of Geffray Chaucer / whiche before had ben
> put in printe / but also to dyuers other neuer tyll nowe imprinted /
> but remaynyng almost vnknowen and in oblyuion. (fol. Aii v)

But Thynne distinguishes his work from the comments of previous editors by
claiming to have sought and examined both printed and manuscript copies
of Chaucer and by emphasizing his own effort in finding these sources; they
were not brought to him. Second, Thynne does not mention that Henry had
a role in helping the edition see the light of day, but instead addresses the
King as if the project were unfamiliar to him, as the following passage makes
clear:

> For this cause most excellent and in all vertues most prestant
> prince / I as humbly prostrate before your kyngly estate / lowly sup-
> ply and beseche the same / that it wol vouch safe to take in good
> parte my poore studye and desyrous mynde / in reducynge vnto
> lyght this so precious and necessary an ornament of the tonge of
> this your realme / ouer pytous to haue ben in any poynt lost / falsi-
> fyed / or neglected: So that vnder the shylde of your most royall
> protectyon and defence it may go forthe in publyke. . . . (fol. Aiii r)

Although hyperbole and false modesty are typical elements of dedicatory
prose, it is noteworthy that the preface indicates that Thynne proceeded in
his task alone and at his own expense simply from a love of Chaucer and a
desire to save his works from obscurity and abuse. This accounts for the fact
that the preface seems to be looking for patronage rather than presenting the
volume as the fruit of patronage already well spent.

Dedicating a work is a gesture of homage. Even though Henry does
not seem to have encouraged Thynne to produce his edition, the preface nevertheless casts Henry as the inspiration for the edition. Thynne writes:

> And deuisyng with my selfe / who of all other were most worthy / to
> whom a thyng so excellent and notable shulde be dedicate / . . .
> none coulde to my thynkyng occurre / that syns / or in the tyme of
> Chaucer / was or is suffycient / but onely your maieste royall /
> whiche by discrecyon and iugement / as moost absolute in wyse-
> dome and all kyndes of doctryne / coulde & of his innate clemence
> and goodnesse / wolde adde or gyue any authorite hervnto. (fol.
> Aiii r)

More simply put, since Chaucer's time, no one except Henry has had suffi-
cient sense to appreciate Chaucer's works. The attributes Thynne claims for
Henry—discretion, judgment and wisdom, which resemble the qualities
Caxton found praiseworthy in Chaucer—are, in Thynne's preface, what enable
Henry to authorize Chaucer.

Caxton's preface focused on language as a tool of poets, clerks and
historians and cast Chaucer as the paragon of practitioners in the English
idiom. Thynne broadened the scope considerably, and the first third of his
preface is a synopsis of the general importance of language, especially writing, as the flower of human intelligence, showing how it developed from a
"confusion of tongues" to the perfection of Greek and Latin, to the Romance
vernaculars, and finally blossomed in English in the works of Chaucer. This
emphasis on language becomes the thread which connects Thynne, Henry
and Chaucer. Thynne's role as conservator of English is limited but still evident when, in another self-referential remark, he writes that just as others
have improved their languages:

> so hath there nat lacked amonges vs Englisshmen / which haue
> right well and notably endeuoyred and employed them selues / to
> the beautifyeng and bettryng of thenglysh tonge. Amonges whom
> moost excellent prynce . . . I your most humble vassall . . . Wylliam
> Thynne . . . moued by a certayne inclynacion & zele . . . haue taken
> great delectacyon . . . to rede and here the bokes of that noble &
> famous clerke Geffray Chaucer. (fol. Aii v)

Thynne portrays his role in respect to English letters as something akin to
Chaucer's and Caxton's; all are preservers and improvers of English. To com-
plete the circle of authority, Thynne connects Chaucer's role as perfector of
English with Henry's role as English king.

The preface links Henry with Chaucer by portraying the printing of
Chaucer's works as an act of patriotism to counter:

> the neglygence of the people / that haue ben in this realme / who
> doutlesse were very remysse in the settyng forthe or auauncement
> either of the histories therof / to the great hynderaunce of the
> renoume of such noble princes and valyant conquerours & capi-
> tayns as haue ben in the same / or also of the workes or memory of
> the famous and excellent clerkes in all kyndes of scyences that haue
> florisshed therin. (fol. Aii v)

Albeit short on details, this passage clearly seeks to distinguish the publication of Chaucer from an earlier dissatisfying abuse of the print medium and
to establish a connection, however tenuous, between the reputation of
"noble princes" (Henry) and the publication of work by "excellent clerkes"

(Chaucer). A little later, the preface expresses the hope that the publication of Chaucer under Henry's protection will:

> preuayle ouer those that wolde blemysshe / deface / and in many thynges clerely abolyssh the laude / renoume / and glorie hertofore compared / and meritoriously adquired by dyuers princes / and other of this said most noble yle / wherevnto nat onely straungers vnder pretexte of highe lernyng & knowlege of their malycious and peruers myndes / but also some of your owne subiectes / blynded in foly and ignorance / do with great study contende. (fol. Aiii r)

It is obvious that the poetic impulse of language expressed in Caxton's preface yielded in Thynne's preface to a political impulse. The early 1530s was a tumultuous period in England as Henry tried to dissolve his marriage to Catherine, and there is no doubt that his behavior did not win universal praise among his subjects.[19] In an act of homage to the King, Thynne did not miss the chance to link detractors of the English language with those who disparaged the King. So, in the fullest expression of Chaucer's authority to date, Thynne used Chaucer as a means of bolstering and authorizing Henry himself.

The first five printed prefaces to Chaucer show that as Chaucer's star rose, more people attached themselves to it by sharing his authority. Caxton expressed his authority in the utilitarian terms of goodness, newness and correctness in order to sell books. Pynson and de Worde, also interested in selling books, found Caxton's approach so serviceable that Caxton's authority virtually outstripped Chaucer's. But this simple approach did not suffice for the large collection Thynne dedicated to Henry VIII. Like Caxton's, Thynne's preface stressed the obvious virtues of Chaucer's works but, by introducing the King into the authorial equation, Thynne's preface acknowledged a more complex shared authority wherein Chaucer's text and reputation were made to serve Henry's propagandistic ends.

Georgia Southern University

NOTES

1. On the price of sixteenth-century folio editions of Chaucer, see Forni.
2. STC numbers and dates are from the revised edition of Pollard and Redgrave, *Short Title Catalogue of English Books*, 1475-1640.
3. I am quoting from the microfilm of Caxton's second edition, Shipment 1 reel 1. The text of this preface can also be found in Blake, *Caxton's Own Prose*, 61-63.
4. The number of differences between Caxton's first and second editions are rather fewer than his preface implies. See Blake, "Caxton and Chaucer," 22-25.
5. These epilogues may be found in Blake, *Caxton's Own Prose*, 58-60,102-103.

6. The epilogue to *Boece* parallels the preface to the second edition of *The Canterbury Tales* insofar as it also pays tribute to a "singuler frende and gossib" for requesting that Caxton print Boethius. Similarly, Caxton also reminds his audience that he has "done [his] debuoir and payne t'enprynte it." Beyond this, Caxton does not emphasize his own editorial and authorial role. See Blake, *Caxton's Own Prose*, 59.

7. In addition to the current meaning of "writer," the OED shows that "author" could also mean more generally 1a) inventor, constructor, founder; 1c) he who gives rise to or causes an action, event, circumstance, state or condition of things: and 3a) one who sets forth written statements; the composer or writer of a treatise or book. Genette also asks "faut-il rappeler encore que le garant, en latin, se disait *auctor*?" (127).

8. All quotations of Chaucer's works are from *The Riverside Chaucer*, ed. Larry Benson.

9. For illuminating discussions of prefatory poetics on which this paragraph depends, see Dunn 1-16; Genette 110-218; and Janson 116-142.

10. Carlson speculates that Pynson printed *The Canterbury Tales* "on a belief that there was business to be done." Carlson also suggests that Pynson might have printed *The Canterbury Tales* before de Worde due to "the lapse of Caxton's business, after his death in the autumn of 1491 and before de Worde's resumption of it about the middle of 1492. . ." (52).

11. See Garbáty.

12. These observations were made by Stephen Partridge in his paper delivered to an Early Book Society session at the 34th International Congress on Medieval Studies, Kalamazoo, 1999.

13. Why de Worde went to the trouble of altering Caxton's text but then did not seek to capitalize on the "improvements" is a subject that merits more attention.

14. Dane also discusses these changes in the language of the 1526 edition that imply an increase in Pynson's authority (44).

15. For a discussion of Pynson's 1526 edition, see Boffey.

16. It is important to note that William Thynne was not a printer but was chief clerk of the kitchen of Henry VIII. The edition itself was printed by Thomas Godfray, a relatively minor player in London printing who in the 1530s appears to have worked as a jobber for Thomas Berthelet, the King's printer. This arrangement introduced a new link in the chain of people involved in preparing Chaucer for print and leaves unclear who made the final decisions concerning the texts in the edition. For an argument in favor of Godfray's association with Berthelet, see Wawn. Elton argues against such a connection in *Policy and Police* (174). An assessment of Thynne's association with Godfray may be found in Donaghey.

The value of the preface as a certain indicator of Thynne's intent is compromised by the assertion that Brian Tuke, Henry VIII's postmaster and treasurer of the King's chamber, wrote the preface, not Thynne. The primary evidence for this assertion is an inscription in the margin above the preface of the Clare College, Cambridge, copy of the 1532 edition, which reads: "This preface I sir Bryan Tuke knight wrot at the request of mr clarke of the kechyn then being / tarying for the tyde at Grenewich." This statement raises many questions. For instance, is it not odd that, after all the work Thynne presumably put into the edition, something as frequent and changeable as the tide should have prevented him from writing a preface? Is it reasonable to accept that Tuke wrote the preface even though, as David Starkey notes, it "is his only known publication" (129)? An unresolved discussion of the problematic authorship of Thynne's preface can be found in Dane (33-49). Tuke's involvement with Thynne's edition is a difficult issue: in this essay, I do not challenge Thynne's authorship.

17. The title-page border used in Thynne's edition can be found in McKerrow and Ferguson, plate 19. The connection between the title page and Holbein is posited in Bätschmann and Griener (177). For a discussion of Holbein's connection with Sir Brian Tuke, also associated with the edition, see Hand.

18. A much-reduced table of contents was also part of the preface to Pynson's 1526 edition.

19. For a discussion of the resistance to Henry's divorce and break with Rome, see Elton, *Reform and Reformation* 126-156, and Guy 116-153.

WORKS CITED

Bätschmann, Oskar and Pascal Griener. *Hans Holbein*. Princeton: Princeton University Press, 1997.

Benson, Larry D., ed. *The Riverside Chaucer*. Boston: Houghton Mifflin, 1987.

Blake, N. F. "Caxton and Chaucer." *Leeds Studies in English* 1(n.s.) (1967): 19-36.

———. *Caxton's Own Prose*. London: André Deutsch, 1973.

Boffey, Julia. "Richard Pynson's *Book of Fame* and *The Letter of Dido*." *Viator* 19 (1988): 339-353.

Brewer, D. S., ed. *Geoffrey Chaucer: The Works 1532*. Menston: Scolar Press, 1969.

Carlson, David R. "Woodcut Illustrations of the *Canterbury Tales*, 1483-1602." *The Library* 6th series, 19 (1997): 25-67.

Dane, Joseph A. *Who is Buried in Chaucer's Tomb?: Studies in the Reception of Chaucer's Book*. East Lansing: Michigan State University Press, 1998.

Donaghey, Brian. "William Thynne's Collected Edition of Chaucer: Some Bibliographical Considerations." In *Texts and Their Contexts: Papers from the Early Book Society*, edited by John Scattergood and Julia Boffey. Dublin: Four Courts Press, 1997.

Dunn, Kevin. *Pretexts of Authority*. Stanford: Stanford University Press, 1994.

Elton, G. R. *Policy and Police*. Cambridge: Cambridge University Press, 1972.

———. *Reform and Reformation: England, 1509-1558*. Cambridge, MA: Harvard University Press, 1977.

Forni, Kathleen. "The Value of Early Chaucer Editions." *Studia Neophilologica* 70 (1998): 173-180.

Garbáty, Thomas J. "Wynkyn de Worde's 'Sir Thopas' and Other Tales." *Studies in Bibliography* 31 (1978): 57-67.

Genette, Gérard. *Seuils*. Paris: Éditions du Seuil, 1987.

Guy, John. *Tudor England*. Oxford: Oxford University Press, 1988.

Hand, John Oliver. "The Portrait of Sir Brian Tuke by Hans Holbein the Younger." *Studies in the History of Art* 9 (1980): 33-49.

Janson, Tore. *Latin Prose Prefaces: Studies in Literary Conventions*. Stockholm: Almquist and Wiksell, 1964.

McKerrow, R. B., and F. S. Ferguson. *Title-Page Borders Used in England and Scotland, 1485-1640*. London: Oxford University Press, 1932.

Pollard, A. W., G. R. Redgrave, W. A. Jackson, F. S. Ferguson and Katherine F. Pantzer, eds. *A Short-Title Catalogue of Books Printed in England, Scotland, and Ireland and of English Books Printed Abroad, 1475-1640*. 3 vols. 2nd ed. London: Bibliographical Society, 1986-1992.

Skeat, W. W., ed. *The Works of Geoffrey Chaucer and Others*. London: Alexander Morning Ltd. and Henry Frowde, n.d.

Starkey, David, ed. *Henry VIII: A European Court in England*. London: Collins and Brown, 1991.

Wawn, Andrew N. "Chaucer, *The Plowman's Tale*, and Reformation Propaganda: the Testimonies of Thomas Godfray and I *Playne Piers*." *Bulletin of the John Rylands University Library of Manchester* 56 (1973): 174-192.

The Prophecies of *Piers Plowman* in Cambridge University Library MS Gg.4.31

BRYAN P. DAVIS

There have been multiple, unpublished versions of this essay, each with new title, and thus my emphases have evolved with each successive draft. "I wole constrewe eche clavse and ken it y̲e̲ on [early modern] englysshe," "Incunabular *Piers Plowman*," and "Proto-Crowleian *Piers Plowman*" are three of my personal favorites among these provisional titles, and they represent my evolving intentions at least as well as Langland's are represented in manuscript or print. From the beginning of this process, I have known that the bibliographical codes in Cambridge University Library MS Gg.4.31 (MS G) make it unique among the manuscripts of *Piers Plowman*, but the reason that these codes are significant, not simply eccentric, has been more difficult to pinpoint. Moreover, a means of expressing the manuscript's significance proved elusive, partially because this specific performance of *Piers Plowman* is enjambed toward the latter end of the shift from manuscript to print, closer to the English Reformation than to Wyclif, and squarely within the popular proliferation of the humanistic learning in England as represented by the likes of William Tyndale, Sir Thomas Elyot and Roger Ascham among others. My purpose has remained clear throughout, however: to show how ill-advised it is to deem that " y̲e̲ table off pyers plowman"[1] "is of no value"[2] and to show how much more the planner of the manuscript did than simply outline the poem.[3] I want to show that MS G is significant not only as a bibliographical curiosity, but as a manuscript in which the bibliographical codes construct a reading of the text that is often different from what I take to be Langland's intention. In addition, the apparatus provides tantalizing hints about what type of person the planner of MS G was and how one individual who lived in the early sixteenth century read the poem. The planner of MS G constructed a reading of *Piers Plowman* that dislocates the poem from its tantalizingly topical context and shifts it closer to the context of reformist, prophetic rhetoric into which the poem was inserted by Bale and Crowley, *et al.*

When one approaches MS G, one approaches a performance of *Piers Plowman* that is unusual even among the many unusual copies of this textually complex poem, and while this reasoning led to the title "I wole constrewe eche clavse and ken it ye on [early modern] englysshe," that title proved to be my least satisfactory attempt. Nonetheless, it bears noting that MS G is unusual within the context of a textual tradition that includes many conjoint or composite copies of *Piers*, such as Huntington Library MS HM 114, that weave together varying configurations of A, B, and C exemplars to construct a single performance of the poem. Because the producer of MS G seems to have been largely satisfied with his exemplar of the B Version of *Piers Plowman*, he did not skillfully, destructively, indifferently, or pragmatically edit the text of the poem as the producers of conjoint copies did, often simultaneously. The planner of MS G was unlike any of the earlier scribes who constructed copies of *Piers Plowman*, and his uniqueness stems largely from the fact that he worked in the early sixteenth century well after the introduction of print, when attitudes towards texts were changing as a result of the way printers were beginning to package their products.

My second draft title, "Incunabular *Piers Plowman*," took account of print culture as a factor in the construction of MS G, but ignored the influence of print culture on the reading of texts in general and this one in particular. By the time that the planner of MS G worked, crucial changes in the culture of reading had begun to take place that were reflected in neither the archetype of *Piers Plowman* B nor the earlier copies produced from it. The planner of MS G worked in the penumbra between manuscript and print cultures, and thus, his copy is Janus-like. This producer seems to have been largely satisfied with the received text but not the received textual apparatus, choosing to exercise his editorial vigor on the periphery of the text and producing a performance of the poem that is partially swaddled in the bibliographical codes characteristic of print culture.

The apparatus of MS G is more than an outline of *Piers Plowman* because it was produced during a time of religious ferment that was quite different from but imaginatively connected with the religious ferment of Langland's time. Thus, the apparatus in MS G constructs a reading of the text that might not have been to Langland's taste, if his C Revisions are any guide to his intentions for the reception of the B Version. At the same time, the planner of MS G read the poem in a way that partially anticipates Crowley's reading in the *editio princeps* of the poem. It is this sense of MS G's intermediacy that led to my last provisional title for this article, "Proto-Crowleian *Piers Plowman.*" The planner of MS G often constructs a misprision of Langland's topical content that transforms the poem into a prophecy of English church reform.

Physically dating MS G as a product of the early sixteenth century is a relatively straightforward yet imprecise endeavor. The scribe of MS G writes in a Tudor secretary hand that employs single compartment graphs for "a" and "g," as well as the graph of "e" that is perhaps the most important shibboleth of the hand. Among manuscripts of *Piers Plowman*, his hand is similar in most ways to the hand of the glossarist of Cambridge University Library Manuscript Ll4.14 (MS C^2) and to Sir Adrian Fortescue's hand, found in MS Digby 145 (Digby). In addition, the scribe employs the graph "y" to represent the allophones "theta" and "eth" only in the initial position of abbreviations such as "y^e" while using the graph "th" under all other conditions. Since the use of the graphs "y" or "þ" survived latest in superscript abbreviations,[4] I conclude that the scribe of MS G was trained toward the end of the fifteenth century or near the beginning of the sixteenth century after the shift to the exclusive use of "th" was well under way but not complete. Placing MS G in this paleographical context suggests a production date circa 1500, but the watermark evidence, the single watermark type in the manuscript resembles Briquet 13396, dated 1514,[5] moves MS G's date much closer to the 1520-30 range that I favor.

This production date fixes MS G well after printing had been established but before it had become dominant as the medium of literature in England. However, an even more precise physical date would be less than informative without some understanding of the publicly available concepts of textuality and other intellectual currents that were circulating at around 1520. Such understanding can be accomplished by closely reading the annotation of *Piers Plowman* in MS G. In the process, we will be able partially to understand how one reader who lived around 1520 thought about Langland's poem, and the conclusions drawn by this reader of the poem.

The planner of MS G does not seem to have manipulated the language of his exemplar much, if at all. This planner did not engage in the energetic editorial activity for which many *Piers Plowman* scribes have been so often censured. Neither did he engage in any of the less energetic types of editing, such as modernization, that were quite common even among non-composite texts. My collation of MS G[6] has produced very few instances of unique variation and thus I conclude that any modernization in the manuscript arose from exemplars constructed prior to the preparation of this manuscript. To be sure, the scribe made unique substitutions, but they were most often unconscious, orthographic ones such as the substitution of "the" for "þe" or "thy" for "youre." MS G is remarkably free of the types of deliberate textual manipulation that may be seen in manuscripts such as Huntington Library MS HM 114 or Corpus Christi College, Oxford, MS 201.[7] The planner of MS G was relatively respectful, compared to many copyists of *Piers Plowman*, towards the text of his received exemplar, although this apparent respect may have had more to do with the already considerably altered state of the textual tradition by the time it reached him than with any scruples about textual integrity.

In the process of annotating the poem, the planner of MS G was more innovative in manipulating the traditions of interpretation he inherited than the earlier performers of *Piers Plowman* had been. Many earlier producers of *Piers Plowman* transmitted not only the text of the poem, but its strategies of *mise-en-page*, as well. Of course, one producer might have remarked a site in the text that was not remarked by another, but most used the commonplace technology of annotation found in vernacular literary texts: the simple marginal note. At the time when the planner of MS G was at work, printers were inventing new strategies of interpretive annotation and redeploying old strategies in new situations. Moreover, reader aids, such as foliation, had become more common by the later fifteenth century even in printed books. For instance, foliation had begun supplanting existing mnemonic systems of navigating a book, such as the Dominican system, with foliation even being added to portable Bibles that were originally produced in the thirteenth and fourteenth centuries.[8] In addition, by 1480, foliation had appeared in German vernacular Bibles in combination with tables that indexed the biblical books.[9] From that point it was a short step to tables that indexed not only books, but also subjects and chapters within books. While it is impossible to determine whether the planner of MS G included an index due the influence of print or manuscript practices, it is noteworthy that he chose the option that would become the standard practice in print culture.

MS G is the only manuscript of *Piers Plowman* textual tradition in which such a large part of its interpretive apparatus is located at the rear of the volume, and this choice effectively concentrates the bulk of its navigational aids for the reader in that one site. This concentration of explanatory information allows easy access while simplifying the job of the annotator; locating the index at the rear of the volume allowed the annotator to explicate the text more extensively than would have been possible in the margins, while simplifying the process of layout. Ultimately, the primary reason that the producer of MS G manipulated and expanded the traditions of interpreting *Piers Plowman* he inherited was that he read the poem differently from earlier readers. However, it is debatable whether late manuscript or early print culture was the primary influence on his reading strategies.

While the apparatus of MS G preserves some of the features of marginalia common to many *Piers Plowman* manuscripts, including the notation of the parliament of the rats and mice and of the seven deadly sins, the manuscript's apparatus introduced marginal notations in many sections of the text that had not been extensively annotated by previous producers. In addition, both the inherited and the innovated marginalia coordinate with the subject index and folio references to produce a manuscript that is uncommonly easy to navigate once you have deciphered its system. As a result of this annotation technology, a person wishing to reread the section on *"ira,"* for instance, need only consult the four leaves of the index to locate the proper folio rather than leafing back and forth through the book scanning the margins. The index not only coordinated with the marginalia, but also with *litterae notabiliore* that marked the beginnings of the sections discursively described in the index. Thus the apparatus simultaneously indexed and explicated the aspects of *Piers Plowman* that were most significant to the planner of MS G.

The planner of MS G may be seen manipulating the received traditions of interpretation most easily in the alterations that were made to the text's rubrication. As has been noted by Robert Adams, multiple traditions of rubrication circulated simultaneously with the text of *Piers Plowman* during its early dissemination.[10] The planner of MS G combined elements of both the major strains of the rubrication tradition to produce a unique scheme that transcends the earlier attempts at combination, many of which had ended in confusion. The planner of MS G maintained the four-part division of the text into the *Visio* and the *Vitas* of Dowell, Dobett, and Dobest, but sidestepped the confusion that reigned in many manuscripts by abandoning any attempt to number the *passus* serially from beginning to end of the entire text. He provided each *passus* with an *explicit; incipits* were supplied at the beginnings of the *visio* and the three *vitas*, and the prologue was regarded as the first *passus* of the *visio*. Thus, MS G contains such rubrics as *"explicit primus passus de visione,"* *"hic incipit primus passus de dowell,"* and *"explicit septimus et vltimus passus de dowell/incipit primus passus de dobett."*[11] The manuscript is divided into the eight *passus* of the *visio*, the seven *passus* of the *vita* of dowell, the five *passus* of the *vita* of dobett, and the single *passus* of the *vita* of dobest.

The subject index to MS G maintains the four-part structure consistent with the rubrication of the text, and each of the four sections is provided with an *incipit* and an *explicit* similar to those provided for the poetic text's divisions. For instance, folio 102v begins *"hic incipit tabula de dowell"* and ends *"explicit tabula de dowell."* The four tables vary in length with the *"tabula de visione"* occupying folios 101v to 102r; the table of Dowell, folio 102v; and the tables of both Dobett and Dobest, folio 103r. The layout and rubrication of the index sincerely flatters the *mise-en-page* of the complete poem by imitation. The left-hand margins of the index contain notations that are largely identical to the notations found throughout the outer margins of the text itself. To the right of these marginal notes in the index is a discursive prose description of the section of the poem being indexed and to the right of these descriptions are folio references. This arrangement allows a reader to locate the subjects in the poem that the planner of MS G deemed most compelling or important. The index summarizes the planner's reading of *Piers Plowman* in a miniature simulacrum of the poetic text. Furthermore, the coordination and integration of MS G's apparatus extends quite a bit beyond the index and rubrics. While the index provides only foliation, a section may be located on its specific page, usually in one of three ways.

In some cases, a marginal note keyed to a similar note in the index marks the section. For instance, on folio 29v, the note "a profecy" appears in the left-hand margin opposite the lines:

> but I warne you workemen wynne whyle ye mowe
> for hongre hydderward hastethe hym fast
> he shall awake with watre wastovrs to chaste
> er fyve be fullfylled seyche famyne shall aryse
> thrugh floddes & fovle wedders fryvtes shall fayle
> and so satarne yat seynt you to warne
> when ye se ye sonne a myd & two monkes heydes
> and a meyde haue ye mastrye & mvltyply by heyght
> yen shall dethe with drawe & derthe be justece
> & daw ye dyker dye for hongre
> but yff god off hys goodnes graunt vs a trewe.[12]

On folio 102, in the left hand margin of the index appears the marginal note "ye profecy off derthe" opposite the description:

> ye xviiii chapter declareth the profecy of derthe
> yat shall come yff yat wastovrs be not
> reformed & corrected.

This entry concludes in the right margin of 102 with the folio reference "29" in arabic numerals.

In other cases, a *litterae notabiliore* marks the subject reference, as on folio 24r where a two-line "L" in black ink begins the line "Leve pyers quod thes pylgrymes & profered hym hyre."[13] In the left-hand margin of the index appears the note "ye way to/trewths/house" opposite the description:

> ye xvii chapter declareth how ye pylgryms
> desyred pyers plowman to shew them ye
> way to trewths dwellyng place,[14]

and the description is followed by a reference to folio 24.

In still other cases, both devices are used to mark the beginning of an indexed section. For example, the marginal note "ira" appears to the left of the line "**N**ow awaketh wrathe with too wyte eyne" on folio 18r—the "N" being a two-line *litterae notabiliore* in black ink. The index contains the identical marginal note opposite the description:

> ye xiii chapter declare how wrathe cam
> to shryft
> & declareth how he reyned in relygyon.[15]

Each of these ways of remarking allows a reader to locate the beginning of the specific section indexed, and they demonstrate more about the way in which the planner of MS G was reinventing the received interpretive apparatus of *Piers Plowman*. Each of the three discursive descriptions quoted as examples refers to a chapter within the text of the poem, and these chapters are often surprisingly distinct from the received *passus* divisions.

While the sense of "chapter" as a major division within a book had been current in English since the thirteenth century, the usage of the term in MS G, like the manuscript itself, occupies a penumbra between traditional manuscript practices and the innovations of print production. On the one hand, the copy of *Piers Plowman* in MS G retains the traditional separation of the B-text into twenty-one divisions designated as *passus*, as well as the larger division into a *Visio* and three *Vitas*. On the other hand, the use of "chapter" in the table of subjects to refer to subdivisions in the text and to the *litterae notabiliore* that mark the beginnings of these subdivisions suggests a scheme of division found in print texts and not in any other manuscript copies of *Piers Plowman*.[16] Furthermore, the "chapters" are numbered 1 to 21 in the *tabula de visione* and then begin again with chapter one in each of the other three parts of the index. In MS G, *Piers Plowman* is indexed as if it were composed of four books, corresponding to the *Visio* and the three *Vitas*, each of which is subdivided into a number of chapters. The traditional division of the text into *passus* has been retained and improved in the rubrics, while a parallel system of describing and dividing the constituent parts of a text has been introduced into the index. These chapter divisions in the index to MS G are a unique feature of the planner's interpretation of the poem.

While the annotation and indexing of MS G is thorough, the planner of the manuscript was unable to reconcile his competing schemes of dividing and describing *Piers Plowman*. At the beginning of the index, the traditional division into *passus* is invoked and then abandoned within the space of a single entry on the first leaf. The index notes that "ye first passus of ye vysyone conteynethe iii chapters"[17] and it goes on to elaborate what each of the three chapters "tretethe" or "declareth." However, the initial line that indicates how many chapters make up the first *passus*, the *passus* that is denoted as the prologue in most manuscripts, is also the only reference to the word "passus" in the entire index. For most of the index, the planner abandons the *passus*, the major element of the traditional division of the poem, in favor of chapters. The eight *passus* of the *Visio* have been divided into twenty-one chapters and only the beginning of the first chapter correlates with the opening of a *passus*. Similarly, the *tabula de dowell* has been divided into eight chapters, when this section of the poem traditionally contains seven *passus*. In the first two sections of the index, the division into chapters supersedes the conventional division into *passus*. By contrast, the last two *tabula* of the index correlate with the traditional division into *passus*, while continuing to designate these divisions "chapters." The *tabulae* of Dobett and of Dobest have five chapters and one chapter respectively, and both of these figures coincide with the number of *passus* typically found in these *Vitae*, but again no mention of *passus* appears in these sections of the index.

The plan for the index in MS G did not successfully integrate the desire to maintain the traditional elements of *Piers Plowman* with the desire to designate new subdivisions within the poem that interpret the subject matter more minutely than the division into *passus* allowed. Moreover, the length of the chapter descriptions in the respective sections of MS G's index increases as the number of chapters in them dwindles, suggesting that, consciously or not, the planner of MS G was more comfortable with the traditional divisions in the later than in the earlier *passus*. Alternatively, it could be that, like many readers of the poem, the planner of MS G simply found the earlier *passus* of *Piers Plowman* more compelling than the later. Or it might be added that there was simply more traditional marginalia to copy and account for in the earlier than in the later *passus*.

The planner of MS G introduced an alternative scheme of dividing the *Visio* and the *Vita de dowell* in the index that contrasts quantitatively with the more traditional strategy of division employed in indexes to the *Vitae* of Dobett and Dobest. None of the chapter descriptions in the *tabula de visione* extend beyond three lines and many of them are no more than two. The descriptions vary from barely two lines of the sixth chapter, "the vi chapter declareth how mater ecclesia declareth/what mede ys," to three lines of the fourth chapter:

> ye iiii chapter declaryth how money oght to be
> bestowed & to whom ytt belongeth & off ye borowys
> yat the church[18] receyvyd off vs at ovr baptyme.[19]

As the number of chapter divisions decreases in the last two *Vitae*, the descriptions become more verbose, finally culminating in the entry that describes the ultimate chapter/*passus* of the poem:

ye fyrst chapter[20] declareth yat nede hathe no
lawe & ys an hygh vertewe & howe in all
our adversytyes we shold resort to ye holy churche
& beleve in ytt & of ye covetyovsnes of prests
& how yat men shrave yem at ye freres & not att
ye parsons & cvratts for.[21]

The planner of MS G found the traditional division of *Piers Plowman* most unsatisfactory in the first eight *passus* of the poem, especially in *Passus* V. As noted above, the *Visio* has been divided into twenty-one chapters in the index, and moreover *Passus* V alone was divided into five chapters. Since the planner retained the traditional division of the last two *Vitae*, while nonetheless exchanging the terminology "chapter" for "*passus*," one may surmise that he found these divisions less problematic. Ultimately, the most problematic thing for the planner of MS G about the poem's later *passus* was that less of the prophetic subject matter he favored could be found there.

Like the book that he designed and constructed, the planner of MS G's interpretation of *Piers Plowman* was situated near a crux in the history of ideas in England. Thus, the interpretation of the poem that emerges from MS G's index advances both typical and uncommon readings of its subject matter. In the earlier sections of the poem, the index of MS G presents a rather stereotypical reading of the text in short descriptive phrases that elaborate on and coordinate with the marginal notes. As the descriptions lengthen in the latter sections of the poem, the reading of the text becomes more selective. The evidence from other B manuscripts, and from the manuscripts of the A and C Versions as well, indicates that the earlier sections of the poem were better known than the later, and, therefore, a more detailed communal reading was circulating with the text in the form of typical marginalia. The planner of MS G elaborated on this typical marginalia by describing his interpretation more vividly in the index than was possible in marginal notes constrained by space. In the later *passus*, the planner of MS G was compelled to select the subjects for annotation, because so few typical marginalia circulated with the later sections of the poem. In addition, there may have been less of the material that interested the planner, or any other reader, in these sections of the poem.

Several of the entries in the subject index of MS G demonstrate that the planner of the apparatus recognized the ambiguity, as well as the deeper figurative aspects of *Piers Plowman's* allegory. As a result, providing interpretive closure for the allegory became part of the function of the apparatus. For instance, the planner of MS G indexed the metaphoric possibilities of the pardon that Piers received from Truth as well as the fictional document's location within the text. The planner observed of "pers pardon" that:

> ye xix chapter declareth what pardone
> was gravnted to pers plowman & to all
> trve dealers & laborers by trewthe,[22]

thus acknowledging Piers' figurative status as a representative of the right-eous. Furthermore, he does not seem to be such a literal reader that he sees the necessity to censure the corruption of the pardon-granting process.

Likewise, he observes interpretations offered within the text itself and incorporates them into his own apparatus as when he describes a passage from *Passus* XIX (*passus quintus de dobettre*) in this way:

> ye vth chapter declareth how ye thre kyngs
> sence gold   myrre[23]
> offered to god reason ryghtyovsnes & ruthe
> wych ys properly called mercy or pytye. . . .[24]

It may be that the planner of MS G recognizes that this interpretation of the gifts of the Magi is unprecedented,[25] but regardless, he consistently attempts to offer interpretive closure for allegory whenever possible.

In the process of stabilizing his allegorical interpretation of *Piers Plowman*, the planner of MS G occasionally has recourse to a rudimentary critical vocabulary that betrays some familiarity with Latin literature or the New Learning. In *Passus* VIII, *primus passus de dowell* in MS G, the planner describes a friar's use of the commonplace image of a storm-tossed boat as the "simili-tudo/off ye bott to/a jvst man."[26] The accurate use of the Latin term for "metaphor," a term that became anglicized as "similitude" in the course of the fifteenth century,[27] illustrates that the planner had some knowledge of Latin rhetorical terminology. Furthermore, he uses the anglicized term later in the subject index when he notes that "ye iijrd chapter declareth the symmylytude of the/trynyte to a hoole fyst.[28] The planner of MS G not only recognized the possibilities of allegory, but also possessed a rudimentary critical vocabulary with which to describe those possibilities.

The index suggests also that the MS G planner's familiarity with literature conditioned him to read the poem in typical ways, while his ideological preoccupations conditioned him to read in more uncommon ways. On one hand, the planner of MS G displays interest in many of the aspects of the poem that commonly made *Piers Plowman* popular, when popularity is gauged by the frequency with which selected passages of the poem were marginally glossed. Included among these conventional interests were estates satire and anticlericalism, and the length of the notes in MS G allows both a closer reading of the text by the planner and a closer reading of the planner's interests than with other manuscripts. On the other hand, the planner of MS G interprets many passages in the poem as prophecies that may come to pass in his historical moment. Since the planner is aware that *Piers Plowman* is not a contemporary poem, he does not, as earlier readers could have and did, read the text as contemporary commentary. The prophetic interpretation of the text that emerges from the MS G index leans in the direction of the later Reformation readings of *Piers Plowman* advanced by reformers and early antiquaries such as John Bale and Robert Crowley, while not being quite as radical. The planner of MS G seems to have sat firmly on the fence between sincere loyalty to Holy Church and complete rejection of the abuses plaguing her.

Among the more common marginalia in *Piers Plowman*, present in the majority of the manuscripts I have examined, are notes that identify the various estates and vocations that Will observes during his initial vision of the middle earth, the tower above, and the dungeon below. A typical sample of such marginal notes might include "plowmen," "ancres," "marchauntz," and "mynstrales" in the right-hand margin of its initial leaf, and similar notes can be found in manuscripts of all three versions of *Piers Plowman*. While there are no similar marginal notes on the initial leaf of MS G, the index articulates a similar interpretive focus when it notes that the *primus passus de visione* "tretethe what he sawe yn mydle yerthe amongest ye lered & ye lewde."[29] While echoing the standard interpretation of the passage, this entry draws upon important alliterative language, "ye lered & ye lewde," which echoes throughout the poem. This alliterative tag highlights one of the key tensions present throughout the poem: the relationship between learning and salvation. Within conventional interpretive contexts such as estates satire, the planner of MS G often subtly relates key concepts from the text by the language he repeats in his apparatus.

The marginalia accompanying the first index entry provides another example of the planner associating language intratextually. The note "pylgrymes" appears to the left of the index entry on "ye lered & ye lewde," indicating that the planner of MS G associates the "fayre feld full of folke/ . . . off all maner off men ye meyne & ye ryche/worchyng & wanderyng as ye world asketh"[30] with the pilgrims in *Passus* V who wander in search of Saint Truth. Indeed, many of the allegorical types described on the first few folios of the poem, such as the wasters and the proud, are represented among the company who take part in the pilgrimage to Saint Truth's house, and they are guided by one who ". . . pvtten [hem] to plogh pleden full selde."[31] Even when his interpretation is firmly rooted in traditional *Piers Plowman* marginalia, the planner of MS G consistently highlights intratextual echoes by mimicking the language of the poem in his apparatus and produces a richly textured reading of the text in the process.

The planner of MS G was influenced by the widespread interest in antifraternalism in *Piers Plowman*, as well as estates satire, but his reading of this aspect of the poem was more subtle than most. Many manuscript producers were as quick to notice the antifraternalism in the first few leaves of the poem as they were the estates orientation. In Huntington Library MS HM 114, for instance, the marginal notes "freres," "pardoners" (1v), and "parsons &/prelates" call attention to the first mention of each of these typological churchmen, and similar marginalia can be found in many other manuscripts including B-texts such as Oriel College, Oxford MS 79, and C-texts such as Huntington Library MS HM 143.[32] In the index to MS G to the right of the marginal note "pardoners/& prelates," the entry states that "ye second chapter declareth ye deceate off pre/lates off holy cherche & off pardoners" (101v). While this entry echoes the common interest in antifraternalism, the planner of MS G also calls attention to Long Will's indictment of bishops for their complicity in the fraudulent practices of pardoners. The planner of MS G has little original insight to offer into the early sections of *Piers Plowman*, but he has nonetheless read the poem carefully and made noticeable interpretive connections. Moreover, he consistently applied his interpretive connections to lesser-known sections of the text.

The index entry describing the third chapter of *Passus* I demonstrates that the planner of MS G was alienated from the poem's original interpretive context, even while establishing the episode as one of the planner's fundamental interests in *Piers Plowman*. As with the first two chapters in *Passus* I, this chapter involves an often-noted episode, the parliament of the rats and the mice, but his interpretation of this episode demonstrates that the allegory was no longer topical for the planner of MS G. The index entry states that "ye thyrd chapter declareth ye profycye of ye/catt ye ratt & ye mysse,"[33] whereas earlier manuscripts typically referred to the episode as a "parlement." These interpretations differ significantly in that a "parlement" would likely be a *fait accompli*, while a "profycye" could be construed as foretold, perhaps occurring but certainly not accomplished. The latter interpretation would, therefore, preclude any association of this allegorical tale with the career of John of Gaunt in a way that the former interpretation does not. Regardless of whether the association of the parliament of the rats and mice with John of Gaunt is accurate, this fiction was not interpreted by the planner of MS G as topical, since he did not associate the assembly of rats and mice with Parliament. Therefore, the designation of this episode as a prophecy rather than a fable is distinctive and indicative of one source of the planner's consistent interests in *Piers Plowman*.

The fundamental appeal of *Piers Plowman* for the planner of MS G was its predictive value. He identified no less than four other chapters as prophetic in addition to "ye/catt ye ratt & ye mysse" suggesting that a substantial percentage of the matter in the poem interested the planner of MS G because he considered it oracular. This interpretation was not wildly different from that of the poem's earlier readers, but the extent of the prophetic material in the MS G planner's view was much greater than in the minds of many of his fellow composers of *Piers Plowman* texts. In the late fourteenth or early fifteenth century, the fable of the belling-of-the-cat may have resonated because it could be read as a satiric comment on contemporary events. Langland's allegory may have lived and breathed in his time; however, to the planner of MS G, the poem was valuable because it could be read as an ancient prophecy predicting the events to come, perhaps in his own time, as the book of Revelation might.

Many of the allegorical moments in *Piers Plowman* that the planner of MS G interpreted as prophetic were intended by Langland as contemporary commentary. Reinterpretation of the allegory may be observed in the planner's handling of the character Hunger during the Plowing-of-the-Half-Acre episode. Toward the end of *septimus passus de visione* in MS G, Piers calls on Hunger to punish the idle pilgrims who are not pulling their weight in the plowing of his half-acre. The *passus* ends with the caution "but I warne you workemen wynne whyle ye mowe/for hongre hydderward hastethe hym fast"[34] and a prediction of famine through foul weather if workmen do not heed the narrator's warning. In MS G, the passage in the text that describes the foul weather was marked out by the marginal note "a profecy,"[35] and this interpretation of prophecy was carried over into the index where an entry for folio 29 is marginally noted as "ye profecy off/derthe." This entry in the index states that:

> ye xviiii chapter declareth the profecy of derthe
> yat shall come yff yat wastovrs be not
> reformed & corrected.[36]

Of course, the passage invites a prophetic interpretation when the voice behind the narrator drops its mask, but a purely prophetic reading of the passage overlooks a topical allusion to the Statute of Laborers that immediately precedes the narrator's direct address to the reader. Before confronting the laborers, Will describes the allegorical figure of Wastovr thusly:

> he grevethe hym ageynst god & gruggethe ageynst reason
> and cavsethe he ye kyng all hys covnseyle after
> seych *lawes to loke laborers* to greve
> but whyle hongre was here master non off yem wold chyde
> ne *struve ageynst yis statvte* so sternleche he loked.[37]

When this passage is read as an allusion to the "Statvte off Laborers," the following lines may be read as the consequences of transgression against a particular law rather than a general warning against sloth. The planner of MS G overlooks this allusion, when he has demonstrated himself perfectly capable of reading astutely in other passages, because the reference is no longer topical as Langland intended.

Although he did not identify the belling-of-the-cat and censure-of-wasters episodes as topical, the planner of MS G did find them especially compelling. Both passages receive marked special treatment in the margins of the text and of the index, because in each case a graphic marker was added to the marginal note in the text that was keyed to an identical graphic in the margin of the index. The graphic that, for the belling-of-the-cat episode resembles a letter "S" with six heavy black dots evenly spaced along its length, and the graphic associated with the censure of wasters resembles a heraldic cross crosslet.[38] Moreover, the planner of MS G accords such special treatment to only three other passages in the poem.

This exceptional denotation of selected passages suggests that some prophecies were especially evocative for the planner of MS G, and after all five which received special treatment have been considered separately, a pattern emerges that I believe guided their selection. Another of the selected prophecies, marked by a pair of small squares arranged bendwise sinister touching at their lower left and upper right hand corners respectively, comes near the end of the debate between Lady Mede and Conscience before the King. In this passage Conscience says:

> and er thys fortune fall fynde men shall the worste
> by syx sonnes & a shyppe & halve a sheyffe off arowes
> & the mydell off a mone shalt make the jves tvrne
> and sarazenes for yat syght shall synge *gloria in excelsis*
> for machomet & mede mysshape shalt that tyme.[39]

The planner labelled this passage as "ye profecy off ye dome to come"[40] in the index, and the apocalyptic nature of the passage is indeed obvious. Schmidt glosses this passage by saying that "riddling prophecies were common at the time" and noting that the particulars of the passage may be interpreted both numerologically and astrologically as signs of the last days.[41] The planner of MS G would agree with Schmidt's gloss, and, as a result of the planner's special treatment of the passage, we may add millenarianism to his list of interests.

The fourth of the five special passages combined two of the MS G planner's interests: millenarian prophecy and the censure of clerical abuses. Unlike the other four passages, however, this one might be read as more topical during Henry VIII's reign than earlier. In the *tercius passus de dowell*[42] of MS

G, Clergie makes the following observation while preaching on the proper conduct of clergy:

> & now ys relygyon a rydre a romer by stretes
> a pricker on a palfray from man<u>er</u> to man<u>er</u>
> a leyder off lovedayes & a land bugger
> an heype off hovndes att hys arse as he a lorde were
> & but yff hys knave knele y<u>at</u> shall hym cvppe brynge
> he lovrethe on hym & askethe wo taght hym covrtysye.[43]

In this instance the MS G index is less explanatory than the marginalia because it only echoes the note found to the left of line 306 of the text, "<u>pro</u>fycy of [r]elygyous,"[44] and reproduces the graphic marker also found on that leaf that resembles a square with trefoils sprouting from its corners. However, the marginal notation alongside the text makes the planner's interpretation of the passage quite plain since, in addition to the aforementioned note, two others appear on folio 42v. The first of these other marginalia is a *nota bene* that appears next to the first line of the following passage:

> but y<u>er</u> shall come a kyng & co<u>n</u>fesse you relygyovse
> & beyte you as y<u>e</u> byble tellethe for breykyng off your rvele
> & amend monales monkes & chanons
> & put y<u>em</u> to theyr penaunce *ad prestinum statu*.[45]

Further down the leaf, the note [t]habbott of/Abyngdou<u>n</u>[46] appears opposite the lines,

> then shall y<u>e</u> abbott off abyndon & hys yssve for eu<u>ere</u>
> haue knocke w<u>ith</u> a kyng & vncvrable y<u>e</u> wovnde
> that is worthe sothe seke ye y<u>at</u> ofte over se ye byble.[47]

To the planner of MS G, this passage prophesies the appearance of a king who will put an end to the abuses in religious houses. While this passage, even given the marginalia in MS G, might be read as a straightforward apocalyptic prophecy in which the king would be the prince of peace, the passage might also be interpreted as topical by a sixteenth-century reader. The king might be read as Henry VIII and the "vncvrable wovnde" might be read as the disendowment of the religious houses. MS G was more than likely produced before the disendowment, but the planner's reading of this passage certainly participates in the air of antifraternalism that preceded and partially sanctioned the disendowment.

The MS G planner's belief in the necessity of royal reform of the Church and Society is repeated in the fifth and final passage chosen for special attention. On folio 95, a passage has been noted by the combination of a marginal note, "a p<u>ro</u>fecy," and a marker that may be best described as a cross *formy quadrate* oriented as though it were a cross of St. Andrew. This prophetic passage involves a king who appears after a long passage in which Conscience discourses to Will on the disorders in and the proper ordering of the world:

> I am kyng w<u>ith</u> crowne the com<u>m</u>vne to revle
> and holy ^churche^ & claregye fro cu<u>r</u>sed men to defend
> & yff me lackethe to lyve by y<u>e</u> lawe wole I take ytt
> there I may hastylyche have ytt for I am heyde off lawe
> for y<u>ei</u> beene but me<u>m</u>bres & I aboven all
> & sythe I am your aller heyde I am your aller heale
> & holy cherche cheffe helpe & chefteyne off y<u>e</u> com<u>m</u>vne
> & what I take off you two I take ytt at y<u>e</u> teachyng
> off *spi<u>ri</u>tus justicie* for I jvgge you all
> so I may bowldlye be howseled for I borowed neu<u>er</u>
> ne crave off my com<u>m</u>vne but as my kynd askethe.[48]

In the subject index this "profecy of a kyng" is described as "what a kyng may do by justece,"[49] suggesting, like the passage discussed immediately above, that a king may be necessary to reform the Church.

In order to read this king's speech as prophetic, the passage must be dislocated from its context within the poem and redeployed in a manner consistent with the ideological preoccupations of the planner of MS G. This ideological (re)interpretation of the text as prophetic rather than topical is the pattern that emerges from the five passages marked out for special attention. Within the context of the *passus* in which his speech appears, there is little or no indication that the king is a prophetic figure. Rather, he represents another illustration of material excess corrupting the proper functioning of worldly institutions that Conscience has been exemplifying for Will throughout the preceding lines of the *passus*. This particular excess, overtaxation by the king, could have been construed as a topical reference by earlier readers during the Hundred Years' War, when friction between the king and the commons over taxation for foreign military adventures was nearly constant. However, the planner of MS G consistently and strongly misreads such potentially topical passages due to his inadequate knowledge of their context, viewing them through the lens of his own interest in millenarian prophecy. He consistently interprets episodes in the poem as projections of a future for which he yearns rather than as reflections of the contemporary scene when *Piers Plowman* was written.

A yearning for reform of the Church through secular political action may also be seen in the indexing of some less well-marked passages. On folio 69v, the note "*no<u>ta</u> hic/de religios*" points out the following excerpt

> yff lewde men knewe thys laten y_ei_ wolde look to gyve
> and auyse y_em_ a fore fyve dayes off or syxe
> er they amortysed to monkes & chanons y_er_ rent
> alas lordes ladyes lewd covnceyle haue ye
> to gyve fro your heyres y_at_ your ayles had
> and gyvethe to bydde for you to soche y_at_ beene ryche
> and beene fovnded & feaffed eke to bydde for other
> who p_er_fovmethe y_is_ p_ro_fecye off y_e_ peeple y_at_ mowe lyvethe
> *dispersit dedit pauperibus*
> yff any peeple perfome y_is_ texte ytt are y_e_ pore freres
> for y_at_ y_ei_ beggen abovte in beeldyng they spende
> on theyre sleve some & on soche as been y_eir_ laborovrs
> & off |theym| y_at_ haue y_ei_ taken and gyve to theym y_at_ ne havethe.[50]

"Thys laten" incorporates Job 6:5, a passage noting that brute beasts will not
call for more sustenance when they are full. The Job quotation is glossed by
an unidentified commentary[51] and states that "*Brutorum animalium natura te
condempnat, quia cum eis pabulum commune sufficiat; ex adipe prodiit iniquitas tua*"
(336-37). It would seem that the planner of MS G finds Anima's gloss of the
Latin congenial partially because it suggests that the Commons could help
correct the avarice of the rich Clergy. Again the planner's interest is piqued
by an Erastian solution to the abuses in the Church.

The planner of MS G believed that only the Commons or a messianic
king could enact religious reform, because the collusion of the *cleros* and the
miles was responsible for the current abuses. When he noted the following
passage on folio 72v as a "p_ro_phycie," he demonstrates his desire that his
time was the time for reform:

> & nowe is warre & wo & who so whye askethe
> ffor covetyse after cros y_e_ crowne stand in golde
> bothe ryche & relygyovse that roode they honoren
> that in y_e_ grote ys lgraue & yn y_e_ golde nobles
> ffor covetyse off y_at_ cros men off holy kyrke
> shall torne as templers dyd y_e_ tyme approcethe fast.[52]

He applauded Anima's call that clergy be disendowed like the Templars were,
and further down on the same folio, he laid the ultimate blame with the hierarchy of the Church. He admonished the reader to "*nota bene p_er_ episcopis*":

> *dos eccle_sia_* thys day hathe dronke wenome
> and yet y_at_ haue petyrs power arre empoysoned all
> a medycyne mvte ys to y_at_ may ame_n_d p_re_lates
> that shold pray for y_e_ pens possessyon y_em_ lettethe.[53]

His note on this passage in the subject index, "ye first chapter declareth . . . how yat by constantynes gift poyson cam in to ye churche yen,"[54] anticipates the polemic of more radical reformers such as Crowley and Bale. Indeed in the second edition of *Acts and Monuments*, John Fox interpreted Constantine's gift as the end of the era of the unblemished Church, as had earlier reformers. Like them, the planner of MS G must place his faith in political reform, since he envisions the Church as too corrupted from within to reform itself.

Ultimately, however sympathetic he was to the cause of religious reform, the planner of MS G was not so radical a reformer as to question the ultimate authority of the Church. He recognized the abuses of the Church's institutions, but that recognition did not arouse in him thoughts of complete overthrow of those institutions. For instance, he recognized that the sacrament of confession had been corrupted in many ways, and this recognition can be seen in his entry on *Passus* III where he notes that "ye viii chapter declareth how mede thurgh hyr gyfts/stopped men off lawys movths & prestes."[55] Similarly, in the final entry in the subject index, he decries "how yat men shrave yem at ye freres & not att/ye parsons & cvratts" (103). Nonetheless, the abuse of the sacrament does not lead the planner of MS G to reject it altogether as many Protestant reformers did. In respect to another crucial dogmatic issue, the MS G planner's position may be gauged by contrasting his description of the beginning of *Passus* XIV with Robert Crowley's. The planner of MS G describes Haukyn's confession thus,

> ye viiith chapter declareth how havkyn ye actyve
> man pourged hys cote with contrytyon confesyon
> & satysfacyon.[56]

and this description is consistent with his description of the confessions of the Deadly Sins. By contrast, Crowley does not explicitly mention the sacrament that he rejects, "It declarith how the labourynge man, excuseth hym/selfe of hys sinne."[57] Unlike Crowley and his ilk, the planner of MS G rejects the abuse of confession but continues to acknowledge the sacrament.

The last entry that the planner of MS G included in his subject index doubly confirms his ultimate belief in the institution of the Holy Church. First, in the left hand margin of folio 103r near the bottom of the leaf, the subjects of the *primus passus de dobest* are described as "ye resort to/holy chvrch/& how freres/hyndred contrytyng." Second, the discursive portion of the entry itself explains "howe in all/our adversytes we shold resort to ye holy churche/& beleve in ytt." This supreme belief in the institution of Holy Church contrasts markedly with Crowley's description of the *passus* in which no mention was made of the Holy Church. While the planner of MS G was committed to religious reform, he was not a revolutionary who rejected the Holy Church's basic institutions because they were abused.

Two things are clear above all about the planner of MS G: both material and intellectual influences of his time may be seen in the text he constructed. The material influences may be seen in his decision to reproduce the text of *Piers Plowman* in ways that are unusual among the extant manuscripts. He handled his received lexical text of the poem gently; whether due to respect for its ancient purity or to unconsciousness of its deficiencies is unclear. In any event, he revised his received bibliographical text drastically in ways that were influenced by the technical changes taking place in both manuscript and print culture. Moreover, his bibliographical text suggests an unusual reading of *Piers Plowman* with respect to both the planner of MS G's interpretive strategies and his interpretations. He brought some of the preoccupations and strategies of a Christian humanist to his reading, he read the poem as a prophetic document, and he took steps to make the principal prophecies easily accessible for repeated perusal.

Georgia Southwestern State University

NOTES

1. Cambridge University Library Manuscript Gg.4.31 101v (hereafter referred to as MS G). All quotations of this manuscript result from my own transcriptions.
2. W.W. Skeat, intro. *The Vision of William Concerning Piers the Plowman Together with Vita de Dowel, Dobet et Dobest Secundum Wit et Resoun: Text B.* by William Langland. Early English Text Society o.s. 38. (London: Oxford University Press, 1869), xxiii.
3. George Kane and E. Talbot Donaldson, intro. *Piers Plowman: The B Version: Will's Visions of Piers Plowman, Do-Well, Do-Better and Do-Best,* by William Langland (London: Athlone, 1988), 8.
4. Michael Benskin, "The letters <þ> and <y> in later Middle English, and some related matters," *Journal of the Society of Archivists* 7(1982): 26.
5. Briquet, C.M. *Les Filigranes,* ed. A.H. Stevenson. 4 vols. (Amsterdam: Paper Society, 1968).
6. My comparison of readings was made primarily with the other members of the so-called GYOC2CbmBoCot group of B witnesses. See Kane and Donaldson *Piers Plowman* 52-54.
7. The planner of Huntington HM 114 combined A-, B-, and C-exemplars to create a nine thousand plus line version of the poem; see Ralph Hanna, III, "The Scribe of Hm 114," *Studies in Bibliography* 42(1989): 120-133. The planner of Corpus Christi Oxford 201 redivided the *passus* of the poem to coincide more closely with the progress of the poem's many dreams; see Sean Taylor, "The F Scribe and the R Manuscript of *Piers Plowman B,*" *English Studies: A Journal of English Language and Literature* 77(1996): 530-548.
8. Paul Saenger, "The Impact of the Early Printed Page on the Reading of the Bible," *The Bible as Book: The First Printed Editions,* eds. Paul Saenger and Kimberly Van Kampen, (London and New Castle, DE: British Library and Oak Knoll Press, 1999), 33.

9. Ibid. 34.

10. Robert Adams, "The Reliability of the Rubrics in the B-Text of *Piers Plowman*," *Medium Ævum* 54(1985): 215.

11. MS G 3v, 32v, and 65r, respectively.

12. Ibid. *passus septimus de visione*.301-311

13. Ibid. *passus sextus de visione*.557.

14. Ibid. 102r.

15. Ibid. 102v.

16. In a typical manuscript from any of the poem's three versions, subdivisions within the *passus* were indicated by paraphs, skipped lines, or both. None of these features are present in MS G. In addition, MS G lacks any indication, typically indicated by a *punctus elevatus*, of the caesura in the alliterative long lines.

17. MS G 101v.

18. This word was inserted using a caret by the scribe who copied the rest of the manuscript.

19. MS G 101v.

20. That is, the first chapter of the *Vita de dobest*.

21. MS G 103r.

22. There is some confusion in the numbering of the chapters at this point in the index. This is actually the twentieth chapter of the *Visio*.

23. These three words were entered interlinearly in the index above the interpretations to which they correspond.

24. MS G 103r.

25. A.V.C. Schmidt *The Vision of Piers Plowman: A Complete Edition of the* B-Text, by William Langland, (Rutland, VT: Everyman, 1978), 353-354.

26. MS G 102v.

27. MED senses 3a and 3b.

28. MS G 103v.

29. Ibid. 101v.

30. Ibid. *primus passus de visione*.17-19.

31. Ibid. *primus passus de visione*.20

32. For example, the notes "hermytis wente/to walsingham" and "hyer prechid frerys" may be found on folio 4r in Huntington Library MS. Hm 143.

33. MS G 101v.

34. Ibid. *septimus passus de visione*.301-302

35. Ibid. 29v.

36. Ibid. 102r.

37. Ibid. *septimus de visione*.296-300—emphasis added.

38. Carl Grindley had suggested to me that this marker resembles one used by legal scriveners.

39. MS G *quartus de visione*.333-337.

40. Ibid. 101v.

41. Schmidt, 313, n.325-330.

42. Usually *Passus* X.

43. MS G *passus tercius de dowell*.318-23.

44. Ibid. 42v.

45. Ibid. *passus tercius de dowell*.329-332.

46. Part of this note has been cropped in rebinding, but "t" is the logical reading for the missing bit.

47. MS G *passus tercius de dowell*.340-342.

48. Ibid. *passus quintus de dobetter*.457-467.

49. Ibid. 103r.

50. Ibid. *primus passus de dobett*.338-350

51. John A. Alford, *Piers Plowman: A Guide to the Quotations* (Binghamton, NY: MTRS, 1992), 95.

52. MS G *passus primus de dobett*.539-544.

53. Ibid. *passus primus de dobett*.559-562.

54. Ibid. 103r.

55. Ibid. 101v.

55. Ibid. 102v.

57. Robert Crowley, ed. *The Vision of Pierce Plowman, nowe the seconde time imprinted by Roberte Crowley dwellynge in Elye rentes Holburne* by William Langland, 2nd ed., (London: 1550), C.iii.

WORKS CITED

Adams, Robert. "The Reliability of the Rubrics in the B-Text of *Piers Plowman*." *Medium Ævum* 54(1985): 208-31.

Alford, John. Piers Plowman: A *Guide to the Quotations*. Binghamton, NY: MTRS, 1992.

Benskin, Michael. "The letters <þ> and <y> in later Middle English, and some related matters." *Journal of the Society of Archivists* 7(1982): 13-30.

Briquet, C.M. *Les Filigranes*. Ed. A.H. Stevenson. 4 vols. Amsterdam: Paper Society, 1968.

Crowley, Robert, ed. and preface. *The Vision of Pierce Plowman, nowe the seconde time imprinted by Roberte Crowley dwellynge in Elye rentes Holburne* by William Langland. 2nd ed. London: 1550. STC 19907.

Hanna, Ralph, III. "The Scribe of Huntington HM 114," *Studies in Bibliography* 42(1989): 120-33.

Kane, George and E. Talbot Donaldson, eds. *Piers Plowman: The B Version: Will's Visions of Piers Plowman, Do-Well, Do-Better and Do-Best*. by William Langland. London: Athlone, 1988.

Langland, William. *Piers Plowman*. Cambridge Univerity Library MS. Gg 4.31. Cambridge.

——. *Piers Plowman*. Huntington Library MS. Hm 143. San Marino, CA.

Saenger, Paul. "The Impact of the Early Printed Page on the Reading of the Bible." *The Bible as Book: The First Printed Editions*. eds. Paul Saenger and Kimberly Van Kampen . London and New Castle, DE: British Library and Oak Knoll Press, 1999. 31-51.

Skeat, Walter W., ed. and intro. *The Vision of William Concerning Piers the Plowman Together with Vita de Dowel, Dobet et Dobest Secundum Wit et Resoun: Text B.* by William Langland. Early English Text Society o.s. 38. London: Oxford UP, 1869.

Schmidt. A.V.C., ed. *The Vision of Piers Plowman: A Complete Edition of the* B-Text. by William Langland. Rutland, VT: Everyman, 1978.

Taylor, Sean. "The F Scribe and the R Manuscript of Piers Plowman B." *English Studies: A Journal of English Language and Literature* 77(1996): 530-48.

The Narrative of Selection in Jean Froissart's Collected Poems: Omissions and Additions in BN MSS fr. 830 and 831

KRISTEN M. FIGG

In his study entitled *Pseudo-Autobiography in the Fourteenth Century*, Laurence de Looze explores a group of writers whose works all seem to encourage what he calls "contrasting, even contradictory readings," responses to text which force the audience to shift between what is perceived as "'true,' 'historical,'" or "'autobiographical'" and what is clearly fictional—that is, constructed in the context of literary convention and intended to be recognized as artistically invented.[1] In this group of writers, de Looze includes Juan Ruiz, Guillaume de Machaut, Geoffrey Chaucer, and Jean Froissart, and he posits theoretical connections between the development of the pseudo-autobiographical text and the growing identification of poetry with the personality of the author. If, as he says, the *Roman de la Rose* is the earliest and most influential example of the "first-person expression of the poet's situation," these later works tended to increase self-referentiality by "revers[ing] the equation" of lover and poet, making the narrator "a poet first and a lover second,"[2] often, as in both Chaucer and Froissart, with an ironic view to the success of the lover in comparison to the expertise and skill of the writer. Likewise, the poet's relationship with his patron encouraged an apparent historical referentiality according to which, in the case of Machaut's *Jugement dou Roi de Behaigne*, Froissart's *Dit dou bleu chevalier*, and Chaucer's *The Book of the Duchess*, the poet becomes an advisor in a semi-real world, offering a kind of consolation that may or may not overlap with events familiar to the reader.

That this tendency towards constructing autobiography is also related to changes in book production has been well documented, for, as Sylvia Huot has shown, during the late thirteenth and the early fourteenth century, not only does the single-author codex come to be organized in a way that emphasizes the identity of the poet as a producer of books, but the ordering of texts often maps, roughly, the chronology of the author's poetic career.[3] The development of this relationship between the organization of the manuscript and the career of the author is significant for a number of reasons, but it is particularly worthy of close examination in the manuscripts of Jean Froissart because of a unique combination of biographical and codicological factors. First, Froissart's identity is complicated by issues of allegiance. He began his writing career in the 1360s in England as secretary to Queen Philippa, and then, after her death in 1369, returned to his native Hainaut and to France under the patronage of a sequence of continental, pro-French patrons. Second, his poetry survives in only two manuscripts, each apparently produced under his own supervision within a period of about one year yet clearly intended for two different audiences, with variations in dialect and in content as well. What these manuscripts would seem to suggest is that Froissart, known in his *Chroniques* for having constructed several different versions of history,[4] was also constructing the narrative of his poetic self along two different lines to comply with the expectations or tastes of distinctly different sets of readers.

The two manuscripts in question are BN fr. 830, completed in 1393 and given the siglum B, and BN fr., completed in 1394 and designated A. The A manuscript has been accepted as the preferred copy text for modern editions both because it is the last completed in the lifetime of the author and because its Picard dialect is closer to Froissart's own language.[5] However, its 201 vellum leaves do not include a number of poems that appear in the B manuscript, which, at 220 leaves, is almost 10 percent longer. With its *francien* dialect, the B manuscript seems to have been destined for use in a French court, while the A manuscript, with its Picard dialect and apparently more selective content, was almost certainly destined for England, where it is known to have been by the beginning of the fifteenth century.

Given the fact that Froissart documents in his *Chroniques* the preparation of a volume of poetry to be presented to Richard II in England in July 1395, it has generally been assumed that MS A is either the very manuscript presented to Richard, or a copy of it.[6] In describing his trip, Froissart explains his plan for the book with a good deal of emphasis on his own role as author and compiler: "And I had, through foresight, caused to be copied, engrossed and illuminated and gathered together all the writing on love and morality which I had composed over thirty-four years by the grace of God and of Love." A few lines later he says, "I had with me this very fine book, nicely decorated, bound in velvet with studs and clasps of silver gilt, which I meant to present to the King by way of introducing myself."[7] The extant manuscript, which is perhaps a bit plainer in its illumination than one might expect from the author's words, has no cover by which to identify it, but it matches Froissart's description insofar as it is clearly a completed book, with a table of contents and continuous text, rather than a collection of gatherings that could have been rearranged before binding. Moreover, there is no evidence that Froissart had with him a second book intended for presentation to another English patron, as Kervyn de Lettenhove conjectured in the nineteenth century,[8] and one can hardly argue that the miniature showing the author reading rather than presenting his book is inappropriate, since this illustration fits the idea of "introducing" the author, foregrounding his role rather than that of a recipient for whom the book had been prepared purely on speculation, with no assurance of how—or even whether—it would be received. In any case, the extant MS's flyleaf identifies it only as the property of Richard Beauchamp, Duke of Warwick, who was thirteen years old at the time of Froissart's visit but inherited his dukedom in 1401 and died in 1439.[9] The B MS, by contrast, has no early history and is not recorded in a catalogue until 1622.[10]

In spite of the uncertainty about ownership, the dating of the manuscripts presents no problem, since each has a dated *explicit* in the hand of the scribe. In MS 831, for example, the text indicates that the book was completed on precisely May 12, 1394:

> Explicit dittiers et traitiers amoureus et de moralité fais, dittés et ordonnés par discret et venerable homme sire Jehan Froissart, priestre, a che tamps tresorier et chanonne de Cymai et cloÿ che dit livre en l'an de grasce Nostre Signeur mil .ccc. iiijxx et .xiiij., le .xije jour dou mois de may. (MS 831, f. 200v)

These closing rubrics (that is, those in both MS 830 and 831) match, in wording and emphasis, the opening passages detailing not only the role of the author in creating and selecting the contents of the book, but also his origins as a native of Valenciennes, his current position as canon and treasurer of the cathedral of Chimay, and his desire to write for the pleasure of his patrons:

> Vous devés sçavoir que dedens ce livre sont contenu pluisour dittié et traitié amourous et de moralité, les quels sire Jehans Froissars, prestres, en ce temps tresoriers et canonnes de Cymai, et de nation de la conté de Haynnau et de la ville de Valenchienes, a fais, dittés et ordonnés à l'aÿde de Dieu et d'Amours, et a le contemplation et plaisance de pluisours haus et nobles signours et de pluisours nobles et vaillans dames. Et les commencha a faire sus l'an de grasce Nostre Signour mil .ccc. lxij. et les cloÿ sus l'an de grasce mil trois cens quatre vins et quatorze; et vous ensagnera

ceste table comment il sont escript ou dit livre par ordenance. (MS 831, f. 1)

In this passage, Froissart invites readers to think of his life consciously as a narrative by providing a span of dates for his career—that he began writing in 1362 and has continued for thirty-three years up to the present time—and he simultaneously constructs himself in a literary manner by giving credit both to God and to Love, who, in the allegorical style of the *Roman de la Rose*, is to become a character in the first verse narrative that follows.

If one were to begin to build the pseudo-autobiographical story of Froissart's life based on an initial examination of these manuscripts, it is their physical similarity that would speak first. Although there are some differences, most notably the single miniature in A and the heavy guidelines in B (see Figs. 1 and 2), they are both designed with two columns of 32 lines each, with the first letter of each line set apart and highlighted in yellow, titles and *explicits* in red, the initial letter of each work in blue or pink on gold, and initial capitals of subdivisions in blue or mauve. In each case a bar border with ivy vines frames the page, though the style of 831 is more graceful. In his edition of 1871, Scheler speculated that the handwriting and ornamentation are similar enough to have come from the same workshop,[11] though the differences in spelling and content, along with the sharing of certain common errors, as noted by Anthime Fourrier, suggest that the two books would have to have been copied from a single exemplum rather than one from the other.[12] Whether they are from a single workshop or not, however, is less important than the fact that they were made to look so similar to each other, in a conservative hand that is reminiscent of the middle of the fourteenth century rather than the end—and, indeed, almost identical in style to manuscripts of the works of Guillaume de Machaut, in whose literary footsteps Froissart was following. No matter which audience Froissart was writing for, he apparently wanted his work and life to be seen, first of all, as a continuation of the courtly tradition, and so the manuscripts were written in *textura* and decorated in a slightly old-fashioned way.

These features of the book's appearance are consistent with Sylvia Huot's analysis of the "poetics" of Froissart as a writer and compiler of lyric poetry. Huot identifies in Froissart's manuscripts the continuation of several patterns initiated by Machaut, including not only the theme of poetic identity itself but also a more specific progression of developmental stages.[13] In Froissart's case, the author begins in *Le Paradis d'Amour* as the youthful performer who is proving his mastery of his craft and, by way of professional reference, making numerous allusions to the works of Machaut; then, in midcareer, with *La Prison amoureuse*, he redefines himself as the author/ compiler, creating an explicit definition of the relationship between poet and patron as well as writer and reader; later, in the *Joli Buisson de Jonece*, he appears as the seasoned poet who manipulates traditions with a high degree of self-reflexivity; and finally, in the *Plaidoirie de la rose et de la violette*, he appears as the retrospective author who is no longer lyric poet or lover, but chronicler of his own lyrical production. As Huot describes it, "the story that we read is the story of the book, and its very existence guarantees that the story is, at least at some level, true."[14] Read this way, the anthology has a strong biographical continuity, though Huot concedes that the depiction of Froissart's career is fragmentary, a quality revealed even within the rubrics of the poems, where Froissart reminds his readers that he, as a man, has had many other experiences not recorded there.

Huot does not deal with the variations between the two manuscripts except to note that 831 omits those pieces that might be politically offensive to an English audience.[15] But the image of Froissart as a writer is, in fact, quite different in the two manuscripts, and the very biographical experiences Huot refers to are more frequently developed in the contents of the *francien* manuscript than in the one prepared for the English court, suggesting that, in his own mind, Froissart's shaping of a literary pseudo-autobiography has taken on dimensions that go beyond creating the story of the book to include a conscious manipulation of the story of the author himself. At this level Froissart, unlike Machaut,[16] has a number of complicating factors to consider. For one thing, by the 1390s he had a dual public identity as poet and historian, with a major shift towards the latter in mid-career. Furthermore, there is the question of nationality. If, for Richard's grandmother, Froissart was a trusted compatriot from her native Hainaut, by the 1390s he was identifiable mostly by his French language, for, as he explains in his chronicles, the English are apt to refer to all speakers of "northern French as Frenchmen, whatever country or nation they belong to."[17] Although Froissart had been present at Richard's birth in Bordeaux, he had been away from England for twenty-eight years, and so his use of his book by way of "introduction" is important. Who is Jean Froissart? Knowing Richard's predilection for courtly entertainment and tastes, it would seem that Froissart has designed his book not only to omit possibly offensive references to pro-French themes, but also to present himself noncontroversially as pure poet, rather than the half-poet, half-participant-in-history that he had really become.

The mixed nature of the longer manuscript can be seen by a quick glance through the combination of genres and subject matter that it contains (see Fig. 3). In both cases, the manuscripts begin with the early dream narrative, the *Paradis d'Amour*, followed by the *Temple d'Honneur*, a kind of mirror for princes composed for the marriage of Humphrey X of Bohun,[18] and the *Joli Mois de May*, a highly conventional lyric piece. Indeed, both manuscripts contain all the long dream narratives with intercalated lyrics, as well as collections of the fixed-form lyrics arranged by genre (a pattern used by Machaut in his manuscripts as well) and the final *Plaidoirie*, which, in its personification of conventional poetic flowers, comments directly on the literary symbolism that Froissart relied upon throughout his lyric career. Certainly, the general lines of his development as a self-conscious poet are visible in both manuscripts, and, in one of his most pronounced pseudo-autobiographical moments, he corroborates the authenticity of the order of major works by allowing the narrator of the *Joli Buisson* to review the chronology of writings leading up to the moment in November 1373 when the events of that poem are said to take place:

> Voirs est qun livret fis jadis
> Quon dist lamoureus paradis
> Et ossi celi del orloge
> Ou grant part del art damours loge
> Apries lespinete amoureuse
> Qui nest pas al oyr ireuse
> Et puis lamoureuse prison
> Quen pluiseurs places bien prise on
> Rondiaus balades virelais
> Grant fuison de dis et de lais (443-52)

> It is true that long ago I wrote a book
> That is called *Paradis amoureux*
> And also the one about the *Orloge*,
> Where there is a great deal about the art of love;
> And after that, the *Espinette amoureuse*,
> Which is not unpleasant to hear;
> And then the *Prison amoureuse*,
> Which is well regarded in quite a few places,
> Rondeaux, ballades, virelays,
> A great collection of dits and lays. . . [19]

But what is not clear from the list in the *Joli Buisson*, where the phrase "grant fuison de dis" groups together all of the shorter independent pieces, is the fact that his complete repertoire of poetry, as represented in the longer MS B, contains not only the kinds of verse with words like "honneur," "amoureus," "May," "Margherite," and "Rose" in the title, but also a debate between a horse and a greyhound (*Le Debat dou cheval et dou levrier*) and a begging poem with a talking coin (*Le Dit dou florin*). While the author who is the poet-narrator of the *Joli Buisson* and the compiler of MS A has consistently maintained his persona as a literary disciple of the god of Love, the author and compiler of MS B is a man who has also analyzed the mechanical workings of an amazing new clock in Paris,[20] toured Scotland with Edward Despenser,[21] and had his purse stolen in Avignon, where he was trying to help negotiate a noble marriage and work out the details of a new benefice with the pope.[22] The contrast in the nature of the man being "introduced" is quite striking.

This is not to say that the standard argument that Froissart created a politically correct manuscript for his English audience has no validity. If one wishes to accept the simple explanation that Froissart omitted only those pieces which could be offensive to Richard, one could look with some assurance at the differences in the collections of *pastourelles*, where the six that appear exclusively in MS B are mainly occasional poems on historical subjects such as the striking of a new French coin or the celebration of a noble marriage, topics that certainly would feel out of place to an English audience.[23] Extending the same line of thinking to the longer pieces, one might argue that the setting in Scotland for the *Debat dou cheval et dou levrier* might be offensive to Richard because he had suffered a great military loss to the Scottish (now allied with the French) in 1388, or that he would not be pleased by Froissart's reliance on French patrons in the *Dit dou florin*.[24] Whether Richard might have known of the French king's special interest in the building of the Parisian clock used metaphorically as the subject of the *Orloge amoureux* is difficult to say, but one aspect of Froissart's strategy in "introducing" himself was certainly to minimize those poetic settings where he might seem to be stepping out of his role as courtly author and reminding his readers of his existence in a physically realistic, place-bound, and politicized world.

Seen in this light, there is some ambiguity to the inclusion of the one poem that reverses the political allegiance, appearing exclusively in the English manuscript and being clearly intended for the ears and eyes of the English audience. In Ballade 31 Froissart celebrates the Trojan origins of Albion, emphasizing his theme with a refrain echoing Diana's promise from the *Roman de Brut*:

> Trop ne se poet Calcas esmervillier
> De ce qu'il voit la generation
> Au roy Bructus ensi fructefiier
> Et raemplir les sieges d'Albion
> De la ligne au fort roi Pharamon.... (1-5)[25]

One could argue that this flattering piece might have been composed while Froissart was still in the English court and that it is intended to fulfill the same role as the often sycophantic *pastourelles* celebrating marriages and royal entrances in MS 830. However, its placement in the collected *ballades* as number 31 out of forty is not, like the placement of the *pastourelles*, strictly chronological, following, as it does, all the ballades that were recopied from the *Paradis*, the *Espinette*, the *Prison*, and the *Joli Buisson*. Indeed, what is interesting about its placement is that it falls within a final grouping of independent *bal-*

lades (that is, poems that were not intercalated into any narrative) which rely on mythological themes. Within this grouping one finds not only the Calcas, Brutus, and Diana of Ballade 31, but also Helen and Medea in 32, the god of sleep, Morpheus, in 33, Priam and Polixena in 35, Jason and Medea in 36, and Achilles, Leander, and Hero in 39. Thus, while Froissart might well have omitted such a poem to avoid offending a French audience (in the same way that he apparently excised the title of the lay that appears as the *Lay de la mort la royne dengleterre* on folio 41a), its placement into the English MS may be more neutral—that is, more purely thematic—than it appears. In any case, the only other poems added to the English MS are four *rondeaux* on standard topics like the sufferings of love or the power of a pair of gray eyes, and a *pastourelle* honoring the feast of St. John the Baptist.[26] The explanation that seems most likely here is not just that Froissart wanted the English court to forget that he had worked for French patrons, but that he wanted to reinforce, through the addition of conventional, timeless lyrics, his reputation as a dignified and courtly author.

The element of time versus timelessness in the two manuscripts is especially intriguing because one can probably assume that the members of the audience for whom Froissart prepared the *francien* manuscript might have heard him recite publically some of the poems that are included only in 830, at least five of which were written in the 1380s. Certainly members of the French court would have been more familiar than the English with all the aspects of Froissart's career and would have known him as the sort of "roving reporter" that he had become in his efforts to gather material for the *Chroniques*. This style of life, which included being sought out by every knight who wished to have his name recorded for posterity, is implied in his list of travels in the *Dit dou florin*[27] and may be one of the autobiographical realities that Froissart chose to suppress in presenting himself to his English audience.

But he does not suppress every historical reference. If one looks not only at what differs in the two MSS but also at what they have in common, the final element that Froissart seems to have chosen to retain in his persona constructed for the English audience is his desire to glorify and defend chivalry. It would perhaps have been too much to expect that the poet who invented the historical *pastourelle* would have left in only stories that were really about shepherds, and so we find in both manuscripts those poems that relate, supposedly from a shepherd's point of view, stories of noble behavior in the face of captivity—King John's voluntary return to London and Wenceslas of Brabant's release from the Castle of Niedeck—and two poems in honor of the highly regarded Gaston de Foix, the self-proclaimed Gaston Fébus, whose neutralist politics and magnificent court dominated the cultural life of the southwest of France.[28] In the third of these poems, for example, the gift of four greyhounds, two of whom are named Tristan and Hector, draws special attention to the noble pursuit of hunting, and the shepherds are above all impressed by the character of the man in question, who has "sens et povoir / Et largece continuee" (lines 63-64). Likewise, in the poem on Wenceslas, the shepherds comment that they must now rejoice because they will be able to watch over their sheep without further care, emphasizing the duke's role as protector and his bravery in defending their homeland.[29] If the compiler of MS B is a man of the world who both knew personally and received payment from Wenceslas and Gaston, the compiler of A was a man of courtly judgment who appreciated nobility of character, both in the life of love and in the field of action. The two narratives of the poet's life are not contradictory, but the emphasis is certainly different.

Indeed, the self-constructed authorial personae implied by these two manuscripts mirror the ambiguities of any autobiographical enterprise, where the process of selection—of image, of incident, of response—necessarily distorts and slants any attempt to tell "the whole truth." What is remarkable in this case is that by having two versions of Froissart's authorial narrative, we have been given not only a set of strong clues to his sense of audience and poetic unity, but also additional tools for understanding the way he envisioned his own individual texts. One might, for example, reconsider a poem that constitutes one of the remaining mysteries of the Froissart corpus, the *Dit dou bleu chevalier*, a poem so like Chaucer's *The Book of the Duchess* that it seems certain one is modeled upon the other. While it is beyond the scope of the present paper to make a case for interpreting this poem, it is worth noting that its appearance in only the longer *francien* manuscript may provide some clues to its dating and to the real-life identity—if there is one—of the unnamed blue knight who is suffering lovesickness for his lady during a period of political captivity. If, as early scholars believed, the poem is correctly placed in chronological order and the *bleu chevalier* was among the hostages in England in the early 1360s,[30] was his identity so recognizable that the poem could appear only in a manuscript that acknowledged the author's political engagement? Or if, as James Wimsatt has contended, the chevalier is Wenceslas and the poem is Froissart's reworking of Chaucer,[31] might Froissart, in developing his myth of himself as the courtly successor to Machaut, have been hesitant to include a poem that would show indebtedness to his younger English contemporary? Most recently, Rupert Pickens has discounted critics' preoccupation with historical referentiality, claiming that the imprisonment of princes was merely a metaphor for a condition of the heart, providing the context for an exploration of the myth of consolation and the workings of literature.[32] And yet, if this is so, it seems remiss not at least to wonder about its absence from a manuscript so carefully shaped to present its author as a man who has spent a career self-consciously exploring the range and subtext of the courtly lyrico-narrative poem.

Such considerations must, of course, remain speculative until further facts regarding intended readership or circumstances of composition emerge, but what seems certain is that these two manuscripts offer a unique testimony to the role of a late-medieval author in analyzing his audience, selecting his texts, and shaping an image of himself as a writer in a politically and culturally complex situation. Combining the skills of poet and historian, Froissart reflects his awareness of the subtle nuances of both genre and perceived reality, leaving us with what are most certainly two very different books and two substantially different stories.

Kent State University—Salem

NOTES

1. Laurence de Looze, *Pseudo-Autobiography in the Fourteenth Century: Juan Ruiz, Guillaume de Machaut, Jean Froissart, and Geoffrey Chaucer* (Gainesville: University Press of Florida, 1997), ix-xi, 2.

2. Ibid. 6-7.

3. Sylvia Huot, *From Song to Book: The Poetics of Writing in Old French Lyric and Lyrical Narrative Poetry* (Ithaca: Cornell University Press, 1987), esp. 39-45 and 232-236.

4. For an example of the subtlety of variation in Froissart's recensions of his historical accounts, see George T. Diller, "Froissart: Patron and Texts" in J. J. N. Palmer, *Froissart: Historian* (Woodbridge, Suffolk: Boydell, 1981), 145-160.

5. For detailed discussions of the manuscripts and of editorial issues, see the introductions in Anthime Fourrier, ed., *L'Espinette amoureuse* (Paris: Klincksieck, 1972) and Peter Dembowski, ed., *Le Paradis d'Amour; L'Orloge amoureus* (Geneva: Droz, 1986).

6. See, for example, the discussion in Auguste Scheler, *Oeuvres de Froissart—Poésies* (Brussels: Devaux, 1871), x-xvi, and Huot, 241.

7. This translation and those that follow are my own unless noted otherwise. The original French reads as follows: "J'avoie de pourvéance fait escripre, grosser et enluminer et recoeillir tous les traités amoureux et de moralité que au terme de trente quatre ans je avoie par la grasce de Dieu et d'Amour fais et compilés...." (C. Buchon, ed., *Chroniques* [Paris: A. Desrez, 1835], 3: 198). In the Penguin Classics edition of the *Chronicles* (London and New York, 1978) , Geoffrey Brereton translates *de pourvéance* as "in preparation for my trip" (p. 403), making the connection between the selection of texts and the intended recipient seem less ambiguous than does the phrasing of the original French. But in any case we know that there were probably at least three such manuscripts (see note 12), so Froissart may be playfully conflating his "foresight" in having made this type of compilation with his "preparation" for the presentation to Richard.

8. Joseph Kervyn de Lettenhove, ed., Œuvres de Froissart (Brussels: Devaux, 1867-1877) 1: 387ff. As the example quoted above suggests, Froissart was generally eager to record his close connections with important people, so it seems likely that he would have mentioned any other person for whom he went to the trouble of preparing a book on this occasion, especially since he makes a point, in his account of the trip, of how few of his old friends are still to be found in England. Richard Beauchamp's father, who was Duke of Warwick at the time of Froissart's visit, is never mentioned by Froissart as a personal acquaintance and was, in fact, in political disfavor by the mid-1390s, so he was almost certainly not the intended recipient of the book, as Kervyn de Lettenhove erroneously surmised. Richard Beauchamp himself, on the other hand, was a godson of King Richard as well as being a favorite of Henry IV, who knighted the young man as part of his coronation celebration; thus one might imagine the book coming to Beauchamp either directly from King Richard or as a later gift from the new king.

9. The flyleaf reads as follows: "Ce livre est a Richart le gentil fauls conte de Warrewych," followed by a series of what appear to be pen trials commenting on contemporary acquaintances, written in a different hand. The wording of the phrase "le gentil fauls conte" has not been commented upon by previous scholars, but the term "fauls" would seem here to be a form of fau / feu, defined by Greimas in the Dictionnaire de l'ancien français as "soumis au destin," derived from the Latin fatum. If this reading is correct, it could be that Richard was identifying himself as being "destined" to become the duke—that is, not yet elevated to the position—which would place his ownership of the book before 1401. With its emphasis on love, the book would indeed have made a suitable and fairly impressive (though not overly luxurious) gift for a young man who was fluent in French and interested in the pursuit of nobility. This dating of his ownership would confirm that the book was in fact given to him in England rather than acquired on his later travels. In any case, the location of MS A is unknown between the time of its ownership by Richard Beauchamp and 1544, when it figures in the inventory of the royal library at Blois at the time of its transfer to Fontainebleau (see Dembowski, 4).

10. MS B is listed in the catalog of the Bibliothèque royale de Paris prepared by Nicolas Rigault in 1622 (see Dembowski, 5).

11. Scheler, x.

12. For examples of errors that the two MSS have in common, see Anthime Fourrier, ed., La Prison amoureuse (Paris: Klincksieck, 1974), where he cites such mistakes as the substitution of Priamus for Piramus in a reference to the story of Piramus and Thisbe. Fourrier concludes that the two manuscripts were copied from the same exemplar "que rien n'empêche d'être l'original rédigé par l'auteur" (p. 7).

13 Huot, 302-327.

14. Huot, 326.

15. See Huot, 241, where she refers to "evidence of political editing." Huot describes the texts omitted from MS 831 as being "those expressing pro-French sentiment, flat-

tering the accomplishments of the French court or alluding to Froissart's relations with Richard II's political adversaries," a characterization which is correct in its broad outlines but does not account for all of the differences.

16. For a recent discussion of Machaut's involvement in the compilation and oversight of his manuscripts, see William W. Kibler and James I. Wimsatt, "Machaut's Texts and the Question of His Personal Supervision," *Studies in the Literary Imagination* 20 (1987): 41-53. In this study, the authors agree with the widely accepted idea, originated by Ernest Hoepffner in his three-volume *Oeuvres de Machaut* (Paris: Firmin-Didot, 1908-1921), that Machaut was actively involved in the selection, style of presentation, and ordering of materials for manuscripts, but they use evidence of the deterioration of certain texts to argue that he did not engage in authorial revision or other close supervision of the copying. Among the studies that claim for Machaut a new concept of poetic identity are Sarah Jane Manley Williams, "Machaut's Self-Awareness as Author and Producer" and Kevin Brownlee, "The Poetic Œuvre of Guillaume de Machaut: The Identity of Discourse and the Discourse of Identity," both in Madeleine Pelner Cosman and Bruce Chandler, eds., *Machaut's World: Science and Art in the Fourteenth Century*, Annals of the New York Academy of Sciences 314 (New York: New York Academy of Sciences, 1978), 189-197 and 219-233.

17. Brereton, trans., 405.

18. For a discussion of the probable dating and occasion of this poem, see the Introduction by Anthime Fourrier, ed., *Dits et Debats* (Geneva: Droz, 1979) and Peter Dembowski, "Li Orloge amoureus de Froissart," L'*Esprit Créateur* 18 (1978): 19-31.

19. This text and translation, as well as others from the narrative dits, are quoted from Kristen M. Figg, ed. and trans., *Jean Froissart: An Anthology of Narrative and Lyric Poetry* (New York and London: Routledge, 2001). It is worth noting, in this passage, that Froissart makes a point of saying that the *Orloge* contains "a great deal about the art of love," as if its subject needs defending. As it turns out, this is one of the works that he chooses not to include in MS A.

20. The *Orloge amoureus*, while allegorical in mode, describes the workings of a real clock, the technologically innovative timepiece built by the German master Heinrich von Wieck (Henri de Vic) for the Palace of Justice in Paris between 1362 and 1370. Froissart's description of this clock is so detailed and accurate that it became the subject of several horological studies. For more on this subject, see Dembowski's edition, as well as John Drummond Robertson, *The Evolution of Clockwork* (London: Cassell, 1931), 52-66; and Paul Zumthor, "Un traité français d'horlogerie du XIVe s.," *Zeitschrift für romanische Philologie* 73 (1957), 274-287.

21. Despenser himself is not mentioned in *Le Debat dou cheval et dou levrier*, but the setting of the poem is clearly Froissart's tour of Scotland undertaken in the company of Despenser under the sponsorship of Queen Philippa in 1365. The poem begins: *Froissars descoce revenoit /Sus un cheval qui gris estoit* (1-2).

22. In the Dit *dou florin*, the narrator of the poem says, "I am now here / In Avignon, in bad straits" (180-181), and the coin replies "You are in good stead / To reap advantage and great wealth: / Aren't you about to get a benefice?" (183-185):

> Et li di je sui ores ci
> En avignon en dure masse
> Pour quoi monseignour sauf vo grasce
> Dist le florin vous estes bien
> Pour avoir pourfit et grant bien
> Ne tendes vous a benefisces (180-185)

Such references to autobiographical incidents are frequent in this poem, where Froissart describes in great detail his three-month visit to the court of Gaston de Foix, including his commission to read aloud each night to his host seven pages of his Arthurian verse romance *Meliador*. The marriage he was helping to negotiate was that of the almost fifty-year-old Jean, Duc de Berry, to the twelve-year-old Jeanne de Boulogne, an event later celebrated in *Pastourelle* 15.

23. The lyrics unique to MS B all fall within the category of the historical *pastourelle*. A brief overview of their subjects reveals their special suitability for a pro-French audience: *Pastourelle* 3 (on the striking of the gold florin by Charles V in 1364), with the refrain *Qui vaudront vint saus de tournois*; *Pastourelle* 5 (on the wines of the Poitou and of Gascony), with the refrain *De Poitevin et de Gascongne*; *Pastourelle* 12 (on the victory of Charles VI at the Battle of Roosebeke, 1382), with the refrain *L'orgoeil de Bruges et de Gand*; *Pastourelle* 14 (on the marriage of the son of Guy de Blois to the daughter of Jean de Berry, 1386), with the refrain *La pastourelle de Berri / Avec le pastourel de Blois*; *Pastourelle* 15 (on the marriage of Jean, Duc de Berry, to Jeanne de Boulogne, 1389), with the refrain *Pour le pastourel de Berri / Et la pastoure de Boulongne*; *Pastourelle* 16 (on the entrance into Paris of Isabella of Bavaria, 1389), with the refrain *Comment la royne de France / Est premiers entree en Paris*. All lyrics are quoted from Rob Roy McGregor, ed., *The Lyric Poems of Jehan Froissart: A Critical Edition*, North Carolina Studies in the Romance Languages and Literatures 143 (Chapel Hill: University of North Carolina Press, 1975).

24. The patrons that the florin lists to Froissart as being the type who "would hardly fail you for ten francs" include "the good lord de la Rivière," "the good count of Sancerre," "the dauphin / Of Auvergne," and "Jean the viscount of Acy" (lines 427-47).

25. "Calcas could not stop marveling / When he foresaw the lineage of King Brutus / Thus come to fruition / And fill the high seats of Albion / Through the line of the strong king Pharamon...."

26. The refrains of the rondeaux are as follows: *Jugiés de moi, amant qui congnissiés/ Que c'est d'amours et des mauls qu'il y a...*(104); *Ou me trairai pour aligance avoir / De la dolour qu'amours me font porter?* (105); *Joie me fuit, Esperance m'esquieue, / Desirs m'assaut et Plaisance m'enflame...*(106); *Vous me tenés, ma dame, en vo prison, / Vostre vair oel m'i ont emprison-*

né...(107). The pastourelle on St. John the Baptist is number 18 of 20 and, unlike most of the *pastourelles*, mentions no specific setting.

27. In the *Dit dou florin*, the narrator mentions having traveled to England, Scotland, Wales, and Rome, as well as having "Looked over the realms of France/ From one end to the other" (219-230).

28. The subjects of these historical *pastourelles* are as follows: *Pastourelle* 2 (on King John's return to London to apologize for the Duke of Anjou's departure, 1364), with the refrain *Chils qui porte les fleurs de lis*; *Pastourelle* 6 (to celebrate the return of Wenceslas of Luxembourg and Brabant from captivity, 1372), with the refrain *De Lussembourch et de Braibant*; *Pastourelle* 8 (in honor of Froissart's visit to Gaston de Foix, 1388), with the refrain *Li biaus, li bons et li jentis*; *Pastourelle* 9 (also in honor of Gaston de Foix, 1388), with the refrain *Les armes de Berne et de Fois*. One might expect that the subject of John the Good's heroic return, with its refrain focusing on the *fleur de lis*, might have been too "French" for an English audience, especially since, as Anne D. Hedeman points out, the incident was so important to the royal family that it was one of only two events meriting a two-column miniature in Charles V's *Grandes Chroniques de France*. (See Anne D. Hedeman, *The Royal Image: Illustrations of the* Grandes Chroniques de France, 1274-1422 [Berkeley: University of California Press, 1991], 109-110). But the *pastourelle* in question was clearly one that Froissart wrote while he was in England, and the noble gesture of a king who would voluntarily give himself up to captivity to compensate for his son's breach of honor was exactly the kind of chivalry that, in Froissart's view, transcended considerations of nationality.

29. The passage in question is near the end of *Pastourelle* 6:

> Dont bien resjoïr nous devons
> Car nos brebis et nos moutons.
> Sans avoir doubte ne soussi,
> Garderons; car, pour voir di,
> De sanc plus noble ne plus grant
> Onques mais dou pays n'issi
> De Lussembourch et de Braibant. (54-60)

30. For a discussion of this point of view, see Normand Cartier, "*Le Bleu Chevalier* de Froissart et *Le Livre de la Duchesse* de Chaucer," *Romania* 88 (1967): 232-252.

31. James I. Wimsatt, "The *Dit dou Bleu Chevalier*: Froissart's Imitation of Chaucer," *Mediaeval Studies* 34 (1972): 388-400.

32. Rupert T. Pickens, "History and Narration in Froissart's *Dits*: The Case of the *Bleu chevalier*" in *Froissart Across the Genres*, ed. Donald Maddox and Sara Sturm-Maddox (Gainesville: University Press of Florida, 1998), 119-152.

WORKS CITED

PRIMARY SOURCES

Froissart, Jean. *Chroniques*. Edited by C. Buchon. Paris: A. Desrez, 1835.

——. *Froissart: Chronicles*. Translated and edited by Geoffrey Brereton. London and New York: Penguin, 1978.

——. *Jean Froissart: An Anthology of Narrative and Lyric Poetry*. Edited and translated by Kristen M. Figg, with R. Barton Palmer. London and New York: Routledge, 2001.

——. *The Lyric Poems of Jehan Froissart: A Critical Edition*. Edited by Rob Roy McGregor, Jr. North Carolina Studies in the Romance Languages and Literatures, 143. Chapel Hill: University of North Carolina Press, 1975.

SECONDARY SOURCES

Brownlee, Kevin. "The Poetic Œuvre of Guillaume de Machaut: The Identity of Discourse and the Discourse of Identity." In *Machaut's World: Science and Art in the Fourteenth Century*, 219-233. Edited by Madeleine P. Cosman and Bruce Chandler. Annals of the New York Academy of Sciences 314. New York: New York Academy of Sciences, 1978.

Cartier, Normand. "*Le Bleu Chevalier* de Froissart et *Le Livre de la Duchesse* de Chaucer." *Romania* 88 (1967): 232-252.

de Looze, Laurence. *Pseudo-Autobiography in the Fourteenth Century: Juan Ruiz, Guillaume de Machaut, Jean Froissart, and Geoffrey Chaucer*. Gainesville: University Press of Florida, 1997.

Dembowski, Peter F. "*Li Orloge amoureus* de Froissart." *L'Esprit Créateur* 18 (1978): 19-31.

——. ed. *Le Paradis d'Amour; L'Orloge amoureus*. Geneva: Droz, 1986.

Diller, George T. "Froissart: Patron and Texts." In *Froissart: Historian*, 145-160. Edited by J. J. N. Palmer. Woodbridge, Suffolk: Boydell, 1981.

Fourrier, Anthime, ed. *Dits et Debats*. Geneva: Droz, 1979.

——. *L'Espinette amoureuse*. 2nd ed. Paris: Klincksieck, 1972.

——. *La prison amoureuse*. Paris: Klincksieck, 1974.

Greimas, Algirdas Julien. *Dictionnaire de l'ancien français: Le Moyen Âge*. Paris: Larousse, 1992.

Hedeman, Anne D. *The Royal Image: Illustrations of the* Grandes Chroniques de France, 1274-1422. Berkeley: University of California Press, 1991.

Hoepffner, Ernest, ed. *Oeuvres de Machaut*. Paris: Firmin-Didot, 1908-1921.

Huot, Sylvia. *From Song to Book: The Poetics of Writing in Old French Lyric and Lyrical Narrative Poetry*. Ithaca: Cornell University Press, 1987.

Kervyn de Lettenhove, J. M. B. C., ed. *Œuvres de Froissart: Publiées avec les variantes des divers manuscrits-Chroniques*. 25 volumes in 26. Brussels: Devaux, 1867-1877.

Kibler, William W., and James I. Wimsatt. "Machaut's Texts and the Question of His Personal Supervision." *Studies in the Literary Imagination* 20 (1987): 41-53.

Palmer, J. J. N., ed. *Froissart: Historian*. Suffolk: Boydell, 1981.

Pickens, Rupert T. "History and Narration in Froissart's *Dits*: The Case of the *Bleu chevalier*." In *Froissart Across the Genres*, 119-152. Edited by Donald Maddox and Sara Sturm-Maddox. Gainesville: University Press of Florida, 1998.

Robertson, John Drummond. *The Evolution of Clockwork*. London: Cassell, 1931.

Scheler, Auguste, ed. *Oeuvres de Froissart—Poésies*. Brussels: Devaux, 1871.

Williams, Sarah Jane Manley. "Machaut's Self-Awareness as Author and Producer." In *Machaut's World: Science and Art in the Fourteenth Century*, 189-197. Edited by Madeleine P. Cosman and Bruce Chandler. Annals of the New York Academy of Sciences 314. New York: New York Academy of Sciences, 1978.

Wimsatt, James I. "The *Dit dou Bleu Chevalier*: Froissart's Imitation of Chaucer." *Mediaeval Studies* 34 (1972): 388-400.

Zumthor, Paul. "Un traité français d'horlogerie du XIVe s." *Zeitschrift für romanische Philologie* 73 (1957): 274-287.

Figure 1. Title page with Author portrait.
Paris, Bibliothèque nationale MS fr. 831, folio 1v.

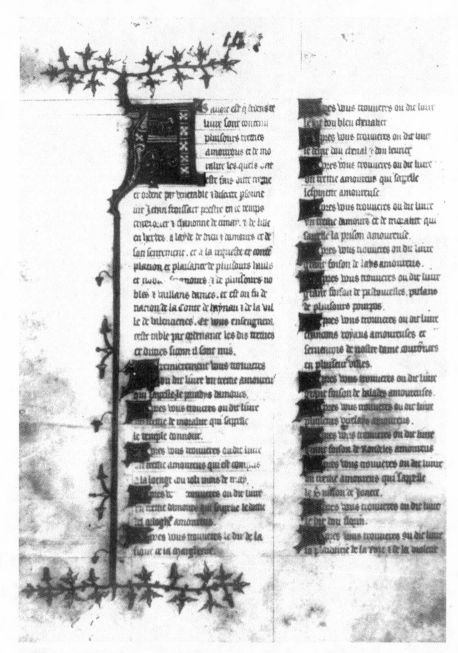

Figure 2. Title page.
Paris, Bibliothèque nationale MS. fr. 830, folio 1v.

MS A **(BN fr. 831,dated May 12, 1394)**	**MS B** **(BN fr. 830, dated 1393)**
1. Le Paradis amourous	Le Paradys d'Amours [c.1361]
2. Le Temple de Honnour	Le Temple d'Onnour [c.1363]
3. Le Joli Mois de May	Le Joli Mois de May
	* L'Orloge amoureus [after 1363]
4. Le Dittie de la Flour de la Margheritte	Le Dit de la Flour de la Margherite [c.1364]
	* Le Dit dou Bleu Chevalier
	* Le Debat dou Cheval et dou Levrier [c. 1365]
5. Lays amourous et de Nostre Dame	[9] L'Espinette amoureuse [c.1369]
6. Pastourielles (+1)	[7] La Prison amoureuse [c. 1372]
7. La Prison amourouse	[5] Lays amoureus
8. Chancons royauls	[6] Pastourelles (+6)
9. L'Espinette amourouse	[8] Chancons royaus
10.Balades (+1)	Balades
11.Virelays	Virelays
12.Rondiauls (+4)	Rondeles
13.Le Joli Buisson de Jonece	Le Joli Buisson de Jonece [1373]
	* Le Dit dou Florin [1389]
14.La Plaidoirie de la Rose et de la Violette	La Plaidoirie de la Roze et de la Violette

Figure 3. Comparison of contents of MSS A and B showing *dits* unique to MS B (*) and numbers of additional lyrics in parentheses

A Book in the Hand:
Some Late Medieval Accounts of
Manuscript Presentations[1]

ERIK INGLIS

In his *Poets and Princepleasers*, Richard Firth Green notes that "Reliable historical accounts of book presentation . . . are not common."[2] Their present rarity is in part due to the fact that they were uncommon in the Middle Ages. But it also results from the fact that the accounts of the ceremony are scattered in a variety of sources—colophons, poems, chronicles and diplomatic letters—and as a result have not attracted much attention. I currently know of seven of these accounts and hope that this article may encourage scholars to uncover others.

Written descriptions of manuscript presentations are interesting for several reasons. They help us understand how readers and viewers physically manipulated their books; they reveal how books could be used to create and/or consolidate political and/or personal relationships; and they complement pictorial depictions of the ritual of book presentation, which have attracted more scholarly attention.

In order to understand what the accounts can offer us, it helps to consider our other major source of information on this ritual: presentation pictures. Presentation pictures depict a person or group presenting a book to another person or group. These pictures are among the best known types of medieval miniature; while the entire tradition has not received the comprehensive study it deserves, it has been discussed in varying levels of detail by a number of scholars.[3] The pictures were produced throughout the Middle Ages, from the sixth to the sixteenth century.[4] According to Evelyn Benesch, whose dissertation is the most thorough study of the French Gothic material, the tradition of painting presentation pictures faded in the early thirteenth century, and was revived in the last quarter of the century.[5] While its new popularity was at first closely associated with the French monarchy, in time presentation pictures spread from royal to aristocratic books, and from the French into the Netherlandish arena. A variety of related factors contributed to their popularity in this time and place, including the rise in lay literacy, the development of vernacular languages, royal patronage of learning and literature, and a desire for lavishly decorated books.[6]

One can get a quick overview of the tradition by examining several representative images from the thirteenth, fourteenth, and fifteenth centuries. According to Benesch, the tradition of painting presentation miniatures was reinaugurated in King Philip III's dedication copy of the *Grandes Chroniques de France* around 1274.[7] The text is an anthology of French chronicles, which were translated from Latin into French by Primat, a monk of St. Denis. The book's presentation picture appears at the end of the book, serving as a pictorial accompaniment to Primat's colophon (Figure 1).[8] The miniature shows Primat kneeling as he offers his book to the enthroned king; the ritual is supervised by the standing Matthew of Vendôme, the abbot of Saint Denis.[9]

The tradition continued into the fourteenth century and is most famously linked to King Charles V. Nicknamed the Wise, Charles ruled France in the turbulent times of the Hundred Years War and looked to learned scholars to support his reign. He founded the first royal library in France and stocked it with a variety of texts on governing.[10] These included classical works in Latin and in French translations commissioned by the King, and several French works written expressly for him. Many of these works open with presentation pictures showing the King receiving the work from its author or translator.[11] Thus in the frontispiece to his copy of *L'information des princes*, Charles receives the translation he commissioned from Jean Golein (Figure 2).[12]

Presentation pictures also appear in books which were given to Charles as gifts. The most famous example is certainly the frontispiece to the *Bible historiale* which Jean de Vaudetar presented to the King in 1372 [new style] (Figure 3).[13] Charles, seated at the left, gestures to the open book in de Vaudetar's hands. An inscription facing the miniature attributes the picture to the *pictor regis* Jean de Bruges, better known as Jean Bondol, and says that it was made at the King's command. As Delaissé was the first to point out, this implies that Charles V commissioned its frontispiece, which occupies an independent bifolium.[14] Benesch makes a convincing argument that the frontispiece was commissioned prior to the completion of the book, so that it was already in place when the volume was presented to Charles.[15] Thus this image—like most presentation pictures—was painted before the event it depicts actually took place; it is an anticipatory commemoration.

Charles V's patronage was widely imitated by rulers and aristocrats of the fifteenth century, which is the highwater mark for presentation pictures. Significantly, these images make the transition from manuscript to printed book. Around 1473 to 1474, William Caxton's translation of Raoul Lefèvre's *The Recuyell of the Historyes of Troye* was printed in Bruges.[16] The book's frontispiece shows Caxton kneeling before Margaret of York, the English-born Duchess of Burgundy, who receives the book from his hands (Figure 4).[17]

The four images are variations on a theme. Some elements vary from one to the next. The book's recipient can appear at the left, the center or the right of the miniature, and receive the book from right or left. The recipient may be alone or accompanied by one or more attendants, and the same is true of the book's presenter. Philip and Charles are seated, while Margaret of York stands. The settings also vary; the canopy above Charles V suggests a formal setting, while Margaret receives her book in a less formal room bustling with activity.

In addition to these variations, there are also some constant elements. Most obvious are the book, its donor and its recipient, the three players required by the ritual. The donor's pose is also strikingly consistent—each one kneels before the recipient. Finally, there is the location of the book, which is always in contact with the donor's hands, though occasionally held by both donor and receiver. Thus, for all the variety in casting and staging, in the end all these miniatures depict the same narrative instant: the moment the book is transferred from the donor's possession to the recipient's.

Given this temporal concentration, it is useful to turn to written reports of the ritual, since most offer a sequential narrative of several events instead of concentrating on a single if crucial moment. Reading these accounts, we gain a better understanding of both the ritual of book presentation, and its illustration in pictures. The accounts can be divided into two categories. The first and smaller group contains those penned before the presentation and included in the given book. These accounts, like the vast majority of presentation miniatures, anticipate the ritual they commemorate.[18] The second category is comprised of accounts written after the presentation.

The two accounts written prior to the manuscript's actual presentation belong to the larger genre of dedication poems, which record the dedication of the work to a patron.[19] They stand out from that genre by the fact that alongside the typical avowals of authorial modesty and patronal prestige, they include a few details about the physical circumstances of the presentation.

The earlier of the two accounts is the scribe Raoulet d'Orléans's poetic colophon at the back of the Vaudetar *Bible historiale*. This famous colophon records the production of the manuscript, with much toing and froing in the rainy streets of Paris, until the manuscript was ready to be presented:

> A vous, Charles, roy plain d'onnour,
> Qui de sapience la flour
> Estes sur tous les roys du monde,
> Pour le grant bien qu'en vous habonde,
> Presente et donne cestui livre,
> Et à genolz cy le vous livre,
> Jehan Vaudetar, votre servant,
> Qui est cy figuré devant.
> C'onques je ne vi en ma vie
> Bible d'ystoires si garnie . . .
> Si fu au prince sus nommé
> Ce livre baillé et donné
> Par ledit Jehan, que je ne mente,
> L'an mil CCCXII et soixante
> De bon cuer, et vausist mil mars,
> XXVIII jours au mois de mars.[20]

> To you, Charles, king full of honor
> who, flower of wisdom
> is above all the kings of the world,
> for the great good which in you abounds
> presents and gives this book,
> and on bended knee delivers it to you
> Jehan Vaudetar, your servant
> Who is depicted thus before.
> Never have I seen in my life
> A bible so decorated with images . . .
> So was to the prince named above
> this book handed over and given
> by the said Jehan, I tell no lie,
> the year 1372
> with good heart, and worth a thousand marks
> the 18th day of the month of March.

There are several points worth mentioning about this account, which is unique in several respects. First of all, it is the only one connected with an extant manuscript. Second, it is the only one to refer directly to a presentation picture. Finally, the poem also lavishly praises the manuscript's decoration, praise which also features in several of the accounts below.

The second account is by John Lydgate. It appears in his *The Fall of Princes*, his translation of Laurent de Premierfait's *Des Cas des nobles hommes et femmes*, which was in turn a translation of Boccaccio's *De Casibus virorum illustrium*. Lydgate's translation had been commissioned by Humphrey, Duke of Gloucester, around 1431 and was probably finished around 1438. At the end of the book, in "Woordis of the translatur un to his book atte ende," Lydgate addresses first his book and then his patron:

> With lettre & leuys go litil book trembling,
> Pray to the Prince to have on the pite,
> Voide of picture & enlumyn|y|ng,
> Which hast of Cithero no corious dite,
> Nor of his gardyn no flour|e|s of beute;
> God graunt|e| grace thi reudnesse nat offende
> The hih noblesse, the magnanymyte
> Of his presence, whan thou shalt up ascende.
>
> And, for my part, of oon hert abidyng,
> Void of chaung and mutabilite,
> I do presente this book with hand shaking
> Of hool affecioun knelyng on my kne,
> Praying the Lord, the Lord oon, too & thre,
> Whos magnificence no clerk can comprehende,
> To sende you miht, grace and prosperite
> Euer in vertu tencresen & ascende.[21]

Lydgate's text is fairly close to that of Raoulet. Like Raoulet, he places his remarks at the back of the book (whereas most presentation pictures come at the beginning). Lydgate also comments on the book's appearance although, contrary to the scribe's praise of the *Bible historiale*, he disparages his undecorated book. Finally, like Raoulet, he says that he presents the book on bended knee, adding that his hand trembles.

Somewhat surprisingly, these are the only two texts I know which mention the donor's kneeling pose, even though this posture is a constant element of presentation pictures. Similarly, both accounts focus on the single moment when the donor kneels, thus sharing the temporal concentration of the pictures. Given these similarities, it is tempting to argue that Lydgate and Raoulet, in imagining the future presentation of their books, relied on a visual vocabulary derived more from presentation pictures than from their familiarity with the actual ceremony. The temptation is all the stronger when one remembers that like these two texts, presentation pictures were produced in anticipation of the event they depict.

My remaining five accounts were written after the presentation of a book. Since they describe a ceremony which has already taken place, it is not surprising that they go into more detail than the two accounts written ahead of time. Four of the five date between c. 1370 and c. 1460. The earliest of these four is a ballad by Eustache Deschamps. In it, Deschamps tells Guillaume de Machaut that he has presented Machaut's *Voir Dit* to Louis de Male, Count of Flanders, and that the work was favorably received.

> Les grans seigneurs, Guillaume, vous ont chier,
> En voz chose prannent esbatement.
> Bien y parut a Bruges devant hier
> A Monseigneur de Flandres proprement
> Qui par sa main reçut benignement
> Vostre *Voir Dit* sellé dessur la range,
> Lire le fist; mais n'est nul vraiement
> Qui en die fors qu'a vostre louenge.
>
> Je lui baillé voz lettres en papier
> Et vo livre qu'il aime chierement;
> Lire m'y fist, present maint chevalier;
> Si adresçay au lieu premierement
> Ou Fortune parla si durement,
> Comment l'un joint a ses biens, l'autre estrange.
> De ce parlent, mais nulz n'en va parlant,
> Qui en die fors qu'a vostre louenge.[22]
>
> The great lords, Guillaume, hold you dear,
> And delight in your pieces.
> It was evident in Bruge the day before yesterday
> To the Lord of Flanders indeed
> Who by his hand kindly received
> Your *Voir Dit* sealed on the strap,
> [and] had it read; but there was truly no one
> who said anything except in your praise.
>
> I handed him your letters on paper
> And your book which he loves dearly;
> He had me read, in the presence of many lords;
> So I turned first to the place
> Where Fortune spoke so harshly,
> How the one esteems his goods, the other disdains them.
> Of this they spoke, but no one goes around talking
> Who said anything except in your praise.[23]

There are several notable details of this account. The text notes that Louis received the volume personally, in his own hand.[24] The text mentions something of the book's appearance by saying that it was sealed on the strap.

This mention of the strap which holds the book shut also suggests that the Count opened the book. He then handed it back to Deschamps, who read a key passage from the text. Deschamps also takes care to note that the whole ceremony unrolls before a prestigious audience of many lords, who discuss the text and praise Machaut's poetry.

My next account involves Charles V, playing not the recipient, as he had with the Vaudetar *Bible historiale*, but the donor. More prosaic than the three preceding poems, it occurs in the *Grandes Chroniques de France*'s record of Emperor Charles IV's visit to France in 1378.[25] During this visit, while staying at Vincennes, the Emperor requested one of Charles V's books of hours, so that he might pray for the King with a book which had once belonged to him. The text records that Charles "lui en envoia deux, unes grans et unes petites, et li manda que il preist les quelles qu'il vouldroit, ou toutes deux s'il plaisoit, le quel les retint toutes deux et en mercia le Roy."[26]

The imperial covetousness displayed here is amusing, but on first reading, this laconic account does not seem particularly enlightening about the actual presentation of the books. However, there are several points worth noting. First, the gift is not the donor's idea but is sparked by the recipient's explicit request. Second, the donor is not actually present at the presentation but sends the books via an intermediary. Finally, and most important, the text implies a conversation about the books, with a choice offered and a decision made. This choice signals that the books were inspected by their recipient, an action absent from most presentation miniatures. The text is mute on how the books were inspected or what qualities the Emperor valued. While the books' value apparently derives less from their appearance than from their royal provenance, it is interesting that Charles chose to send books whose difference lay in their size, not their contents.[27]

The inspection implied by the *Grandes Chroniques* is explicitly described in the fifth report I know, Froissart's account in his *Chronicles* of giving a book to King Richard II.[28] Froissart had traveled to England to renew old acquaintances and make new ones. Prior to setting out, he equipped himself with a "very beautiful book" of his collected love poetry "to make a present and an *entrée* to the King."[29]

Upon meeting Richard, Froissart does not at once present the book to him, for the King is preparing for an important council. Indeed, he waits over a week to find the proper moment. Once the council is over, Richard's men tell the King that Froissart has a book to present to him, and Richard grants him an audience. Froissart writes that:

> voulut voir le roi le livre que lui avois apporté. Si le vit en sa cham-
> bre, car tout pourvu je l'avois; et lui mis sus son lit. Il l'ouvrit et
> regarda dedans et lui plut très grandement; et plaire bien lui devoit,
> car il étoit enluminé, escript et historié, et couvert de vermeil

velours à dix cloux d'argent dorés d'or, et roses d'or au milieu, et à deux grands fremaulx dorés et richement ouvrés au milieu de rosiers d'or. Donc me demanda le roi de quoi il traitoit, et je lui dis: "D'amours!" De cette réponse fut-il tout rejoui; et regarda dedans le livre en plusieurs lieux, et y legy, car moult bien parloit et lisoit françois; et puis le fit prendre par un sien chevalier, qui se nommoit messire Richard Credon et porter en sa chambre de retrait, et me fit de plus en plus bonne chère.[30]

the king asked to see the book I had brought him. So he saw it in his chamber, for I had it ready with me, and laid it on his bed. He opened it and looked inside and it pleased him greatly. Well it might, for it was illuminated, written and illustrated, with a cover of crimson velvet, with ten studs of silver gilt, and golden roses in the middle, and two large gilded clasps richly worked at their centres with golden rose trees. The King asked me what it was about and I told him: "About love!" He was delighted by this answer, and looked into the book in several places, and read from it, for he spoke and read French very well. Then he had it taken by one of his knights, who was called Messire Richard Credon and carried to his private room, and was more cordial than ever to me.[31]

There are several elements worth considering here. First is Froissart's desire for a propitious opportunity to make his presentation; the chronicler waits patiently for the time when his gift will receive the attention it merits. When the moment is ripe, messengers go back and forth between author and King, some telling Richard about the book, and one from the King inviting Froissart to his chamber. When Froissart arrives in the chamber, he does not hand the book directly to Richard but lays it on the bed for Richard to pick up. Beds are present in several presentation miniatures; Green has related this text to the room depicted in the frontispiece of her collected works which Christine de Pizan offered to Isabelle of Bavaria (Figure 5), and also to the one shown in the presentation picture from Jean Miélot's *Traité sur l'oraison dominicale* (Figure 6).[32] However, the placement of the book on the bed before the King takes it in hand is a very different procedure from the direct transfer of the book from donor to recipient that we see in the vast majority of presentation miniatures. Like Charles IV, Richard inspects the book, his inspection providing Froissart the opportunity to describe the gift for his readers. Pleased by the book's appearance, the King asks about its content, and then again returns to it, reading some passages. Although not stated explicitly, it seems most likely that that the King reads out loud, sharing Froissart's gift with the others present. He then hands the book to one of his auditors, who takes it to the King's private room.

There is a very similar, though still more detailed, account relating to Charles VII. In 1457, Francesco Sforza, the Duke of Milan, sent Charles a pair of medical treatises written by the King's physician, Thomas Le Franc. Sforza had originally intended the books as a gift to Le Franc himself.[33] However, because Le Franc died before the books were finished, Sforza offered them instead to Charles VII, while apologizing for the gift's humble nature.[34]

In a letter written from Lyons on February 14, 1457, Sforza's ambassador, Tomasso Tebaldi, reported the proceedings: "I went to His Majesty the King . . . . [and after offering your] compliments, as Your Lordship had instructed me to do, I presented him with the books."[35] Tebaldi delivered the Duke's apology as well:

> Here I sought, by apt words and gracious manner, to make two points: first, that the present had not been ordered by Your Lordship for direct dispatch to his majesty, since you did not consider it worthy enough nor suitable for him; second, to demonstrate the reverence and affection that you bear him and your goodwill.

According to Tebaldi, Charles VII liked the gift very much:

> The King replied to me very graciously, first, that he did not remember Master Thomas' having ever spoken to him about the books but that he was most pleased with what Thomas had done, for he is very happy to have the books and will treasure them; and that he is very grateful to Your Lordship and there was no need to make any excuse because there could not be any books more handsome or more beautifully ornamented, he once again thanking Your Lordship for your goodwill and intentions toward him, of which he is most certain. And this was his reply, made, I promise you, happily.
>
> Then he opened the books and wanted me to show him the illuminations and the way of finding them by the rubric, and so I read him some of the headings and showed everything to him; and I can tell you that he and his courtiers could not praise them enough—and rightly so for in truth I believe that never have been seen such handsome books nor ones so beautifully ornamented. I have since learned from many that the King and others who have seen them say marvelous things about the books and that the King keeps them continually in his chamber, and the other day when his council went there he wanted them to see them. And this is what happened to the books.

It must have been particularly gratifying to Tebaldi to report Charles VII's continued interest in the books, since there were no guarantees that, once given, a book would be looked at again. Gerald of Wales in the early thirteenth century complained of men who "show so great a contempt of literature, that they immediately shut up within their book-cases the excellent works with which they are presented, and thus doom them . . . to perpetual imprisonment."[36] Cerquiglini-Toulet has noted a similar remark in Martin Le Franc's *Complainte du livre du champion des dames a maistre Martin Le Franc son auteur*. In this pathetic text, a fictional dialogue between Le Franc and his own work, the *Champion des Dames*, the book laments the neglect which followed its presentation to Duke Philip the Good of Burgundy. After being honored by the Duke's touch in the ceremony, "when all was said and done I was left all alone, as if moulting, covered with moss and dust like an old board that no one stirs."[37]

In contrast to this sad tale, Tebaldi's account offers a vivid picture of a successful book presentation, one which is both a diplomatic act and an aesthetic experience. Apologizing, the giver denigrates the gift; waving away the apologies, the recipient praises it lavishly. This ritual exchange finished, the giver demonstrates the books' highlights to the recipient, who praises them and shows them off to the others in the room. The books are then stored away, although they are soon displayed again to still more admirers.

Reviewing these accounts, it is particularly noteworthy that both Tebaldi and Froissart give detailed descriptions of a moment which is significantly lacking from most presentation pictures: the recipient, book in hand, leafing through its pages.[38] The same action is implied in the *Grandes Chroniques*, though not stated explicitly. Machaut also says that Louis took the book in hand, implying that he inspected it, and notes that he had it read aloud.

My last account is the only one I know of from the thirteenth century and is somewhat irregular, as it records an involuntary presentation, a confiscation rather than a gift. The source is the Franciscan William of Rubruck's report to Louis IX of his travels in the Far East.[39] Rubruck brought several books with him on his mission, and the books feature prominently in Rubruck's August 1253 visit to Sartach, a Mongol prince and son of Baatu, the Mongol King.[40] Preparing for his audience, Rubruck is told by one of the Prince's retainers to bring his liturgical objects and books. Before arriving, Rubruck writes:

> I . . . put on the more expensive vestments, and held against my breast a very fine cushion, the Bible you had given me, and a most beautiful psalter given me by my lady the Queen, containing very fine illuminations. My colleague took the missal and the cross, while the clerk . . . took the thurible. In this fashion we arrived

before his |Sartach's| residence, and they lifted up the felt hanging
in front of the doorway so that he could see us.

|They enter| singing the *Salve regina* . . . . All his wives were assem-
bled, and the Mo'als who had entered with us were crowded against
us. Coiac |one of Sartach's men| handed him the thurible with the
incense, and he held it carefully while examining it. Next he took
him the psalter, which he and the wife sitting next to him scruti-
nized closely; and after that, the Bible. He asked if it contained the
Gospel. "Yes," I said, "and the complete Holy Scripture." He also
took the cross in his hand, and inquired whether the image on it
was that of Christ. I replied that it was . . . . Then he made the people standing round us draw back, so that he could have a better
view of our finery.

After further discussion, Sartach accepts some bread, wine and fruit offered
by Rubruck, "and had us take the vestments and books back to our lodging."

   Rubruck was not permitted to keep the books, however. The next
day, Coiac's brother demands that they leave the vestments and the books,
since Sartach "wants a closer look at them." On the following day, a
Nestorian priest comes to collect:

appropriating them—the books and vestments—as if they were his
. . . . Then did I have need of patience, since we had no right of
access to Sartach and there was nobody to do us justice . . . . I had
one consolation, in that anticipating their greed I had removed
from among the books the Bible, the *Sentences*, and other volumes
to which I was more attached. But my lady the Queen's psalter I had
not dared remove, as it had attracted too much attention by reason
of the gold illuminations it contained.

   This admittedly irregular account shares several features with the
more normative ones above. There is first of all the sense of ceremony which
dominates the scene—Rubruck and his fellows in their ecclesiastical finery,
entering in procession while singing a hymn. As in the earlier accounts, the
books are displayed, discussed, and admired—indeed, admired so much that
Rubruck loses the psalter for good.
   Apart from their evident anecdotal appeal, these five accounts have
two chief merits. First, they remind us that illuminated manuscripts could be
semipublic objects, that their audience reached beyond their owner to his or
her circle of familiars.[41] The showy display of the books to others features
also in Eustache Deschamps's famous *Mirror of Marriage* (c. 1381-1389), in
which a greedy wife desires a book of hours in order to impress her friends.
She anticipates a book of hours so fine that "those who will see them may

everywhere say and recount that one could not have [an Hours] more beautiful."[42] This semipublic display of illuminated manuscripts has obvious consequences for any consideration of the function of miniatures in late medieval society.

Second, and more directly related to the topic of presentation pictures, the accounts make us reconsider the ritual we have seen depicted so often. Unlike the pictures, which focus on a single moment in time, the texts describe a series of events. One of these events is shown in all the pictures: the donor presenting the book. All the accounts imply or describe a second stage of the ceremony, the recipient's inspection of the book, and two mention a third step: storage. In the most detailed of the accounts, the recipients—Richard II and Charles VII—proceed in an almost identical fashion: delighting in the books they receive, flipping through their pages, and then sending them to their private chamber. The similarities between the accounts suggest that the procedure is almost conventional, involving three steps: presentation, examination, storage.[43]

Though these tripartite rituals are not surprising—anyone who has ever received a coffee-table book will have done much the same thing—they contribute significantly to our understanding of presentation pictures. The accounts reveal that an artist charged with designing a presentation scene had the choice of several distinct moments to depict. Strikingly, though presentation and examination are each eminently depictable, artists consistently choose to show only the first step. The great majority of presentation scenes show the donor presenting the book and never, to my knowledge, the recipient alone holding the book.

There are occasional attempts made to present a more complete picture of the ceremony. The Vaudetar *Bible historiale* is a case in point (Figure 3): it condenses two moments of the presentation into a single picture, as Charles is shown looking and pointing at the picture in the book, illustrating the admiration which was an important part of the presentation ritual. As Benesch notes, the King has also removed one of his gloves as a prelude to turning the pages himself.[44] Similarly, in the *Traité sur l'oraison dominicale* which Jean Miélot presented to Philip the Good, the Duke rather aggressively flips through the pages of the manuscript (Figure 6).[45] However, even in these two pictures, the book has not yet left the donor's hands.[46]

The most compelling evidence that artists self-consciously preserved the book in the donor's hands comes in images which illustrate Froissart's account of his gift to Richard II. Thanks to Laetitia Le Guay's recent monograph, we know that this event is depicted in three extant copies of Froissart's text.[47] All were painted in Flanders between 1450 and 1475; one belonged to Lodewijk van Gruuthuse,[48] one belonged to the courtier and historian Philippe de Commynes,[49] and the third belonged to Anthony, bastard of

Burgundy.[50] In the first two manuscripts, the artists painted conventional presentation scenes, even though this contradicts the text. In van Gruuthuse's Froissart, the author kneels before the enthroned king (Figure 7). In the Commynes copy, Froissart again kneels, but here Richard stands outside a castle wall (Figure 8). In both cases the King is about to receive the book directly from the author's hands, instead of picking it up from a bed as the text specifies.

It would be possible to argue that these artists did not read the text and that, told to paint a presentation picture, they simply turned to the conventional depiction. However, the miniature in Anthony's copy hews much more closely to Froissart's specific account of the ceremony and at the same time uses the conventional, and contradictory, iconography (Figure 9). The miniature is divided into two halves, an exterior on the left, and an interior on the right. In the background on the right the artist depicts several different moments so that, like the text, it represents a sequential narrative. In the back room of the interior, Richard stands next to a bed holding Froissart's book, while the author kneels before him. The close agreement between picture and text demonstrates that the artist or his adviser had read Froissart closely. However, even here the conventional iconography is present; the artist paints Froissart in the donor's traditional kneeling pose, although the text says nothing of his posture. More striking still is the fact that the miniature also includes a redundant depiction of the presentation in the foreground. Here the depiction is completely conventional, contradicting all the textual details: the King is enthroned, and Froissart kneels before him, handing the open book to him directly. This redundant presentation is very significant, for it demonstrates the power of the conventional presentation picture, which is included here despite the artist's evident knowledge that it does not conform to the text.

How can we explain the power of this convention? The easiest explanation would be that the images derive from other images, that tradition is powerful simply because it is tradition. This explanation is insufficient. First of all, the miniature in Anthony of Burgundy's manuscript demonstrates that artists could add innovation to tradition when they wanted. More importantly, because "to persevere is harder than to start afresh,"[51] traditions are not passively but actively maintained, and will endure only so long as they satisfy needs.

So what needs did the conventional depiction satisfy? The textual accounts can help us answer this question. As noted above, they suggest that presenting a book involved three key moments: presentation, perusal, storage. Both presentation and perusal are eminently depictable. The realization that artists had a range of moments to depict and that they almost universally put the book in the hands of the donor helps us recapture the meaning of these conventional scenes: they stress the object's origin, not its beauty or destination. Though the ritual has three conspicuous players—a beautiful book, a deserving recipient, and a generous giver—the picture's real hero is the giver. It is easy to see why. Simply imagine a presentation scene with the book already in the hands of the recipient. Immediately all the other people in the picture become no more than witnesses, and it becomes difficult to determine which of them is the book's donor.[52]

Now, no donor wished to be anonymous in his or her own presentation picture because the gifts commemorated in these pictures established a relationship between the donor and the recipient of the book. Charles V offered his books to the Emperor as part of a campaign to win Charles IV to the French cause against the English, Froissart hoped to earn the approval of Richard II, and Sforza sent books to Charles VII to smooth relations between Milan and France.

Presentation pictures commemorate and confirm such relationships. As depicted, the ritual recalls homage, perhaps explicitly so. Take, for example, the presentation picture in an exemplar of Noël de Fribois's *Abrégé des chroniques de France* (Figure 10).[53] The manuscript was painted in the 1480s; it holds a text which Fribois presented to Charles VII of France in 1459, and probably copies the now lost presentation manuscript.[54] In the book's opening miniature, Charles sits enthroned as Noël de Fribois presents him with the book. Strikingly, the miniature is virtually identical to a miniature in Fouquet's *Grandes Chroniques*, showing the English king Edward I doing homage to Philip the Fair (Figure 11).[55] Both ceremonies employ similar gestures and postures to similar ends: to formalize ties between two parties.[56]

Commemorating the presentation of a book to a ruler could also be a way of advancing claims to authority or prestige.[57] Fribois hoped that Charles VII would give him more work; his text includes suggested areas for the King's patronage.[58] His offering seems to have succeeded; three months after he presented his text, he received further payment from the King for work associated with "le fait des chroniques de France."[59] The miniature also stakes a claim for the French chancellery: Fribois was a royal secretary in the office, and he is joined here by his colleagues. Fribois wrote his history at a time when the chancellery was usurping the historiographic role traditionally filled by the monks of Saint Denis.[60] Indeed, Fribois's image appears as a secretarial translation of the presentation picture in Philip III's *Grandes Chroniques*, where the monk Primat was accompanied by his abbot and other monks from Saint Denis (Figure 1). It is also very interesting to note that two copies of the text, one from the 1460s, the other from the 1480s, eliminate Fribois and the chancellery staff from the presentation scene, and instead depict Benedictine monks giving the book to the king (Figure 12).[61] Little is known about these books' provenance; the substitution of monks for bureaucrats may simply indicate the strong association of royal history with Saint Denis. On the other hand, if the manuscripts were produced within the orbit of the monastery, the substitution might be a more explicit pictorial attempt to reclaim historiographic authority.

Fribois was not the only author who hoped to benefit from his gift. On a similar note, Froissart records that he benefited from Richard II's warm reception of his book, earning an informant for his chronicle:

> Ce propre dimanche que le roi eut retenu et reçu en grand amour mon livre, un écuyer d'Angleterre étoit en la chambre du roi et étoit nommé Henry Crystède, homme de bien et de prudence grandement et bien parlant françois; et s'acointa de moi pour la cause de ce qu'il eut vu que le roi et les seigneurs me eurent fait bonne chère; et avoit vu le livre lequel j'avois présenté au roi. Et imagina, si comme je vis les apparences par ses paroles, que j'étois un historien, et aussi il lui avoit été dit de messire Richard Sturry, et parla à moi. . . .[62]

> That same Sunday when the king received and retained my book with great love, an English squire was in the king's room, named Henry Crystède, a good man and prudent, and a good French speaker; and he introduced himself to me because he had seen that the king and the lords had made me welcome; and he had seen the book which I had presented to the king. And he imagined, as I saw from his words, that I was a historian, as he had also been told by Richard Sturry, and he spoke to me [about Richard's Irish campaign].

To sum up, a comparison of presentation pictures with accounts of actual presentations reveals that the pictures are highly selective. They are designed above all to remind a book's recipient of the person who had given the book, and this involved emphasizing the donor's role over every other stage of the ceremony. At times, the donor enjoyed this flattery more than perhaps was proper. Thus when Jean Germain prepared a moralized world map for the Duke of Burgundy, he commissioned two copies of the text (Figure 13).[63] He offered the Duke the copy with no pictures and kept the one with the presentation picture for himself!

Oberlin College

NOTES

1. An earlier version of this paper was delivered at "Reading the Middle Ages: Book, Object, Image," the 8th Annual Columbia Medieval Guild Conference on November 1, 1997. I have benefited from the comments of Jonathan Alexander, William Diebold, Dale Kinney and Heather Galloway, and the assistance of Joseph Romano and Julee Holcombe of Oberlin's College's Slide Library. I thank the Office of the Dean of Oberlin College for its generous support in purchasing reproductions.

2. Richard Firth Green, *Poets and Princepleasers: Literature and the English Court in the Late Middle Ages* (Toronto: University of Toronto Press, 1980), 93.

3. There are three extended analyses: Joachim Prochno, *Das Schreiber- und Dedikationsbild in der deutschen Buchmalerei*, 800-1100 (Leipzig: B. G. Teubner, 1929), esp. XIX-XXIV; Evelyn Benesch, "Dedikations- und Präsentationsminiaturen in der pariser Buchmalerei vom spaten dreizehnten bis zum frühen fünfzehnten Jahrhundert" (doctoral dissertation, University of Vienna, 1987); and Cyriel Stroo, "Bourgondische presentatietaferelen: boeken en politiek ten tijde van Filips de Goede en Karel de Stoute," in *Boeken in de late Middeleeuwen: verslag van de Groningse Codicolgendagen* 1992, ed. by Jos. M. M. Hermans and Klaas van der Hoek (Groningen: Egbert Forsten, 1994), 285-298, derived from his dissertation in progress at Louvain, "De celebratie van de macht. Presentatieminiaturen en aanwerwante voorstellingen in handschriften van filips de Goede (1419-1467) en Karel de Stoute (1467-1477)," which I have not seen. For brief definitions of presentation iconography, see E. Lachner, "Dedikationsbild," in *Reallexikon zur deutschen Kunstgeschichte* (Stuttgart: J. B. Metzler, 1937-), III, 1189-1197; Michelle Brown, *Understanding Illuminated Manuscripts: A Guide to Technical Terms* (Malibu: J. Paul Getty Museum, 1994), 102. For an excellent discussion of late medieval courtly gift-giving rituals including but not limited to manuscripts, see Brigitte Buettner, "Past Presents: New Year's Gifts at the Valois Courts, ca. 1400," *Art Bulletin* 83/4 (December 2001): 598-625. In addition to the works cited below, the following include brief but valuable discussions of presentation scenes within larger contexts: Elizabeth Salter and Derek Pearsall, "Pictorial Illustration of Late Medieval Poetic Texts: The Role of the Frontispiece or Prefatory Picture," in *Medieval Iconography and Narrative: A Symposium*, ed. by Flemming G. Andersen *et al.* (Odense, Denmark: Odense University Press, 1980), 100-123; Natalie Zemon Davis, "Beyond the Market: Books as Gifts in Sixteenth-Century France," *Transactions of the Royal Historical Society* 5th series, 33 (1983): 69-88; Eberhard König, "The History of Art and the History of the Book at the Time of the Transition from Manuscript to Print," in *Bibliography and the Study of 15th-Century Civilisation*, ed. by Lotte Hellinga and John Goldfinch (London: British Library, 1987), 154-184, esp. 154-157; Colette Beaune and François Avril, *Le miroir de pouvoir* (Paris: Editions Hervas, 1989), 14-26; John Lowden, "The Royal/Imperial Book and the Image or Self-Image of the Medieval Ruler," in *Kings and Kingship in Medieval Europe*, ed. by Anne J. Duggan (London: King's College London Centre for Late Antique and Medieval Studies, 1993), 213-240, esp. 213-220; Richard Gameson, "The Gospels of Margaret of Scotland and the Literacy of an Eleventh-Century Queen," in *Women and The Book:*

Assessing the Visual Evidence, ed. by Lesley Smith and Jane H. M. Taylor (London: British Library, 1996), 158-160; and Anne D. Hedeman, "Constructing Memories: Scenes of Conversation and Presentation in Pierre Salmon's *Dialogues*," *The Journal of the Walters Art Gallery Essays in Honor of Lilian M. C. Randall*, 54 (1996): 119-134. For an anthropological overview of gift-giving rituals, see Raymond William Firth, *Symbols Public and Private* (Ithaca: Cornell University Press, 1973), 368-402: "Symbolism in Giving and Getting."

4. The earliest extant image occurs in the Vienna Dioscurides (Vienna, Osterreichische Nationalbibliothek, Codex Vindobonensis med. gr. 1, fol. 6v); dating to c. 512-513, it shows Anicia Juliana receiving the book from a *putto*. On the manuscript, see Kurt Weitzmann, *Late Antique and Early Christian Book Illumination* (New York: George Braziller, 1977), 60-71; for a brief discussion of Anicia Juliana, with further bibliography, see Martin Harrison, *A Temple for Byzantium* (Austin: University of Texas Press, 1989), 36-41, 145 n.12.

5. Benesch, "Dedikations- und Präsentationsminiaturen," 5-7.

6. Brigitte Buettner, "Profane Illuminations, Secular Illusions: Manuscripts in Late Medieval Courtly Society," *Art Bulletin* 74/1 (March 1992): 75-90.

7. Benesch, "Dedikations- und Präsentationsminiaturen," 5-6. The manuscript is now Paris, Bibliothèque Sainte-Geneviève, ms. 782; the text is published in *Les Grandes Chroniques de France*, ed. by Jules Viard (Paris: Société de l'histoire de France, 1920-1953).

8. Paris, Bibliothèque Sainte-Geneviève, ms. 782, fol. 326v. The image is discussed in Benesch, "Dedikations- und Präsentationsminiatur," 5-6; and Anne D. Hedeman, *The Royal Image: Illustrations of the* Grandes Chroniques de France *1274-1422* (Berkeley and Los Angeles: University of California Press, 1991), 15.

9. The book's opening initial on folio 1 depicts a monk kneeling before an enthroned king with a single book held by both figures simultaneously (reproduced in Hedeman, *Royal Image*, fig. 3). Hedeman interprets the image as a less elaborate presentation miniature, with the book being handed to the king (*Royal Image*, 15). However, Benesch offers a convincing argument that it actually depicts Louis commissioning Primat to prepare the *Grandes Chroniques*, a commission mentioned in the text's prologue. The initial would thus show Louis handing Primat a Latin source ("Dedikations- und Präsentationsminiaturen," 19-20). On the potential difficulty of interpreting images where the book is held by both parties, see Emmanuèle Baumgartner, "La 'Premiere page' dans les manuscrits du 'Tristan en prose,'" in *La Présentation du Livre: Actes du colloque de Paris X-Nanterre (4,5, 6 décembre 1985)*, ed. by Emmanuèle Baumgartner and Nicole Boulestreau (Paris: Université de Paris X-Nanterre, 1987), 58.

10. On Charles V's library, see Leopold Delisle, *Recherches sur la librairie de Charles V* (Paris: H. Champion, 1907); Bibliothèque nationale, *La Librairie de Charles V* (Paris: Bibliothèque nationale, 1968); and the following more specialized studies: Claire Richter, *The Portraits of Charles V of France (1338-1380)* (New York: New York University Press, 1969); *idem, Imaging Aristotle: Verbal and Visual Representation in Fourteenth-Century France* (Berkeley and Los Angeles: University of California Press, 1995); Hedeman,

Royal Image, 93-133; and Catherine Sparta, "Le manuscrit 434 de la Bibliothèque municipale de Besançon. Culture antique et latinité sous le règne de Charles V," *Histoire de l'art*, 45 (December 1999): 13-23.

11. For the corpus of his dedication pictures, see Sherman, *Portraits of Charles V*, 17-32; and Benesch, "Dedikations- und Präsentationsminiaturen," 43-99.

12. Paris, Bibliothèque nationale de France, MS. fr. 1950, fol. 2. See Bibliothèque nationale, *Librairie de Charles V*, no. 183, 105; Sherman, *Portraits of Charles V*, 31-32; and Benesch, "Dedikations- und Präsentationsminiaturen," 80, 162.

13. The Hague, Rijksmuseum Meermanno-Westreenianum Ms. 10 B 23, fol. 2. On this manuscript, see Bibliothèque nationale, *Librairie de Charles V*, no. 168, 94-95; Sherman, *Portraits of Charles V*, 25-28; François Avril, *Manuscript Painting at the Court of France The Fourteenth Century*, trans. by Ursule Molinaro (New York: George Braziller, 1978), 110-111; *Les Fastes du Gothique: Le siècle de Charles V* (Paris: Réunion des musées nationaux, 1981), no. 285, 331-332; and Benesch, "Dedikations- und Präsentationsminiaturen," 62-68, 96, 159, V-VI.

14. L. M. J. Delaissé, "Enluminure et peinture dans les Pays-Bas; À propos du livre de E. Panofksy, *Early Netherlandish Painting*," *Scriptorium*, XI (1957), 110-111. Delaissé argued against Panofsky, who said that *istud opus* referred to the whole manuscript, not simply the frontispiece; *Early Netherlandish Painting* (Cambridge: Harvard University Press, 1953), 37. Delaissé objected on the grounds that the other miniatures in the book had little to do with Bondol's style. Millard Meiss supports Panofsky, *French Painting in the Time of Jean de Berry: The Late Fourteenth Century and the Patronage of the Duke* (London: Phaidon, 1967), 21, while Sherman, *Portraits of Charles V*, 26, n.53, and Benesch "Dedikations- und Präsentationsminiaturen," 65-67, agree with Delaissé, whose thesis also convinces me.

15. Her argument rests on two supports; first, a careful reckoning of the dates in the book's opening inscription, which faces the miniature, and its concluding colophon, and second, the colophon's reference to "Jean de Vaudetar, votre servant/qui es cy figuré devant," a reference which would make little sense if the book did not already bear its frontispiece; Benesch, "Dedikations- und Präsentationsminiaturen," 65-67.

16. Lotte Hellinga-Querido, "Reading an Engraving: William Caxton's dedication to Margaret of York, Duchess of Burgundy," in *Across the Narrow Seas: Studies in the History of Bibliography and the Low Countries Presented to Anna E. C. Simoni*, ed. by Susan Roach (London: British Library, 1991), 1-15; and Martin Lowry, "Sister or Country Cousin? The Huntington *Recuyell* and the Getty *Tondal*," in *Margeret of York, Simon Marmion, and* The Visions of Tondal, ed. by Thomas Kren (Malibu: J. Paul Getty Museum, 1992), 103-110.

17. San Marino, CA, Huntington Library.

18. Buettner, "Past Presents," 617.

19. For examples of this genre, see Karl Julius Holzknecht, *Literary Patronage in the Middle Ages* (Philadelphia, 1923),156-164.

20. Delisle, *Recherches sur la librairie de Charles V*, I, 75-76.

21. *Lydgate's Fall of Princes*, ed. by Henry Bergen, Early English Text Society, Extra Series, no. 123 (London: Oxford University Press, 1924-1927), III, 1021, lines 3589-3604. The passage is cited in Holzknecht, *Literary Patronage*, 160.

22. "Ballade CXXVII," in *Oeuvres complètes de Eustache Deschamps*, ed. by Le Marquis de Queux de Saint-Hilaire and Gaston Raynaud, Société des anciens textes français (Paris: Librairie de Firmin Didot et Cie, 1878-1903), I, 249. For the ballad's date, see Daniel Poirion, *Le Poète et le prince: L'évolution du lyrisme courtois de Guillaume de Machaut à Charles d'Orléans* (Paris: Presses Universitaires de France, 1965), 225; and Lawrence Earp, *Guillaume de Machaut* A *Guide to Research* (New York: Garland Publishing, 1995), 57. This ballad is also discussed in Holzknecht, *Literary Patronage*, 157; and Sarah Jane Manley Williams, "Machaut's Self-Awareness as Author and Producer," in *Machaut's World: Science and Art in the Fourteenth Century*, ed. by Madeleine Pelner Cosman and Bruce Chandler, Annals of the New York Academy of Sciences, 314 (New York: New York Academy of Sciences, 1978), 195.

23. I thank Janice Zinser for her help with this paraphrase.

24. For the frequent use of intermediaries between donor and noble recipient, see Buettner, "Past Presents," 613 and fig. 17.

25. *Les Grandes Chroniques de France. Chroniques des règnes de Jean II et de Charles V*, ed. by R. Delachenal (Paris: Société de l'histoire de France, 1910-1916), II, 193-277. The visit is extensively illustrated in Charles V's own copy of the text, Paris, Bibliothèque nationale de France, ms. fr. 2813. For a discussion of this cycle, see Hedeman, *Royal Image*, 129-133. The account of the Emperor's visit puts contemporary French art and architecture in an interesting diplomatic context, and I am planning to translate it.

26. "sent him two [books], one big and one small, and asked the emperor to take the one he wanted, or both if it pleased him, and the emperor kept both books and thanked the king for them," *Chroniques des règnes de Jean II et de Charles V*, II, 264. I do not know if these books survive. These were the only books the Emperor received on this visit, but he was also presented with metalwork on two occasions; 227-228, 268-269. It is interesting that the gift of the books is not illustrated in Charles V's copy of the text, while the gifts of metalwork are (Paris, Bibliothèque nationale de France, ms. fr. 2813, fols. 472, 478v). This may be because the bearers of the metalwork had significant status (the City of Paris, and the Dukes of Berry, Burgundy and Bourbon), while the bearer of the manuscript is an unnamed household official. For these gifts of metalwork, and the status of giver and receiver, see Buettner, "Past Presents," 613. For a discussion of how presentation miniatures enhance the donor's role, see below.

27. A book's size is a distinguishing factor in documents of the period. One of Charles V's inventories cites his "très belles grans Heures" (formerly Turin E V 47); see Delisle, *Recherches*, pp. 208-213. The Duke of Berry's *Grandes* and *Petites Heures* (Paris, BNF, mss. lat. 919 and 18014) are also worth noting; while the latter name is modern, the Duke's inventory of 1413 calls the former the *très grans moult belles et riches heures*. For the inventory descriptions of both manuscripts, see Meiss, *Late Fourteenth Century*, 155, 256-257.

28. The account's art-historical interest is cited by Sandra Hindman, "Iconography of Queen Isabeau de Bavière: An Essay in Method," *Gazette des Beaux-Arts*, 6th period, 102, no. 1377 (October 1983): 107; Benesch, "Dedikations- und Präsentationsminiaturen," 1; and Buettner, "Profane Illuminations, Secular Illusions," 76-78. The text is also discussed in Holzknecht, *Literary Patronage*, 158-159; Green, *Poets and Princepleasers*, 64-5, 70, 77, 93, 95-6, 98, 130, 205; Joyce Coleman, *Public Reading and the Reading Public in Late Medieval England and France* (Cambridge: Cambridge University Press, 1996), 132, 138; and Jacqueline Cerquiglini-Toulet, *The Color of Melancholy: The Uses of Books in the Fourteenth Century*, trans. by Lydia G. Cochrane (Baltimore: Johns Hopkins University Press, 1997), 157. I thank Adam Cohen for this last reference.

29. "un très beau livre et bien aourné, couvert de velours, garni et clos d'argent doré d'or, pour faire présent et entée au roi," *Chroniques de sire Jean Froissart*, Book IV, chap. 40, ed. by J.-A.-C. Buchon (Paris: Desrez, 1837), III, 198. I do not know if this volume has survived.

30. *Chroniques*, Book IV, chap. 41, III, 207.

31. This translation is based closely on that of Geoffrey Brereton in Jean Froissart, *Chronicles* (Harmondsworth: Penguin, 1978), 408.

32. London, British Library ms. Harley 4431, fol. 3, and Brussels, Bibliothèque Royale Albert Ier, ms. 9092, fol. 1; Green, *Poets and Princepleasers*, 64-65. For more on Christine's manuscript, see Millard Meiss, *French Painting in the Time of Jean de Berry: The Limbourgs and Their Contemporaries* (New York: George Braziller, 1974), esp. 38-41, 292-296; Sandra Hindman, "The Composition of Christine de Pizan's Collected Works in the British Library: A Reassessment," *British Library Journal* 9 (1983): 93-123; and *idem*, "Iconography of Queen Isabeau de Bavière." For more on Miélot's manuscript, see L. M. J. Delaissé, *De Vlaamse Miniatuur Het Mecenat van Filips de Goede 1445-1475* (Brussels: Paleis voor Schone Kunsten, 1959), no. 90, 93.

33. G. du Fresne de Beaucourt, *Histoire de Charles VII* (Paris: A. Picard, 1881-1891), VI, 236, 408. Thomas Le Franc, also called Thomas Coroneus or Greci, was a significant enough personality at the court that the Italian humanist Francesco Filelfo corresponded with him and the chancellor Guillaume Jouvenel des Ursins in an attempt to gain entry to Charles VII's circle. See one of Filelfo's letters to Le Franc in *Cent-dix lettres grecques de François Filelfe*, ed. by Émile Legrand (Paris: École des langues orientales vivantes, 1892), 73-77, and discussion of him in Diana Robin, *Filelfo in Milan: Writings, 1451-1477* (Princeton: Princeton University Press, 1991), 84; Ernest Wickersheimer, *Dictionnaire biographique des médecins en France au Moyen Âge* (Geneva: E. Droz, 1936, rpt. Geneva, Librairie Droz, 1979), II, 762; and Danielle Jacquart, *Dictionnaire biographique des médecins en France au Moyen Age. Supplément* (Geneva: Droz, 1979), 274.

34. I do not know whether the manuscripts presented to Charles VII have survived.

35. The letter is printed and translated in *Dispatches with Related Documents of Milanese Ambassadors in France and Burgundy, 1450-1483*, ed. by Paul M. Kendall and Vincent Ilardi (Athens, OH: Ohio University Press, 1970-1981), I, 258-265. It is cited but not discussed in detail in Charles M. Rosenberg, "The Bible of Borso d'Este: Inspiration and

Use," in *Cultura figurativa ferrarese tra XV e XVI secolo: in memoria di Giacomo Bargellesi* (Venice: Corbo e Fiore, 1981), 60, and Léopold Delisle, *Le Cabinet des manuscrits de la Bibliothèque nationale* (Paris: Imprimerie nationale, 1881), III, 341.

36. Gerald of Wales, Second Preface to *The Description of Wales*, in *The Historical Works of Giraldus Cambrensis*, ed. and trans. by Thomas Wright (London: H. G. Bohn, 1863; rpt. New York: AMS Press, 1968), 474.

37. Quoted in Cerquiglini-Toulet, *Color of Melancholy*, 157-158, and further discussed in Green, *Poets and Princepleasers*, 98, 205-207 and Buettner, "Past Presents," 616-617. Le Franc had first presented the text to the Duke in 1442, complete with a presentation picture. Apparently it attracted little attention, and Le Franc's poem was included in the second, more lavishly illustrated copy of the text which he offered the Duke ten years later. The manuscripts, Brussels, Bibliothèque royale Albert Ier, MS. 9466 and Paris, Bibliothèque nationale de France, MS. fr. 12476, are discussed in Pascale Charron, "Les réceptions du *Champion des dames* de Martin Le Franc à la cour de Bourgogne. 'Tres puissant et tres humain prince [. . .] veullez cest livre humainement recepvoir,'" *Bulletin du Bibliophile*, 2000, no. 1, 9-31; François Avril and Nicole Reynaud, *Les Manuscrits à peintures en France 1440-1520* (Paris: Flammarion, 1993), no. 112, 205, and no. 50, 101-102. Le Franc's poem is printed in G. Paris, "Un poème inédit de Martin Le Franc," *Romania* XVI (1887): 383-437. On the general difficulties facing court writers, see Green, *Poets and Princepleasers*, 203-211.

38. On the importance of the recipient's touch, see Firth, *Symbols*, 377-378.

39. *The Mission of Friar William of Rubruck. His journey to the court of the Great Khan Möngke, 1253-1255*, trans. by Peter Jackson, with an introduction and notes by Peter Jackson and David Morgan (London: Hakluyt Society, 1990). I thank Professor Jonathan Alexander for bringing this text to my attention.

40. *Mission*, 116-120.

41. For further discussion of group interactions with books, see Coleman, *Public Reading*, especially 109-147.

42. "ceuls qui les verront/puissent par tout dire et compter/qu'om ne puet plus belles porter"; in *Oeuvres complètes*, IX, 46, lines 1320-1322. These interesting lines have been unduly ignored, as they are omitted from the oft-quoted translation by Panofsky, *Early Netherlandish Painting*, 68.

43. See also Buettner, "Past Presents," 602.

44. Benesch, "Dedikations- und Präsentationsminiaturen," 63.

45. Brussels, Bibliothèque Royale Albert Ier, MS 9092, fol. 1; reproduced in color in Edwin Hall, *The Arnolfini Betrothal: Medieval Marriage and the Enigma of Van Eyck's Double Portrait* (Berkeley and Los Angeles: University of California Press, 1994), plate 11. For another example, see Buettner's persuasive interpretation of the famous presentation miniature in Jean sans Peur's *Livre des merveilles*, Paris, BNF, ms. fr. 2810, fol. 226, "Past Presents," 602.

46. These are not the only times an open book is presented to its recipient, though this does not happen as often as one might expect. Sherman, *Portraits of Charles V*, 23,

points out that Charles is presented an open book in his copy of the *Cité de Dieu*, Paris, Bibliothèque nationale de France, MS. fr. 22912, fol. 3. For a similar example from the tenth century, see the Gospel book which Count Dietrich of Holland and his wife Hildegard presented to the monastery of Egmont, in which the presentation picture shows the couple placing an open book on the monastery's altar; The Hague, Koninklijke Bibliotheek, MS. 761/1, fol. 214v, reproduced in Henry Mayr-Harting, *Ottonian Book Illumination: An Historical Study* (London: Harvey Miller Publishers, 1991), II, plate 33. Presentation miniatures may also imply the future opening of the book; Sherman, *Imaging Aristotle*, 51, notes that in a presentation picture from the Charles V's copy of Aristotle's *Ethics* (Brussels, BR, ms. 9505-9506, fol. 2v) the work's translator appears to unclasp the work with his left hand while he presents it with his right. This image can be linked to Deschamp's ballad, which mentions the strap on Machaut's book.

47. Laetitia Le Guay, *Les Princes du Bourgogne Lecteurs de Froissart Les Rapports entre le texte et l'image dans les manuscrits enluminés du livre* IV *des* Chroniques (Paris and Brussels: CNRS Editions and Brepols, 1998).

48. Paris, BNF, mss. fr. 2643-2646. For van Gruuthuse's patronage, see Maximilian P. J. Martens, *Lodewijk van Gruuthuse: Mecenas en Europees Diplomaat ca.* 1427-1492 (Bruges: Stichting Kunstboek, 1992), whose brief mentions of the Froissart place it in the context of van Gruuthuse's large library, 121, 129, 136, 140, 142, 146.

49. London, BL, Harley mss. 4379-4380.

51.   Peter the Venerable to Bernard of Clairvaux, quoted in Wolfgang Braunfels, *Monasteries of Western Europe: The Architecture of the Orders*, trans. by Alaistair Lang (London: Thames and Hudson, 1972), 51.

50. Berlin, Staatsbibliothek Preussischer Kulturbesitz, Breslau deposit I, ms. Rhediger 4.

52. The need to identify the donor probably explains why Froissart is shown kneeling by Richard's bed in Anthony's manuscript.

53. Paris, Bibliothèque nationale de France, MS. fr. 10141, fol. 1.

54. Paris, Bibliothèque nationale de France, MS. fr. 10141. On this text, see Kathleen Daly, "Histoire et politique à la fin de la guerre de Cent Ans: l'*Abrégé des Chroniques* de Noël de Fribois," in *La "France Anglaise" au Moyen Âge. Actes du 111e congrès national des sociétés savantes. Section d'histoire médiévale et de philologie. Poitiers,* 1986 (Paris: Comité des travaux historiques et scientifiques, 1988), 91-101; and *idem*, "Noël de Fribois," in *Dictionnaire des lettres françaises Le Moyen Âge,* ed. by Geneviève Hasenohr and Michel Zink (Paris: Fayard, 1992), 1078. On the relationship of fr. 10141 to the lost presentation copy, see Erik Inglis, "Noël de Fribois and a Lost Work by Jean Fouquet," *Bulletin du Bibliophile,* 2000, no. 1, 32-56.

55. Paris, Bibliothèque nationale de France, MS. fr. 6465, fol. 301v. On this manuscript, see François Avril, Marie-Thérèse Gousset and Bernard Guenée, *Les Grandes Chroniques de France* (Paris: Philippe Lebaud, 1987); and Avril and Reynaud, *Manuscrits à*

peintures, no. 70, 139-140. I discuss the relationship between these two miniatures in "Noël de Fribois and a Lost Work by Jean Fouquet."

56. Sherman notes the similarity of presentation and homage scenes in *Portraits of Charles V*, 18 n.4, and there are relevant remarks in Stroo, "Bourgondische presentatietaferelen," 285-289.

57. See Holzknecht, *Literary Patronage*, ch. X, "Rewards," 170-190.

58. He suggests a translation of Salic Law and a treatise on how to recognize traitors, BN Ms. fr. 10141, fols. 3v-4, 17.

59. This record is contained in BN Ms. fr. 32511, fol. 210v, quoted in François Avril, "Jean Fouquet, illustrateur des *Grandes Chroniques de France*" in Avril, Gousset, Guenée, *Grandes Chroniques de France*, 22-23.

60. Kathleen Daly, "Mixing Business with Leisure: Some French Royal Notaries and Secretaries and their Histories of France, c. 1459-1509," in *Power, Culture and Religion in France, c.* 1350-1550, ed. by Christopher Allmand (Woodbridge, UK: Boydell Press, 1989), 99-115; and Bernard Guenée, "Chancelleries et monastères. La mémoire de France au Moyen Age," in *Les Lieux de mémoire*. II. *La Nation*, ed. by Pierre Nora (Paris: Gallimard, 1986), I, 5-30.

61. Paris, Bibliothèque nationale de France, ms. fr. 4943, fol. 1, and Geneva, Bibliothèque publique et universitaire, MS. fr. 83. On the latter, see Bernard Gagnebin, *L'enluminure de Charlemagne à François Ier: Les manuscrits à peintures de la Bibliothèque publique et universitaire de Genève* (Geneva: Bibliothèque publique et universitaire and Musée d'art et d'histoire, 1976), 141-142.

62. Froissart, *Chroniques*, Book IV, chap. 41, 207.

63. Lyon, Bibliothèque municipale, P.A. 32, fol. 1. See Avril and Reynaud, *Manuscrits à peintures en France*, no. 107, 196.

WORKS CITED

ORIGINAL TEXTS

Deschamps, Eustache. *Oeuvres complètes de Eustache Deschamps*. Edited by Le Marquis de Queux de Saint-Hilaire and Gaston Raynaud. Société des anciens textes français. Paris: Librairie de Firmin Didot et Cie, 1878-1903.

Dispatches with Related Documents of Milanese Ambassadors in France and Burgundy, 1450-1483. Edited by Paul M. Kendall and Vincent Ilardi. Athens, OH: Ohio University Press, 1970-1981.

Filelfo, Francesco. *Cent-dix lettres grecques de François Filelfe*. Edited by Émile Legrand. Paris: École des langues orientales vivantes, 1892.

Froissart, Jean. *Chroniques de Sire Jean Froissart*, ed. J.-A.-C. Buchon (Paris: Desrez, 1835-1837)

———. *Chronicles*. Trans. Geoffrey Brereton. Harmondsworth: Penguin, 1978.

Gerald of Wales. *The Historical Works of Giraldus Cambrensis.* Edited and trans. by Thomas Wright. London: H. G. Bohn, 1863; rpt. New York: AMS Press, 1968.

Les Grandes Chroniques de France. Edited by Jules Viard. Paris: Société de l'histoire de France, 1920-1953.

Les Grandes Chroniques de France. Chroniques des règnes de Jean II et de Charles V. Edited by R. Delachenal. Paris: Société de l'histoire de France, 1910-1916.

Lydgate, John. *Lydgate's Fall of Princes.* Edited by Henry Bergen, Early English Text Society, Extra Series, no. 123. London: Oxford University Press, 1924-1927.

William of Rubruck. *The Mission of Friar William of Rubruck. His journey to the court of the Great Khan Möngke, 1253-1255.* Trans. Peter Jackson. Introduction and notes by Peter Jackson and David Morgan. London: Hakluyt Society, 1990.

SECONDARY LITERATURE

Avril, François. *Manuscript Painting at the Court of France: The Fourteenth Century.* Trans. Ursule Molinaro. New York: George Braziller, 1978.

———. Gousset, Marie-Thérèse, and Guenée, Bernard. *Les Grandes Chroniques de France.* Paris: Philippe Lebaud, 1987.

———. and Reynaud, Nicole. *Les Manuscrits à peintures en France 1440-1520.* Paris: Flammarion, 1993.

Baumgartner, Emmanuèle. "La 'Premiere page' dans les manuscrits du 'Tristan en prose,'" in *La Présentation du Livre: Actes du colloque de Paris X-Nanterre (4,5, 6 décembre 1985),* edited by Emmanuèle Baumgartner and Nicole Boulestreau, 51-63. Paris: Université de Paris X-Nanterre, 1987.

de Beaucourt, G. du Fresne. *Histoire de Charles VII.* Paris: A. Picard, 1881-1891.

Beaune, Colette and Avril, François. *Le Miroir de Pouvoir.* Paris: Editions Hervas, 1989.

Benesch, Evelyn. "Dedikations- und Präsentationsminiaturen in der pariser Buchmalerei vom spaten dreizehnten bis zum frühen fünfzehnten Jahrhundert." Doctoral dissertation, University of Vienna, 1987.

Bibliothèque nationale. *La Librairie de Charles V.* Paris: Bibliothèque nationale, 1968.

Brown, Michelle. *Understanding Illuminated Manuscripts: A Guide to Technical Terms.* Malibu: J. Paul Getty Museum, 1994.

Buettner, Brigitte. "Profane Illuminations, Secular Illusions: Manuscripts in Late Medieval Courtly Society." *Art Bulletin* 74/1 (March 1992): 75-90.

———. "Past Presents: New Year's Gifts at the Valois Courts, ca. 1400." *Art Bulletin* 83/4 (December 2001): 598-625.

Cerquiglini-Toulet, Jacqueline. *The Color of Melancholy: The Uses of Books in the Fourteenth Century*. Trans. Lydia G. Cochrane. Baltimore: Johns Hopkins University Press, 1997.

Charron, Pascale. "Les réceptions du *Champion des dames* de Martin Le Franc à la cour de Bourgogne. 'Tres puissant et tres humain prince [...] veullez cest livre humainement recepvoir.'" *Bulletin du Bibliophile* 2000, no. 1: 9-31.

Coleman, Joyce. *Public Reading and the Reading Public in Late Medieval England and France*. Cambridge: Cambridge University Press, 1996.

Daly, Kathleen. "Histoire et politique à la fin de la guerre de Cent Ans: l'*Abrégé des Chroniques* de Noël de Fribois." In *La 'France Anglaise' au Moyen Âge. Actes du 111e congrès national des sociétés savantes. Section d'histoire médiévale et de philologie. Poitiers, 1986*, 91-101. Paris: Comité des travaux historiques et scientifiques, 1988.

——. "Mixing Business with Leisure: Some French Royal Notaries and Secretaries and their Histories of France, c. 1459-1509." In *Power, Culture and Religion in France, c. 1350-1550*, edited by Christopher Allmand, 99-115. Woodbridge, [UK]: Boydell Press, 1989.

——. "Noël de Fribois." In *Dictionnaire des lettres françaises: Le Moyen Âge*, edited by Geneviève Hasenohr and Michel Zink, 1078. Paris: Fayard, 1992.

Davis, Nathalie Zemon. "Beyond the Market: Books as Gifts in Sixteenth-Century France." *Transactions of the Royal Historical Society* 5th series, 33 (1983), 69-88.

Delaissé, L. M. J. "Enluminure et peinture dans les Pays-Bas; À propos du livre de E. Panofksy, *Early Netherlandish Painting*." *Scriptorium* XI (1957), 109-18.

——. *De Vlaamse Miniatuur Het Mecenat van Filips de Goede 1445-1475*. Brussels: Paleis voor Schone Kunsten, 1959.

Delisle, Léopold. *Le Cabinet des manuscrits de la Bibliothèque nationale*. Paris: Imprimerie nationale, 1868-1881.

——. *Recherches sur la librairie de Charles V*. Paris: H. Champion, 1907.

Earp, Lawrence. *Guillaume de Machaut A Guide to Research*. New York: Garland Publishing, 1995.

Les Fastes du Gothique: Le siècle de Charles V. Paris: Réunion des musées nationaux, 1981.

Firth, Raymond William. *Symbols Public and Private*. Ithaca: Cornell University Press, 1973.

Gameson, Richard. "The Gospels of Margaret of Scotland and the Literacy of an Eleventh-Century Queen." In *Women and The Book: Assessing the Visual Evidence*, edited by Lesley Smith, Jane H. M. Taylor, 148-71. London: British Library, 1996.

Green, Richard Firth. *Poets and Princepleasers: Literature and the English Court in the Late Middle Ages*. Toronto: University of Toronto Press, 1980.

Guenée, Bernard. "Chancelleries et monastères. La mémoire de France au Moyen Age." In Les Lieux de mémoire. II. La Nation, edited by Pierre Nora, vol. I, 5-30. Paris: Gallimard, 1986.

Hall, Edwin. The Arnolfini Betrothal: Medieval Marriage and the Enigma of Van Eyck's Double Portrait. Berkeley and Los Angeles: University of California Press, 1994.

Harrison, Martin. A Temple for Byzantium. Austin: University of Texas Press, 1989.

Hedeman, Anne D. The Royal Image: Illustrations of the Grandes Chroniques de France 1274-1422. Berkeley and Los Angeles: University of California Press, 1991.

——. "Constructing Memories: Scenes of Conversation and Presentation in Pierre Salmon's Dialogues." The Journal of the Walters Art Gallery Essays in Honor of Lilian M. C. Randall 54 (1996), 119-34.

Hellinga-Querido, Lotte. "Reading an Engraving: William Caxton's dedication to Margaret of York, Duchess of Burgundy." In Across the Narrow Seas: Studies in the history of bibliography and the Low Countries presented to Anna E. C. Simoni, edited by Susan Roach, 1-15. London: British Library, 1991.

Hindman, Sandra. "The Composition of Christine de Pizan's Collected Works in the British Library: A Reassessment." British Library Journal 9, no. 2 (1983): 93-123.

——. "Iconography of Queen Isabeau de Bavière: An Essay in Method." Gazette des Beaux-Arts 6th period, 102, no. 1377 (1983): 102-10.

Holzknecht, Karl Julius. Literary Patronage in the Middle Ages. Philadelphia, 1923.

Inglis, Erik. "Noël de Fribois and a Lost Work by Jean Fouquet." Bulletin du Bibliophile, 2000, no. 1, 32-56.

Jacquart, Danielle. Dictionnaire biographique des médecins en France au Moyen Age. Supplément. Geneva: Librairie Droz, 1979.

König, Eberhard. "The History of Art and the History of the Book at the Time of the Transition from Manuscript to Print." In Bibliography and the Study of 15th-Century Civilisation, edited by Lotte Hellinga and John Goldfinch, 154-84. London: British Library, 1987.

Lachner, E. "Dedikationsbild." In Reallexikon zur deutschen Kunstgeschichte, vol. III, 1189-97. Stuttgart: J. B. Metzler, 1937-.

Le Guay, Laetitia. Les Princes du Bourgogne Lecteurs de Froissart: Les Rapports entre le texte et l'image dans les manuscrits enluminés du livre IV des Chroniques. Paris and Brussels: CNRS Editions and Brepols, 1998.

Lowden, John. "The Royal/Imperial Book and the Image or Self-Image of the Medieval Ruler." In Kings and Kingship in Medieval Europe, edited by Anne J. Duggan, 213-40. London: King's College London Centre for Late Antique and Medieval Studies, 1993.

Lowry, Martin. "Sister or Country Cousin? The Huntington *Recuyell* and the Getty *Tondal.*" In *Margeret of York, Simon Marmion, and* The Visions of Tondal, edited by Thomas Kren, 103-10. Malibu: J. Paul Getty Museum, 1992.

Martens, Maximilian P. J. *Lodewijk van Gruuthuse Mecenas en Europees Diplomaat ca. 1427-1492.* Bruges: Stichting Kunstboek, 1992.

Mayr-Harting, Henry. *Ottonian Book Illumination: An Historical Study.* London: Harvey Miller Publishers, 1991.

Meiss, Millard. *French Painting in the Time of Jean de Berry: The Late Fourteenth Century and the Patronage of the Duke.* London: Phaidon, 1967.

———. *French Painting in the Time of Jean de Berry: The Limbourgs and Their Contemporaries.* New York: George Braziller, 1974.

Panofsky, Erwin. *Early Netherlandish Painting.* Cambridge: Harvard University Press, 1953.

Paris, G. "Un poème inédit de Martin Le Franc." *Romania* XVI (1887): 383-437.

Poirion, Daniel. *Le Poète et le prince: L'évolution du lyrisme courtois de Guillaume de Machaut à Charles d'Orléans.* Paris: Presses universitaires de France, 1965.

Prochno, Joachim. *Das Schreiber- und Dedikationsbild in der deutschen Buchmalerei, 800-1100.* Leipzig: B. G. Teubner, 1929.

Robin, Diana. *Filelfo in Milan: Writings, 1451-1477.* Princeton: Princeton University Press, 1991.

Rosenberg, Charles M. "The Bible of Borso d'Este: Inspiration and Use." In *Cultura figurativa ferrarese tra XV e XVI secolo: in memoria di Giacomo Bargellesi,* 51-73. Venice: Corbo e Fiore, 1981.

Salter, Elizabeth and Pearsall, Derek. "Pictorial illustration of late medieval poetic texts: the role of the frontispiece or prefatory picture." In *Medieval Iconography and Narrative: A Symposium,* edited by Flemming G. Andersen *et al.,* 100-123. Odense [Denmark]: Odense University Press, 1980.

Sherman, Claire Richter. *The Portraits of Charles V of France (1338-1380).* New York: New York University Press, 1969.

———. *Imaging Aristotle: Verbal and Visual Representation in Fourteenth-Century France.* Berkeley and Los Angeles: University of California Press, 1995.

Sparta, Catherine. "Le manuscrit 434 de la Bibliothèque municipale de Besançon. Culture antique et latinité sous le règne de Charles V." *Histoire de l'art,* 45 (December 1999), 13-23.

Stroo, Cyriel. "Bourgondische presentatietaferelen: boeken en politiek ten tijde van Filips de Goede en Karel de Stoute." In *Boeken in de late Middeleeuwen: verslag van de Groningse Codicolgendagen 1992,* edited by Jos. M. M. Hermans and Klaas van der Hoek, 285-98. Groningen: Egbert Forsten, 1994.

Weitzmann, Kurt. *Late Antique and Early Christian Book Illumination.* New York: George Braziller, 1977.

Wickersheimer, Ernest. *Dictionnaire biographique des médecins en France au Moyen Âge*. Geneva: E. Droz, 1936, rpt. Geneva, Librairie Droz, 1979.

Williams, Sarah Jane Manley. "Machaut's Self-Awareness as Author and Producer." In *Machaut's World: Science and Art in the Fourteenth Century*, edited by Madeleine Pelner Cosman and Bruce Chandler, 188-97. Annals of the New York Academy of Sciences, 314. New York: New York Academy of Sciences, 1978.

Figure 1. "Primat presents the book to Philip III," *Grandes Chroniques de France.*
Paris, Bibliothèque Ste.-Geneviève, ms. 782, fol. 326v.

Figure 2.   "Jean Golein presents the book to Charles V," Jean Golein, L'*Information des princes*. Paris, Bibliothèque nationale de France, ms. fr. 1950, fol. 2. Cliché Bibliothèque nationale de France, Paris.

Figure 3. "Jean de Vaudetar presents the book to Charles V," *Bible historiale*. The Hague, Museum Meermanno-Westreenianum, ms. 10 B. 23, fol. 2.

Figure 4. "William Caxton presents the book to Margaret of York," Raoul Lefèvre, *The Recuyell of the Historyes of Troye*. San Marino, CA, Huntington Library. Reproduced by permission of *The Huntington Library, San Marino, California*.

Figure 5. "Christine de Pizan presents the book to Isabelle of Bavaria," Christine de Pizan, *Collected Works*. London, British Library, ms. Harley 4431, fol. 1. By permission of the British Library.

Figure 6. " Jean Miélot presents the book to Philip the Good," Jean Miélot, *Traité sur l'oraison dominicale*. Brussels, Bibliothèque Royale Albert Ier, ms. 9092, fol. 1.

Figure 7. "Jean Froissart presents the book to Richard II," Froissart, *Chronicles*. Paris, Bibliothèque nationale de France, ms. fr. 2646, fol. 194v. Cliché Bibliothèque nationale de France, Paris.

Figure 8. "Jean Froissart presents the book to Richard II," Froissart, *Chronicles*. London, British Library, ms. Harley 4380, fol. 23v. By permission of the British Library.

FIGURE 9. "Jean Froissart presents the book to Richard II," Froissart, *Chronicles*. Berlin, Staatsbibliothek Preussischer Kulturbesitz, Breslau deposit I, ms. Rhediger 4, fol. 174.

Figure 10. "Noël de Fribois presents the book to Charles VII," Noël de Fribois, *Abrégé des Chroniques*. Paris, Bibliothèque nationale de France, ms. fr. 10141, fol. 1. Cliché Bibliothèque nationale de France, Paris.

FIGURE 11. "Edward I does homage to Philip the Fair," *Grandes Chroniques de France*. Paris, Bibliothèque nationale de France, ms. fr. 6465, fol. 301v. Cliché Bibliothèque nationale de France, Paris.

Figure 12. "Two Benedictine monks present the book to the King," Noël de Fribois, *Abrégé des Chroniques*. Geneva, Bibliothèque publique et universitaire, ms. fr. 83, fol. 3.

Figure 13. "Jean Germain presents the map to Philip the Good," Jean Germain, *Mappemonde spirituelle*. Lyon, Bibliothèque municipale, P.A. 32, fol. 1.

A Small Library for Pastoral Care and Spiritual Instruction in Late Medieval England[1]

R. N. SWANSON

Pott Shrigley, near Macclesfield in Cheshire, has few claims to fame. Yet it boasts a fine early-Tudor church,[2] a relic of an ambitious commemorative enterprise which epitomizes the devotionalism and memorialism of pre-Reformation England. Geoffrey Downes, a member of a local family of gentry, established the chapel as his chantry, to be served not as a benefice through formal amortization but as a tenure with the endowments held through feoffment to uses.[3] The key document providing evidence on the chantry is dated June 20, 1492; often misleadingly described as Downes's "will," it is essentially a statement of the regulations concerning the selection, duties, and behavior of the chapel priests.[4] The document implies that Downes was the chapel's chief founder, although recognizing some involvement by a Dame Jane Ingoldthorpe, who was the other leading beneficiary of the prayers.

In fact, the process of establishing the chantry may have been more complex. The chapel and its wardens are mentioned as existing in 1472.[5] The will (this time a real will) of Jane Ingoldthorpe also survives, dated June 18, 1494, and probated on the 25th; in it she refers to Pott chapel "of the which I am foundresse." In that document Geoffrey Downes, identified as an esquire, is nominated as her executor, and was actually awarded the administration.[6] This emphasizes the uncertainty surrounding the document of 1492 and leaves the date of Downes's death rather unsatisfactorily open-ended.[7] Overall, the terms of Jane Ingoldthorpe's will suggest some sleight of hand by Downes when creating the chantry at Pott, and a substantial part of the endowment may well have derived from her in the first place: she left the revenues of certain lands to Pott to be received until two years after Geoffrey Downes's death;[8] he was named as the executor responsible for dealing with the residue of her estate for the benefit of her soul. It seems quite likely that he also used these resources to benefit his own soul; and he was accorded sole responsibility for the establishment of the chapel in a commemorative inscription at Pott.[9] This was not the only instance in which he and Jane Ingoldthorpe worked together to guarantee *post mortem* commemoration for their souls. In 1491, when she endowed a fellowship at Queens' College, Cambridge, this Geoffrey Downes was among those who benefited from the chantry element of the foundation. Their souls were also commemorated by St. Augustine's abbey at Canterbury.[10]

Geoffrey Downes's so-called "will" is an excellent indication of the strategies for eternity adopted in late-medieval England. Liturgical arrangements included celebration of the mass of Jesus—tying it in with the Christocentric strand in late medieval devotion—and special prayers to the Virgin. Prayers were also encouraged by the establishment of a formal devotional fraternity whose subscription arrangements are laid out (apparently involving some charitable element, because levels of subscription were to be means-tested). It seems a reasonable presumption that, as with those of other chapels, the fraternity was to have a part in the physical maintenance of the building.[11] Especially notable among the document's stipulations is the tight control established over the chapel clergy, regulating their conduct, dress, and liturgical performances in ways characteristic of the concern to uphold priestly dignity often expressed in late-medieval and early-Tudor England.[12]

These liturgical and functional features encapsulate the traditional religion which Eamon Duffy has identified: lay directed, concerned with Purgatory, devotional, Christ- and Mary-centred, and social.[13] Particularly striking in Downes's "will" is the emphasis on continuing familial domination of the institution, with the chaplains being treated almost as domestic chaplains. Despite the charitable and inclusive features of the fraternity, the social hierarchy was clearly to be maintained.

One further comment is needed on the background to these events. As noted, Geoffrey Downes and Jane Ingoldthorpe cast their nets wide to secure *post mortem* commemoration, including the endowment of a fellowship at Queens' College, Cambridge. At precisely this time another Geoffrey Downes, who it seems reasonable to assume to have been a relative, was a Fellow of that College.[14] The chantry-founding Geoffrey Downes was almost certainly a layman: he is styled "esquire" in Jane Ingoldthorpe's will, and elsewhere calls himself a gentleman of London.[15] The Queens' Fellow would have been a cleric; but so far his career after Cambridge is elusive.[16] The distinction between the two men is important with respect to at least one of the volumes associated with the chapel at Pott.

For present purposes, Pott Shrigley chapel merits attention for something largely ignored in both Jane Ingoldthorpe's will and Geoffrey Downes's ordinance: its books. A surviving inventory of the chantry's possessions, imprecisely datable but probably drawn up in the first years of the chantry's existence, provides identification, detailing the books alongside the lands and jewels.[12] The tally of volumes is, for a mere chantry chapel, impressive:

> In primis - ij masse bookes . . .
> Item - ij port howses, a manuell, & a processionarye
> Item - a boke calde legenda aurea & an oþer calde pergrinacio humane vite
> Item - a boke calde dives & pauper, an oþer calde þe cordyall
> Item - a boke calde þe boke ryall, an oþer calde þe pylgremage of þe saule
> Item - a boke calde speculum vite Christi, an oþer calde gode maners
> Item - a boke calde gestus romanorum, an oþer calde crede michi
> Item - a boke of the brother hode and a quayre of the masse of Jhesu with the servys that longes þerto & xj tabuls with prayers.

This list has not received much attention hitherto. None of the volumes are known to survive.[18] Their provenance is nowhere indicated, but it is a reasonable and almost inescapable presumption that they reached the chapel via the founder Geoffrey Downes, either directly or as intermediary. The presence of books at the chapel is mentioned in his "will" of 1492, although none are identified apart from a mass book and the "boke of the brother hode."

Lists of medieval books owned by local churches are not commonly found, and the concept of the "parish library" seems to be primarily a post-Reformation phenomenon. The reports of medieval episcopal visitations sometimes note books in parish inventories, but these are usually liturgical works, whose possession and maintenance was obligatory and necessary for the functioning of the benefice.[19] Nonliturgical books are rarely noted in official records. This, admittedly, may be a problem of the source material: if the parish libraries were technically in lay ownership, the lists would probably be maintained by the churchwardens rather than incumbents, and nonliturgical volumes would probably not be investigated at visitation.[20]

While the main focus here is on the books which might be considered the "chapel library," the Pott inventory mentions other texts, which reveal "the book" functioning at different levels. First, there is the book as the embodiment of liturgy, indicated by the two mass books, two breviaries ("port howses"), a manual, and a processional as the primary liturgical texts. In addition there is a detached quire containing the Jesus mass, "with the servys that longes þerto." None of this is particularly surprising. Presumably the texts were of Sarum use, given the location within Lichfield diocese. Whether they were manuscripts or printed is not indicated. As other volumes probably were printed, it is likely that some liturgical volumes also reflected the new technology—yet as no printed Sarum processional is known from before 1500, the Pott volume was almost certainly a manuscript; the manual probably was as well.[21] That the Jesus mass existed as a separate quire is noteworthy. This was probably a relatively recently introduced mass, the most likely candidate being the mass of the Name of Jesus. Printed versions of that mass, and of the mass for the equally new feast of the Transfiguration, were produced in England in the 1480s and 1490s.[22] The inclusion of this mass in the Pott Shrigley book list shows the chapel attempting to keep up with the latest liturgical trends.

The quire of the Jesus mass was not, however, the chapel's smallest textual unit. The inventory records eleven "tabuls" with prayers; Downes's "will" also mentions a prayer "written in table."[23] This presumably means a prayer written on a board (or on paper or parchment affixed to a board) to be held for recital. A similar table and the same prayer are mentioned in a document revealing Downes's devotional benefactions in nearby Taxal.[24]

Beyond the book as liturgy, the document also shows it acting as memorial record. The "boke of the brother hode" must be a membership register for the fraternity attached to the chantry, possibly also including a statement of its rules. It may have also included accounts. Probably equivalent registers survive from assorted fraternities across the country, several being little more than lists of names.[25] Downes's ordinance shows this register functioning as memorial: not only does inclusion in the register grant participation in the prayers offered by the chaplain and his congregation at mass; it also required that the full list be publicly read out annually on the first Sunday of Lent.[26] This immediately suggests some comparison with a parish bederoll.[27]

The final function of the books is the most important one when the Pott volumes are considered as a library: their role in a process of spiritual development. Speculation is unavoidable in what follows, but the listed works at Pott do suggest a deliberate concern to encourage spiritual growth in a way fully consonant with the rather puritanical and disciplinary appreciation of priestly office indicated in Downes's regulations. Of course, the list being just a list, and with no surviving volumes, uncertainties abound. Not indicated is the format of the volumes: are these manuscripts or printed works? Several of the titles match those of Caxton's output, potentially making the library a significant collection of his work and, accordingly, evidence of the new technology's immediate impact and swift diffusion. The northward movement need not be a surprise: as a London gentleman, Geoffrey Downes could presumably patronize Caxton at Westminster. Some of the volumes may have belonged to Jane Ingoldthorpe, being distributed by Downes in his administration for the good of her soul. Admittedly, her will does not mention books, yet it is highly devotional and was actually dated at the London Blackfriars.[28] Both he and she certainly fit into the social and economic groups which have been identified as characteristic owners of Caxton's products.[29] Indeed, there is a possibility that any link with Caxton could have been through Jane Ingoldthorpe rather than through Geoffrey Downes. She was, after all, the daughter of that earl of Worcester whose translations of Cicero's *De amicitia* and Buonaccorso de Montemagno's *Controversia de nobilitate* were printed by Caxton in 1481, almost a decade after the earl's death. How Caxton came into possession of the works is unknown,[30] but family contact is not an impossible route.

One major uncertainty with the Pott list is whether it records all the works in the collection: the habit of citing a composite volume by the title of its first item may conceal a larger collection.[31] An analysis of the Pott list may aim to derive the maximum from it but is unavoidably based on minimal information. One final point must be made, about language. For books with English titles, it seems certain that the texts were in the vernacular. What, though, of books with Latin titles, the *Legenda aurea*, *Peregrinatio humane vite*, *Speculum vite Christi*, *Gesta Romanorum*, and *Crede michi*? While Latin texts cannot be discounted, and the last appears never to have been translated, the collection's function in a parochial and guild context and expectation of wider distribution of copies based on these volumes,[32] suggest that several of the Latin titles applied to works in English. Certainly all except the *Crede michi* existed in English versions by 1494. Such English texts would therefore be viable candidates for identification with the books on the Pott list, although this does not mean that *Crede michi* was definitely the only nonliturgical text on that list which was in Latin.

The Latinity of the *Crede michi* immediately separates it from the other works; so might its function. It falls at the borderline, and arguably should be counted among the liturgical material. Composed in the 1450s, it served to clarify uncertain points in the Sarum Use.[33] It was aimed specifically at the clergy, so that, the rules being learnt, "vix potest errare in servicio divino."[34] It seems that only one manuscript is known (contained in British Library MS Add. 25456); although the work was printed, there is no evidence that it was circulated as an independent printed text. All the early printed versions (including two editions by Caxton in c. 1484 and 1489) appeared as appendices to Clement Maydeston's *Directorium sacerdotum*. This might suggest that the Pott copy was a manuscript; but that need not be the case. The collations of the printed volumes are such that *Crede michi* could have been easily divorced from the larger work to circulate on its own.[35]

The rest of the collection is a good cross section of the didactic and devotional material used for spiritual formation and personal modeling in Middle English religious writing.[36] The most straightforward text is the *Legenda aurea*, the standard collection of saints' lives formulated by Jacobus da Voragine in the thirteenth century and thereafter disseminated widely throughout Europe. Over the next two centuries it developed numerous regional variants. Its fate as a vernacular work in England was compromised by the existence of a local legendary tradition, epitomized in the "South English Legendary," which integrated some of the *Legenda aurea* material. In the fifteenth century a closer translation became available in the *Gilte Legende*, with additions dealing with specifically English cults. Caxton produced his own translation into English of a French version of the *Legenda aurea*, published in 1483, but also incorporating some material from the *Gilte Legende*. Where the Pott volume fits into this fluid tradition is a matter of guesswork, although the possibility that it was a copy of the Caxton volume or of the later edition of Wynkyn de Worde cannot be rejected.[37]

Dives and pauper was another didactic text, being perhaps the longest commentary on the Ten Commandments produced in late-medieval England.[38] A mendicant product of the early fifteenth century,[39] it works methodically and exhaustively through the Decalogue, meticulously dissecting sins in a dialogue of guidance which was presumably meant to feed into the annual confessional process. Notoriously, it was also considered suspect by some of the ecclesiastical authorities, its possession once being advanced as grounds for suspicion of heresy.[40] However, there is little in it to justify such suspicions, unless it was doctored as "Lollards" doctored other orthodox texts. While the Pott text might have been printed—and therefore fairly new, being printed by Pynson only in 1493 and by de Worde in 1496[41]—a manuscript is perhaps more likely.

Linked in genre to *Dives and pauper* is the book here listed as "þe boke ryall," a work translated by Caxton and published in 1485 to 1486.[42] A version of Lorens d'Orleans's *Somme le roi*, originally written for King Philip IV of France in the late thirteenth century, it deals with the Ten Commandments, the Creed, and sins,[43] and falls squarely into the genre of late-medieval catechetical works which ultimately derive from the "pastoral revolution" initiated at the Fourth Lateran Council of 1215.[44] The *Somme*, in various manifestations, fed into the making of Middle English sermons (although apparently to an extent not fully appreciated).[45] The *Book royal* could have served a similar purpose, although it has been claimed that it was intended for "a relatively educated and sophisticated laity," and is less suitable as a pastoral aid than another Caxton product of the 1480s, the *Doctrinal of Sapience*, a work not on the Pott list.[46]

Similar in genre was the *Book of Good Manners*, a translation of a fifteenth-century work by the French Augustinian Jacques Legrand. Replete with exempla, this too considered the seven deadly sins and their corresponding virtues, dwelt on death and judgment, and discussed the conduct appropriate for various ranks in society.[47] Like other Pott books, it was probably printed; incunable editions were issued by Caxton, Pynson, and de Worde.[48] However, three other late-medieval English translations are known, and even though each survives in only a single manuscript, it remains possible that the Pott text was also a manuscript.[49]

If the titles considered so far provide source materials for the preaching of *pastoralia* in pre-Reformation Pott,[50] the two works by Guillaume de Deguileville, the *Peregrinatio humane vite* and *Pylgremage of þe saule*, offer a more devotional (yet still didactic) focus. The former—Englished in two different versions, the better known being by Lydgate—describes an allegorical journey in which the traveling soul confronts the several sacraments and theological virtues.[51] Again, it meshes into the catechetical program derived from Lateran IV, perhaps at a deeper level than most parishioners would need. The second work moves into the afterlife, journeying through Purgatory to the Last Judgment.[52] That English text has sometimes also been ascribed to Lydgate, sometimes Thomas Hoccleve has been suggested as the translator, but neither ascription can be proved.[53] Only the *Pilgrimage of the Soul* appeared in print in English, being issued by Caxton in 1483.[54] The translation itself has been associated with the assertion of orthodoxy against Lollardy in the early fifteenth century, thereby having affinities with the anti-Lollard facets of Nicholas Love's *Mirror of the Blessed Life of Jesus Christ* (a copy of which may also have been among the Pott volumes).[55] The *Pilgrimage of the Soul* accordingly provided "an attractive vehicle for bolstering orthodox religious beliefs among readers of the vernacular."[56] The Latin title of its companion volume at Pott may hide a manuscript English text or a continental printed copy. If the latter, it would probably have been in French, there being no Latin version; which may increase the likelihood that Pott had an English text in manuscript.[57]

Of the more devotional works at Pott, that most immediately recognizable, even if not precisely identifiable, is the *Speculum vite Christi*. This must be related to the pseudo-Bonaventuran text, which provides a narrative of the life of Christ based on the Gospels and supplemented with apocryphal tales, written as a basis for meditation and devotion within a structured framework.

Its Christocentric concern was characteristic of late-medieval devotion, particularly in its stress on the Passion and the resulting connections created
between God and Man. The imprecision of the Pott inventory is such that the
text could have been in Latin or an English version of any of the several deriv-
atives of the work available at the time. However, its identity can probably be
narrowed down. The most likely candidate is Nicholas Love's *Mirror of the
Blessed Life of Jesus Christ*, produced c. 1410.[58] By 1493 Caxton had already
printed two editions; others were soon issued by Wynkyn de Worde (1494)
and Richard Pynson (c. 1494).[59] If *Dives and pauper* sometimes carried the whiff
of heresy, Love's work was explicitly anti-Lollard and vigorously orthodox in
its interpretations.[60]

Of the remaining works, the *Gesta Romanorum* (setting aside the
unlikely possibility that it was actually a version of some Latin Roman chronicle) also fits into the category of potential preaching tools.[61] Comprising a
series of stories, usually set in the Roman past and suitably moralized,[62] like
the *Legenda aurea* it provides exempla which could be adapted for inclusion in
sermons—and John Mirk exploited both the *Gesta* and the *Legenda* to provide
material for his *Festial* in the early fifteenth century.[63] With the *Gesta*, however,
no clear identification is possible for the Pott text: the original version developed into so many variants that a mere title gives insufficient information.
Versions existed of varying lengths and in different traditions. Most important, there were distinct English and continental traditions. Of these, the
latter was the first into print, in Latin, and apparently so dominated the
market that it effectively pushed the English tradition aside.[64] If the Pott
volume was printed, it would probably have been a continental version, as no
English edition is recorded before 1502.[65] It could still be a Caxton volume,
as he printed a version at Cologne in 1472.[66] Alternatively, if the Pott text was
a manuscript, it probably reflected the text's English tradition.

The last title on the list was almost certainly printed, again probably
a Caxton product. *The Cordyall* was the translation by Antony, Earl Rivers, of a
French version of Gerard van Vliederhoven's *Cordiale quattuor novissimorum*, and
was printed in 1479.[67] Concerned with physical death, the Day of Judgment,
Hell, and Heaven, it functions primarily as a call to self-control and repen-
tance. As such, it ties in with the *Pilgrimage of the Soul* and the concerns of the
Book of Good Manners and yet again fits well with the concern for effective pastoral care which permeates the collection.

The books at Pott are part of a pattern that appears characteristic of
England around 1500. Here printed religious works were "overwhelmingly traditional and orthodox [in] character" and largely replicated the mentality of
the manuscript world.[68] Indeed, the lack of distinction between the worlds of
print and manuscript is explicit in Geoffrey Downes's ordinance, for the Pott
library was not to be static and inaccessible. Downes expected the books to

be used, allowing gentlemen to borrow texts for up to thirteen weeks so that they could be read or copied—with the specific exception of the mass book.[69] Here the diffusion of print is clearly implied (at least for the works which were printed), but via a manuscript culture—a process of bookmaking rather than book-buying, which seems characteristic of the transitional phase before print became the dominant literary medium.[70]

The arrangements for dissemination are important, but so is the principle of retention. The books were to stay at Pott—those borrowed for copying had to be returned within thirteen weeks. Clearly they were meant to be useful for the clergy; whether ordinary parishioners (or, perhaps, fraternity members) had access to them is less certain. Yet as a collection they also show the institutionalization and stabilization of the concept of the "common-profit" volume or library. Such common-profit arrangements usually specified a procedure for transmitting book(s) from owner to owner, but without tying them to a particular location. The formality of Pott's library takes the concept a stage further, integrating it into the wave of library foundations in fifteenth-century England for similar purposes. The Pott arrangements, however, are much less grandiose than others, such as London's Guildhall Library, or Bishop John Carpenter's libraries at Worcester and Bristol.[71] One obvious difference is that the Pott library was a rural rather than urban foundation.

One more book needs attention: an extant volume not in the Pott inventory but linked to the chapel by an inscription. British Library MS Add. 41175 was owned successively by two graduates of the Downes family, Geoffrey and James, passing from one to the other on condition that it revert to Pott on James's death.[72] That Geoffrey must be the Fellow of Queens', not the gentleman of London.

This volume is very different in character from those in the inventory, being a typically well-produced late-fourteenth-century text of the Wycliffite glossed gospels of Matthew and Mark. Arguably its acquisition would help to fill a gap in the Pott collection, which lacks anything explicitly biblical. However, that gap may be illusory: substantial parts of the New Testament were paraphrased in Love's Mirror, while if the version of the Legenda aurea was by Caxton, its preliminary matter would have given access to "one of the most interesting and complete prose biblical paraphrases to be produced in the fourteenth [sic] century."[73] The implications of these glossed gospels are significant if they ever reached Pott. They would thereby provide a channel for Wycliffite ideas to spread in the area; but that the volume was meant to join the chapel possessions suggests that it was not seen by the academic Geoffrey Downes as an overtly heretical or threatening text. Indeed, two earlier owners clearly considered it so unthreatening that they passed it on with requests for prayers for their souls.[74]

Whether these glossed gospels actually reached Pott is unknown. The will of James Downes was proved early in 1529,[75] perhaps sufficiently before the onset of the Reformation and the production of printed English Bibles for it to have been considered worth sending to Pott. Yet as James Downes apparently died in Kent and did not mention Pott in his will, and the inscription in the volume required its delivery to a chapel of Pott in Shropshire, distance and confusion may have worked against its transfer. It is intriguing to speculate about its possible reception, particularly at so critical a point in the development of the English Church.

The books associated with Pott chapel, other than the glossed gospels, are now merely a list of titles. Yet that list, set alongside the stipulations made by Geoffrey Downes in 1492, gives an insight into the multiple functions of the book in pre-Reformation English religion. Liturgical and memorial functions were important—and may be understated here. What stands out is the book's role as a channel of communication, repository for ideas, and means of instruction. If these volumes were mainly printed, the list also shows the immediate impact of the new technology and its intermediary function when volumes provided the basis for both oral instruction through sermons and exemplars for further manuscript dissemination in early-Tudor Cheshire.

University of Birmingham

NOTES

1. A version of this paper was delivered at the Ecclesiastical History Society conference on "The Church and the Book" at Lampeter in July 2000. I am grateful to Dr Valerie Edden for comment on an earlier draft. Archival research at Chester was funded by the Leverhulme Trust.

2. For a description of the building see F. H. Crossley, "The Renaissance of Cheshire Church Building in the Late Fifteenth and Early Sixteenth Centuries," *Journal of the Chester and North Wales Architectural, Archaeological and Historic Society*, 34 (1939-1940), pp. 134-138.

3. On such arrangements, which make it especially difficult to trace some chapels and their incumbents because they do not need to appear in official records, see A. Kreider, *English Chantries: the Road to Dissolution*, Harvard Historical Studies, 97 (Cambridge, MA, and London: Harvard University Press, 1979), pp. 77-79.

4. The document is fully printed (with some defects) in *Cheshire Sheaf*, 2 (1880), pp. 46-48, 51-52; a reduced version is in J. P. Earwaker, *East Cheshire: Past and Present; or a History of the Hundred of Macclesfield in the County Palatine of Chester, from Original Records*, 2 vols.

(London: privately printed, 1877-1880), 2, pp. 325-327. The original no longer survives. For comment, see J. McN. Dodgson, "A Library at Pott Chapel (Pott Shrigley, Cheshire), c. 1493," The Library, 5th ser., 15 (1960), pp. 47-48. As a "will" it is generically different from the modern notion of such a document, which would focus primarily on the distribution of bequests—the function performed in the medieval "testament" (on this distinction see E. F. Jacob, The Register of Henry Chichele, Archbishop of Canterbury, 1414-43, 4 vols., Canterbury and York Society, 42, 45-47 |Oxford: Oxford University Press, 1937-1947|, 2, pp. xix-xxi). Downes's "will" bears no sign of probate, names no witnesses, and specifies no personal or other bequests. It has clear affinities with other documents making provision to regulate chantries and their endowments which survive from this period without being formally testamentary; see, e.g., R. N. Swanson, Catholic England: Faith, Religion, and Observance before the Reformation (Manchester: Manchester University Press, 1993), pp. 234-241; R. N. Swanson, "Medieval English Liturgy: What's the Use?," Studia liturgica, 29 (1999) pp. 181-183. The fact that the "will" is not what would now be considered such creates problems in determining how far its provisions were implemented (although corroborative evidence shows that some were); in particular, the date at which it was put into effect cannot be adequately deduced. Its wording suggests that the feoffees were already in possession of the endowments as trustees, so there would have been nothing to prevent its provisions being acted on immediately. Certainly, there are no real grounds to challenge its reliability.

5. Chester, Cheshire Record Office, DDS 3/37.

6. Her will is London, Public Record Office, Prob.11/10, f.97r-v. She was the sister of Edward Tiptoft, earl of Worcester, who died in 1485, and wife to Sir Edmund Ingoldthorpe of Wickhambreux in Kent (and also of Cambridgeshire). Several members of the Downes family are mentioned in her will; it was through her patronage that James Downes became rector of Wickhambreaux in 1493, dying there in 1529. (For his appointment, see C. Harper-Bill, The Register of John Morton, Archbishop of Canterbury, 1486-1500, vol. 1, Canterbury and York Society Publications, 75 |Leeds: Duffield Printers, 1987|, no. 565. For other aspects of James Downes's career, see pp. 112-13.)

7. Cheshire Record Office, DDS 15/4, dated February 12, 1492/3, suggests that Downes's will was then being implemented. For the chapel founder to be dead by this date would require the postulation of two people of the same name (in fact, three; see below) operating within a nexus centered on Jane Ingoldthorpe.

8. The lands are not named in the will, but appear from her inquisitions postmortem: Calendar of Inquisitions Post Mortem and other Analogous Documents, Henry VII, vol. 1 (London: Her Majesty's Stationery Office, 1898), nos 1085-1092, esp. no. 1092.

9. F. Renaud, Contributions towards a History of the Ancient Parish of Prestbury in Cheshire, Chetham Society Publications, 97 (Manchester: Charles Simms and Co., 1876), p. 13; Earwaker, East Cheshire, 2, p. 328. Joan Ingoldthorpe was commemorated as the donor of a window in an inscription recorded in 1589: Earwaker, East Cheshire, 2, p. 327; G. Ormerod (rev. T. Helsby), The History of the County Palatine and City of Chester, 2d ed., 3 vols. (London: G. Routledge, 1882), 2, p. 774.

10. W. G. Searle, *The History of the Queens' College of St Margaret and St Bernard in the University of Cambridge*, 1446-1560, Cambridge Antiquarian Society Octavo Publications, 9 (Cambridge: Cambridge University Press, 1867), pp. 119-120.

11. V. R. Bainbridge, *Gilds in the Medieval Countryside: Social and Religious Change in Cambridgeshire, c.* 1350-1558, Studies in the History of Religion, 10 (Woodbridge: Boydell Press, 1996), pp. 127-129. There are hints that Downes may have modeled his foundation on one at Taxal: see Chester, Cheshire Record Office, DDS 15/5. Taxal was in Downes family patronage but held by a different branch of the family: Renaud, *Prestbury*, p. 166.

12. P. Marshall, *The Catholic Priesthood in the English Reformation* (Oxford: Clarendon Press, 1994), pp. 51-53, 129-137.

13. E. Duffy, *The Stripping of the Altars: Traditional Religion in England, c.* 1400-*c.* 1580 (New Haven and London: Yale University Press, 1992), Part 1.

14. For the Cambridge Fellow, A. B. Emden, *A Biographical Register of the University of Cambridge to* 1500 (Cambridge: Cambridge University Press, 1963), p. 193. Dodgson assumes that the two Geoffreys are one: "Library at Pott," p. 49.

15. London, Public Record Office, Prob.11/10, f.97r; Chester, Cheshire Record Office, DDS 2/6 (dated 1492).

16. According to J. Venn and J. A. Venn, *Alumni Cantabrigienses*, Part 1, 4 vols. (Cambridge: Cambridge University Press, 1922-1927), 2, p. 60, he died in 1529, but this date is not recorded in Emden.

17. For discussion of the inventory, Dodgson, "Library at Pott," pp. 47-49. He suggests that it was "drawn up not long after February 1493" (p. 49). I would be less precise but still suggest a date in the 1490s, but probably not before 1494.

18. The books are briefly identified, without commentary other than indication of possible printed editions, in Dodgson, "Library at Pott," pp. 50-52. The list does not appear in N. R. Ker, *Medieval Libraries of Great Britain: a List of Surviving Books*, 2d ed., Royal Historical Society Guides and Handbooks, 3 (London: Royal Historical Society, 1964), or in the *Supplement* to that work, ed. A. G. Watson, Royal Historical Society Guides and Handbooks, 15 (London: Royal Historical Society, 1987).

19. E.g., the inventories in T. C. B. Timmins, ed., *The Register of John Chandler, Dean of Salisbury*, 1404-17, Wiltshire Record Society Publications, 39 (Devizes: Wiltshire Record Society, 1984), nos 116-187, passim. Books also appear in the lists in A. Watkin, ed., *Archdeaconry of Norwich: Inventory of Church Goods, Temp. Edward III*, 2 vols., Norfolk Record Society, 19 (n.p.: Norfolk Record Society, 1947-1948), see also ibid., 2, pp. xxv-xlix.

20. The books of All Saints', Derby, are listed in the churchwardens' accounts: Matlock, Derbyshire Record Office, D3372/91/1 (unfoliated); see J. C. Cox and W. H. St. John Hope, eds, *The Chronicles of the Collegiate Church or Free Chapel of All Saints, Derby* (London and Derby: Bemrose and Sons, 1881), pp. 175-177.

21. For printed Sarum liturgical works up to 1500, see A.W. Pollard and G.R. Redgrave (rev. W.A. Jackson, F.S. Ferguson, and K.F. Pantzer), *A Short-Title Catalogue of Books Printed in England, Scotland, and Ireland, and of English Books Printed Abroad* (1475-1640), 3 vols. (2d

ed., London: Bibliographical Society, 1976-1991) |hereafter cited as STC| 15794-15805 (breviaries), 16138-16139 (manuals, dated 1498-1500), 16164-16175 (missals). The first recorded printed processional is at 16232.6.

22. R. W. Pfaff, *New Liturgical Feasts in Late Medieval England* (Oxford: Clarendon Press, 1970), pp. 62-83; STC, 15851-15855.

23. Dodgson, "Library at Pott," p. 50; *Cheshire Sheaf*, p. 51; Earwaker, *East Cheshire*, 2, p. 326.

24. Dodgson, "Library at Pott," p. 52; Cheshire Record Office, DDS 15/5.

25. For characteristic registers see, e.g., W. B. Bickley, *The Register of the Guild of Knowle in the County of Warwick*, 1451-1535 (Walsall: W. H. Robinson, 1894); J. H. Bloom, *The Register of the Gild of the Holy Cross, the Blessed Mary, and St. John the Evangelist of Stratford-upon-Avon* (London: Phillimore and Co., 1907); R. H. Scaife, *The Register of the Guild of Corpus Christi in the City of York*, Surtees Society Publications, 57, Durham, Andrews and Co. (1872); M. D. Harris, *The Register of the Guild of the Holy Trinity, St. Mary, St. John the Baptist, and St. Katherine of Coventry*, 2 vols., Dugdale Society Publications, 13, 19 (London: Oxford University Press, 1935-1944). At Walsall in Staffordshire, the guild accounts can function as a register, noting annual admissions, but they are in a lengthy roll and could not easily be read out in the manner prescribed in Downes's will. An early sixteenth-century register, without financial information, could be so used, despite its somewhat scrappy maintenance: R. N. Swanson, "A Medieval Staffordshire Fraternity: The Guild of St. John the Baptist, Walsall," in *Staffordshire Histories: Essays in Honour of Michael Greenslade*, edited by Philip Morgan and A.D.M. Phillips, Collections for a History of Staffordshire, 4th ser., 19 (Stafford and Keele: Staffordshire Record Society and The Centre for Local History, University of Keele, 1999), pp. 47-65 (esp. 51-52); Walsall, Local History Centre, 276/89.

26. *Cheshire Sheaf*, p. 47; Earwaker, *East Cheshire*, 2, p. 326.

27. On this, see Duffy, *Stripping of the Altars*, pp. 134, 153-154, 334-337.

28. The will's silence on the books is not a legitimate challenge to the possibility that they did originally belong to Jane Ingoldthorpe. Wills, despite their importance as sources, are notoriously incomplete records of possessions. See, in general, A. M. Dutton, "Passing the Book: Testamentary Transmission of Religious Literature to and by Women in England, 1350-1500," in *Women, the Book and the Godly: Selected Proceedings of the St Hilda's Conference, 1993, volume I*, edited by L. Smith and J. H. M. Taylor (Cambridge and Rochester, NY: D. S. Brewer, 1995), pp. 41, 43-44.

29. M. L. Ford, "Private Ownership of Printed Books," in *The Cambridge History of the Book in Britain, Volume III: 1400-1557*, edited by L. Hellinga and J. B. Trapp (Cambridge: Cambridge University Press, 1999), pp. 213-218.

30. R. J. Mitchell, *John Tiptoft* (1427-1470) (London, New York, and Toronto: Longmans, Green, and Co., 1938), pp. 172-178, 185; R. E. Lewis, N. F. Blake, and A. S. G. Edwards, *Index of Printed Middle English Prose* (New York and London: Garland, 1985), nos. 555, 830.

31. For composite volumes including Caxton prints, P. Needham, *The Printer and the Pardoner: an Unrecorded Indulgence Printed by William Caxton for the Hospital of St. Mary*

Rounceval, Charing Cross (Washington, DC: Library of Congress, 1986), App. B; also comment at p. 19. For composite volumes uniting manuscripts and printed works (to add a further complication), see N. F. Blake, "Manuscript to Print," in his *William Caxton and English Literary Culture* (London and Rio Grande, OH: Hambledon Press, 1991), p. 277 (originally in *Book Production and Publishing in Britain, 1375-1475*, edited by J. Griffiths and D. Pearsall, Cambridge: Cambridge University Press, 1989).

32. see pp.111-12.

33. C. Wordsworth, ed., *The Tracts of Clement Maydeston, with the Remains of Caxton's Ordinal*, Henry Bradshaw Society, 7 (London: Harrison and Sons, 1894), pp. xxxi-xxxviii, 27-89.

34. Wordsworth, *Tracts*, p. 81.

35. Incunable prints are STC 17720-17726. For the collations, see E. G. Duff, *Fifteenth-Century English Books: A Bibliography of Books and Documents Printed in England, and of Books for the English Market Printed Abroad*, Bibliographical Society Illustrated Monographs, 18 (Oxford: Oxford University Press, 1917), nos. 290-296.

36. When considered in relation to the categories advanced by Dutton, "Passing the Book," pp. 48-49, almost every type is repesented. The only absence is of her Group 5, "The writings of mystics or visionaries." When set alongside Dutton's work, the Pott books might appear a representative selection of the types of works read or owned by women; but there is nothing exclusively female-oriented about the collection.

37. On the development of this material in England, see M. Görlach, *Studies in Middle English Saints' Legends*, Anglistische Forschungen, 257 (Heidelberg: C. Winter, 1998), pp. 25-32, 55-56, 71-76, 137-145. For early printed editions, see STC, 24873-24876. For the Caxton print, see Lewis, Blake, and Edwards, *Index*, no. 682.

38. See Lewis, Blake, and Edwards, *Index*, no. 156. Edited in P. H. Barnum, *Dives and Pauper*, 2 vols., Early English Text Society, OS 275, 280 (Oxford: Oxford University Press, 1976-1980).

39. A. Hudson, *The Premature Reformation: Wycliffite Texts and Lollard History* (Oxford: Clarendon Press, 1989), p. 418; A. Hudson and H. L. Spencer, "Old Author, New Work: The Sermons of MS Longleat 4," *Medium Ævum*, 53 (1984), pp. 220, 228, 230-233.

40. Hudson, *Premature Reformation*, pp. 417-420.

41. STC 19212-19213.

42. STC 21429; Lewis, Blake, and Edwards, *Index*, no. 824.

43. See W. N. Francis, ed., *The Book of Vices and Virtues: A Fourteenth-Century English Translation of the* Somme le roi *of Lorens d'Orléans*, Early English Text Society, OS 217 (London: Oxford University Press, 1942), pp. xxxvii-xxxviii; R. H. Wilson, "Malory and Caxton," in *A Manual of the Writings in Middle English, 1050-1500*, 3, edited by A. E. Hartung (New Haven, CT: Connecticut Academy of Arts and Sciences, 1972), pp. 794-795, 942.

44. Useful introductory surveys in L. E. Boyle, "The Fourth Lateran Council and Manuals of Popular Theology," in *The Popular Literature of Medieval England*, edited by T. J. Heffernan, Tennessee Studies in Literature, 28 (Knoxville, TN: University of Tennessee

Press, 1985), pp. 30-43; also J. Shaw, "The Influence of Canonical and Episcopal Reform on Popular Books of Instruction," ibid., pp. 45-60.

45. F. N. M. Diekstra, *Book for a Simple Devout Woman: A Late Middle English Adaptation of Peraldus's* Summa de vitiis et virtutibus *and Friar Laurent's* Somme le roi, *edited from British Library MSS Harley 6571 and Additional 30944*, Mediaevalia Groningana, 24 (Groningen: Egbert Forsten, 1998), p. viii.

46. J. E. Gallagher, "The Source of Caxton's *Royal Book* and *Doctrinal of Sapience*," *Studies in Philology*, 62 (1965), p. 62.

47. See Duffy, *Stripping of the Altars*, p. 78; Wilson, "Malory and Caxton," pp. 795, 942-943. For a brief discussion of the French text and outline of its development, and list of exempla, see J. Rychner, "Les sources morales des *Vigiles de Charles VII*: le *Jeu des échecs moralisé* et le *Livre de bonnes moeurs* des *exempla* à la fin du moyen âge," *Romania*, 77 (1956), pp. 447-448, 457-487.

48. STC 15394-15397; Lewis, Blake, and Edwards, *Index*, no. 820.

49. For these other versions, and an assessment of Caxton's text, see B. Lindström, "Some Remarks on Two English Translations of Jacques Legrand's *Livres de bonnes meurs*," *English Studies*, 58 (1977), pp. 304-311. See also B. Lindström, "The English Versions of Jacques Legrand's *Livres de bonnes meurs*," *The Library*, 6th ser., 1 (1979), pp. 247-254; M. Connolly, *John Shirley: Book Production and the Noble Household in Fifteenth-Century England* (Aldershot, Brookfield, Singapore, and Sydney: Ashgate, 1998), pp. 120-126.

50. For a generic discussion of preaching of pastoralia, see H. L. Spencer, *English Preaching in the Late Middle Ages* (Oxford: Clarendon Press, 1993), pp. 201-227.

51. The Lydgate version is in F. J. Furnivall and K. B. Locock, eds, *The Pilgrimage of the Life of Man, Englisht from the French of Guillaume de Deguileville, AD 1330, 1355*, 3 vols., Early English Text Society, ES 77, 83, 92 (London: K. Paul, Trench, Trübner and Co., 1899-1904); see also W. F. Schirmer, *John Lydgate: a Study in the Culture of the XVth Century* (London: Methuen, 1961), pp. 120-121, 123-126. The Lydgate ascription has recently been debated: see K. Wells, "Did Lydgate translate the 'Pèlerinage de vie humaine'?," *Notes and Queries*, 222 (1977), pp. 103-105; R. F. Green, "Lydgate and Deguileville once more," *Notes and Queries*, 223 (1978), pp. 105-106. Another version of the work is in A. Henry, ed., *The Pilgrimage of the Lyfe of the Manhode*, 2 vols., Early English Text Society, OS 288, 292 (Oxford: Oxford University Press, 1985-1988). On the work, see also R. Tuve, *Allegorical Imagery: Some Medieval Books and Their Posterity* (Princeton, NJ: Princeton University Press, 1966), ch. 3; S. K. Hagen, *Allegorical Remembrance: A Study of* The Pilgrimage of the Life of Man *as a Medieval Treatise on Seeing and Remembering* (Athens, GA, and London: University of Georgia Press, 1990).

52. R. M. McGerr, *The Pilgrimage of the Soul: a Critical Edition of the Middle English Dream Vision*, Garland Medieval Texts, 16 (New York and London: Garland, 1990). This is the only volume yet published of a projected two-volume edition. It contains the edition of Book 1 and an Introduction.

53. McGerr, *Pilgrimage*, pp. xxvi-xxix; Schirmer, *Lydgate*, pp. 121-122 (but with a confused argument); M. C. Seymour, ed., *Selections from Hoccleve* (Oxford: Clarendon Press, 1981), pp. xiv-xv, n. 12; J. A. Burrow, *Thomas Hoccleve* (Aldershot and Brookfield, VT: Ashgate, 1994), p. 24.

54. STC 6473-6474; Lewis, Blake, and Edwards, *Index*, no. 72. See also W. L. Hare, "A Newly Discovered Volume Printed by William Caxton: Pylgremage of the Sowle," *Apollo*, 14 (July-Dec. 1931), pp. 206, 213. The text also circulated quite extensively in manuscript: McGerr, *Pilgrimage*, pp. lv-xcii. These texts, unlike Caxton's print, had (or were generally expected to have) illustrations: ibid., pp. xlv-lv.

55. McGerr, *Pilgrimage*, pp. xlii-xlv. For Nicholas Love, see p. 111.

56. McGerr, *Pilgrimage*, p. xliv.

57. For the dissemination of the *Pilgrimage of the Life of Man* see Tuve, *Allegorical Imagery*, pp. 146-147; M. Camille, "Reading the Printed Image: Illuminations and Woodcuts of the *Pèlerinage de la vie humaine* in the Fifteenth Century," in *Printing the Written Word: the Social History of Books circa 1450-1520*, edited by S. Hindman (Ithaca, NY, and London: Cornell University Press, 1991), pp. 260-261.

58. M. G. Sargent, ed., *Nicholas Love's Mirror of the Blessed Life of Jesus Christ: A Critical Edition based on Cambridge University Library Additional MSS 6578 and 6686* (New York and London: Garland, 1992). For problems in identifying this work, especially in distinguishing between Latin and English versions when only the title is given, C. M. Meale, "'Oft siþis with grete deuotion I þought what I mi3t do plesyng to god': The Early Ownership and Readership of Love's *Mirror*, with Special Reference to its Female Audience," in *Nicholas Love at Waseda: Proceedings of the International Conference, 20-22 July 1995*, edited by S. Oguro, R. Beadle, and M. G. Sargent (Cambridge: D. S. Brewer, 1997), pp. 30-34. See also M. C. Erler, "Devotional Literature," in Hellinga and Trapp, *Cambridge History*, pp. 516-518.

59. STC 3259-3262; Lewis, Blake, and Edwards, *Index*, no. 553. See also L. Hellinga, "Nicholas Love in Print," in Oguro, Beadle, and Sargent, *Love at Waseda*, pp. 145-156 (and pp. 143-144 for discussion of the printing of the Latin text).

60. Hudson, *Premature Reformation*, pp. 437-440.

61. S. J. H. Herrtage, ed., *The Early English Versions of the Gesta Romanorum*, Early English Text Society, ES 33 (London: N. Trübner and Sons, 1879); see comment on potential confusion caused by the title at p. vii n. 1.

62. Although one of the English MSS lacks moralizations: Herrtage, *Early English Versions*, p. xx.

63. Görlach, *Studies*, pp. 67-70.

64. Herrtage, *Early English Versions*, pp. xiv-xv, xvii. See also E. P. Goldschmidt, *Medieval Texts and their First Appearance in Print*, Supplement to the Bibliographical Society's Transactions, 16 (London: Oxford University Press, 1943), pp. 9-10.

65. STC 21286.2; Lewis, Blake, and Edwards, *Index*, no. 172.

66. L. Hellinga, "Printing," in Hellinga and Trapp, *Cambridge History*, pp. 66-67.

67. Lewis, Blake, and Edwards, Index, no. 47. The Caxton edition (STC 5748) is reprint-
ed with a limited historical commentary in J. A. Mulders, ed., The Cordyal by Anthony
Woodville, Earl Rivers, edited from M 38 A1, the Museum Meemanno Westreenianum, The Hague
(Nijmegen: Centrale Drukkerij N. V., 1962); see esp. pp. xv-xix, xxi-xxxv. De Worde produced another edition in ?1496: STC 5759.

68. Duffy, Stripping of the Altars, pp. 77-82, esp. 78.

69. Cheshire Sheaf, p. 52; Earwaker, East Cheshire, 2, p. 326.

70. For manuscript copies of early printed books (especially Caxton volumes), see
Blake, "Manuscript to Print," pp. 285-293.

71. J. A. H. Moran, "A 'Common Profit' Library in Fifteenth-Century England and Other
Books for Chaplains," Manuscripta, 28 (1984), pp. 17-25; W. Scase, "Reginald Pecock,
John Carpenter and John Colop's 'Common Profit Books': Aspects of Book Ownership
and Circulation in Fifteenth-Century London," Medium Ævum, 61 (1982), pp. 261-274.

72. London, British Library, MS Add. 41175, f.1. For James Downes, see A. B. Emden,
A Biographical Register of the University of Oxford to 1500, 3 vols. (Oxford: Clarendon Press,
1957-1959), 1, p. 590. There is a remote possibility that another volume could also
have been destined for Pott. London, British Library MS Add. 11475 contains only
Matthew and Mark; Oxford, Bodleian Library, MS Bodley 243, is its companion to complete the New Testament, but lacks provenance. Precisely when its history was
divorced from that of the companion volume is unknown. (I am grateful to Prof. Anne
Hudson for discussing this volume with me.)

73. J. H. Morey, Book and Verse: a Guide to Middle English Biblical Literature (Urbana and
Chicago: University of Illinois Press, 2000), p. 154. The Biblical content is summarized
ibid., pp. 155-158; for that in Love, ibid., pp. 338-343.

74. London, British Library, MS Add. 41175, f. 1, has a request for prayers for the soul
of M. John Crowlond, Fellow of Queens' College, Cambridge, "gyver of this boke;" at ff.
2r, 164r, are requests, "Orate pro anima domini Hugonis Blyth." For Crowlond see
Emden, Cambridge, p. 170. A Hugh Blyth died as rector of Abbess Roding, Essex, in
1455: see R. Newcourt, Repertorium Ecclesiasticum Parochiale Londinense, 2 vols. (London:
Benj. Mothe, 1708-1710), 2, p. 498.

75. London, Public Record Office, Prob. 11/23, ff. 59r-60r.

WORKS CITED

Bainbridge, V. R. Gilds in the Medieval Countryside: Social and Religious Change in
    Cambridgeshire, c. 1350-1558, Studies in the History of Religion, 10.
    Woodbridge: Boydell Press, 1996.

Barnum, P. H. Dives and Pauper, 2 vols., Early English Text Society OS 275, 280.
    Oxford: Oxford University Press, 1976-1980.

Bickley, W. B. The Register of the Guild of Knowle in the County of Warwick, 1451-1535.
    Walsall: W. H. Robinson, 1894.

Blake, N. F. "Manuscript to Print." In his *William Caxton and English Literary Culture*. London and Rio Grande, OH: Hambledon Press, 1991. (Originally in J. Griffiths and D. Pearsall, eds, *Book Production and Publishing in Britain, 1375-1475*. Cambridge: Cambridge University Press, 1989)

Bloom, J. H. *The Register of the Gild of the Holy Cross, the Blessed Mary, and St. John the Evangelist of Stratford-upon-Avon*. London: Phillimore and Co., 1907.

Boyle, L. E. "The Fourth Lateran Council and Manuals of Popular Theology." In *The Popular Literature of Medieval England*, edited by T. J. Heffernan. Tennessee Studies in Literature, 28. Knoxville, TN: University of Tennessee Press, 1985.

Burrow, J. A. *Thomas Hoccleve*. Aldershot and Brookfield, VT: Ashgate, 1994.

Calendar of Inquisitions Post Mortem and other Analogous Documents, Henry VII, vol. 1. London: Her Majesty's Stationery Office, 1898.

Camille, M. "Reading the Printed Image: Illuminations and Woodcuts of the *Pèlerinage de la vie humaine* in the Fifteenth Century." In *Printing the Written Word: the Social History of Books circa 1450-1520*, edited by S. Hindman. Ithaca, NY, and London: Cornell University Press, 1991.

Cheshire Sheaf, 2. 1880.

Connolly, M. *John Shirley: Book Production and the Noble Household in Fifteenth-Century England*. Aldershot, Brookfield, Singapore, and Sydney: Ashgate, 1998.

Cox, J. C., and W. H. St. John Hope, eds. *The Chronicles of the Collegiate Church or Free Chapel of All Saints, Derby*. London and Derby: Bemrose and Sons, 1881.

Crossley, F. H. "The Renaissance of Cheshire Church Building in the Late Fifteenth and Early Sixteenth Centuries." *Journal of the Chester and North Wales Architectural, Archaeological and Historic Society* 34 (1939-1940): 53-160

Diekstra, F. N. M. *Book for a Simple Devout Woman: A Late Middle English Adaptation of Peraldus's* Summa de vitiis et virtutibus *and Friar Laurent's* Somme le roi, *edited from British Library MSS Harley 6571 and Additional 30944*, Mediaevalia Groningana, 24. Groningen: Egbert Forsten, 1998.

Dodgson, J. McN. "A Library at Pott Chapel (Pott Shrigley, Cheshire), c. 1493." *The Library* 5th ser. 15 (1960): 43-53

Duff, E. G. *Fifteenth-Century English Books: A Bibliography of Books and Documents Printed in England, and of Books for the English Market Printed Abroad*, Bibliographical Society Illustrated Monographs, 18. Oxford: Oxford University Press, 1917.

Duffy, E. *The Stripping of the Altars: Traditional Religion in England, c. 1400-c. 1580*. New Haven and London: Yale University Press, 1992.

Dutton, A. M. "Passing the Book: Testamentary Transmission of Religious Literature to and by Women in England, 1350-1500." In *Women, the Book and the Godly: Selected Proceedings of the St Hilda's Conference, 1993, volume I*, edited by L. Smith and J. H. M. Taylor. Cambridge and Rochester, NY: D. S. Brewer, 1995.

Earwaker, J. P. *East Cheshire: Past and Present; or a History of the Hundred of Macclesfield in the County Palatine of Chester, from Original Records*, 2 vols. London: privately printed, 1877-1880.

Emden, A. B. *A Biographical Register of the University of Oxford to 1500*, 3 vols. Oxford: Clarendon Press, 1957-1959.

—— *A Biographical Register of the University of Cambridge to 1500*. Cambridge: Cambridge University Press, 1963.

Erler, M. C. "Devotional Literature." In *The Cambridge History of the Book in Britain, Volume III: 1400-1557*, edited by L. Hellinga and J. B. Trapp. Cambridge: Cambridge University Press, 1999.

Ford, M. L. "Private Ownership of Printed Books." In *The Cambridge History of the Book in Britain, Volume III: 1400-1557*, edited by L. Hellinga and J. B. Trapp. Cambridge: Cambridge University Press, 1999.

Francis, W. N., ed. *The Book of Vices and Virtues: A Fourteenth-Century English Translation of the* Somme le roi *of Lorens d'Orléans*, Early English Text Society, OS 217. London: Oxford University Press, 1942.

Furnivall, F. J., and K. B. Locock, eds. *The Pilgrimage of the Life of Man, Englisht from the French of Guillaume de Deguileville, AD 1330, 1355*, 3 vols., Early English Text Society, ES 77, 83, 92. London: K. Paul, Trench, Trübner and Co., 1899-1904.

Gallagher, J. E. "The Source of Caxton's *Royal Book* and *Doctrinal of Sapience*." *Studies in Philology* 62 (1965): 40-62

Goldschmidt, E. P. *Medieval Texts and their First Appearance in Print*, Supplement to the Bibliographical Society's Transactions, 16. London: Oxford University Press, 1943.

Görlach, M. *Studies in Middle English Saints' Legends*, Anglistische Forschungen, 257. Heidelberg: C. Winter, 1998.

Green, R. F. "Lydgate and Deguileville once more." *Notes and Queries* 223 (1978): 105-106

Hagen, S. K. *Allegorical Remembrance: A Study of* The Pilgrimage of the Life of Man *as a Medieval Treatise on Seeing and Remembering*. Athens, GA, and London: University of Georgia Press, 1990.

Hare, W. L. "A Newly Discovered Volume Printed by William Caxton: *Pylgremage of the Sowle*." *Apollo* 14 (July-Dec. 1931): 205-213

Harper-Bill, C., ed. *The Register of John Morton, Archbishop of Canterbury, 1486-1500*, vol. 1, Canterbury and York Society Publications, 75. Leeds: Duffield Printers, 1987.

Harris, M. D. *The Register of the Guild of the Holy Trinity, St. Mary, St. John the Baptist, and St. Katherine of Coventry*, 2 vols., Dugdale Society Publications, 13, 19. London: Oxford University Press, 1935-1944.

Hellinga, L. "Nicholas Love in Print." In *Nicholas Love at Waseda: Proceedings of the International Conference, 20-22 July 1995*, edited by S. Oguro, R. Beadle, and M. G. Sargent. Cambridge: D. S. Brewer, 1997.

——. "Printing." In *The Cambridge History of the Book in Britain, Volume III: 1400-1557*, edited by L. Hellinga and J. B. Trapp. Cambridge: Cambridge University Press, 1999.

Henry, A., ed. *The Pilgrimage of the Lyfe of the Manhode*, 2 vols., Early English Text Society, OS 288, 292. Oxford: Oxford University Press, 1985-1988.

Herrtage, S. J. H., ed. *The Early English Versions of the Gesta Romanorum*, Early English Text Society, ES 33. London: N. Trübner and Sons, 1879.

Hudson, A. *The Premature Reformation: Wycliffite Texts and Lollard History*. Oxford: Clarendon Press, 1989.

—— and H. L. Spencer. "Old Author, New Work: The Sermons of MS Longleat 4." *Medium Ævum* 53 (1984): 220-238

Jacob, E. F. *The Register of Henry Chichele, Archbishop of Canterbury*, 1414-43, 4 vols, Canterbury and York Society, 42, 45-47. Oxford: Oxford University Press, 1937-1947

Ker, N. R. *Medieval Libraries of Great Britain: a List of Surviving Books*, 2d ed., Royal Historical Society Guides and Handbooks, 3. London: Royal Historical Society, 1964.

Kreider, A. *English Chantries: the Road to Dissolution*, Harvard Historical Studies, 97. Cambridge, MA, and London: Harvard University Press, 1979.

Lewis, R. E., N. F. Blake, and A. S. G. Edwards, *Index of Printed Middle English Prose*. New York and London: Garland, 1985.

Lindström, B. "Some Remarks on Two English Translations of Jacques Legrand's *Livres de bonnes meurs*." *English Studies* 58 (1977): 304-311

——. "The English Versions of Jacques Legrand's *Livres de bonnes meurs*." *The Library* 6th ser. 1 (1979): 247-254

McGerr, R. M. *The Pilgrimage of the Soul: a Critical Edition of the Middle English Dream Vision*, Garland Medieval Texts, 16. New York and London: Garland, 1990.

Marshall, P. *The Catholic Priesthood in the English Reformation*. Oxford: Clarendon Press, 1994.

Meale, C. M. "'Oft siþis with grete deuotion I þought what I mi3t do plesyng to god': The Early Ownership and Readership of Love's *Mirror*, with Special Reference to its Female Audience." In *Nicholas Love at Waseda: Proceedings of the International Conference, 20-22 July 1995*, edited by S. Oguro, R. Beadle, and M. G. Sargent. Cambridge: D. S. Brewer, 1997.

Mitchell, R. J. *John Tiptoft (1427-1470)*. London, New York, and Toronto: Longmans, Green, and Co., 1938.

Moran, J. A. H. "A 'Common Profit' Library in Fifteenth-Century England and Other Books for Chaplains." *Manuscripta* 28 (1984): 17-25

Morey, J. H. *Book and Verse: a Guide to Middle English Biblical Literature.* Urbana and Chicago: University of Illinois Press, 2000.

Mulders, J. A., ed. *The Cordyal by Anthony Woodville, Earl Rivers, edited from M 38 A1, the Museum Meemanno Westreenianum, The Hague.* Nijmegen: Centrale Drukkerij N. V., 1962.

Needham, P. *The Printer and the Pardoner: an Unrecorded Indulgence Printed by William Caxton for the Hospital of St. Mary Rounceval, Charing Cross.* Washington, DC: Library of Congress, 1986.

Newcourt, R. *Repertorium Ecclesiasticum Parochiale Londinense,* 2 vols. London: Benj. Mothe, 1708-1710.

Ormerod, G. (rev. T. Helsby). *The History of the County Palatine and City of Chester.* 2d ed., 3 vols. London: G. Routledge, 1882.

Pfaff, R. W. *New Liturgical Feasts in Late Medieval England.* Oxford: Clarendon Press, 1970.

Pollard, A. W., and G. R. Redgrave (rev. W. A. Jackson, F. S. Ferguson, and K. F. Pantzer), A *Short-Title Catalogue of Books Printed in England, Scotland, and Ireland, and of English Books Printed Abroad* (1475-1640), 3 vols. 2d ed. London: Bibliographical Society, 1976-1991)

Renaud, F. *Contributions towards a History of the Ancient Parish of Prestbury in Cheshire.* Chetham Society Publications, 97. Manchester: Charles Simms and Co., 1876.

Rychner, J. "Les sources morales des *Vigiles de Charles VII*: le *Jeu des échecs moral-isé* et le *Livre de bonnes moeurs* des *exempla* à la fin du moyen âge." *Romania* 77 (1956): 39-65, 446-487

Sargent, M. G., ed. *Nicholas Love's Mirror of the Blessed Life of Jesus Christ: A Critical Edition based on Cambridge University Library Additional MSS 6578 and 6686.* New York and London: Garland, 1992.

Scaife, R. H. *The Register of the Guild of Corpus Christi in the City of York.* Surtees Society Publications, 57. Durham: Andrews and Co., etc., 1872.

Scase, W. "Reginald Pecock, John Carpenter and John Colop's 'Common Profit Books': Aspects of Book Ownership and Circulation in Fifteenth-Century London." *Medium Ævum* 61 (1982): 261-274

Schirmer, W. F. *John Lydgate: a Study in the Culture of the XVth Century.* London: Methuen, 1961.

Searle, W. G. *The History of the Queens' College of St Margaret and St Bernard in the University of Cambridge, 1446-1560,* Cambridge Antiquarian Society Octavo Publications, 9. Cambridge: Cambridge University Press, 1867.

Seymour, M. C., ed. *Selections from Hoccleve.* Oxford: Clarendon Press, 1981.

Shaw, J. "The Influence of Canonical and Episcopal Reform on Popular Books of Instruction." In *The Popular Literature of Medieval England*, edited by T. J. Heffernan. Tennessee Studies in Literature, 28. Knoxville, TN: University of Tennessee Press, 1985.

Spencer, H. L. *English Preaching in the Late Middle Ages*. Oxford: Clarendon Press, 1993.

Swanson, R. N. *Catholic England: Faith, Religion, and Observance before the Reformation*. Manchester: Manchester University Press, 1993.

———. "Medieval English Liturgy: What's the Use?" *Studia liturgica* 29 (1999): 159-190

———. "A Medieval Staffordshire Fraternity: The Guild of St. John the Baptist, Walsall." In *Staffordshire Histories: Essays in Honour of Michael Greenslade*, edited by Philip Morgan and A.D.M. Phillips. Collections for a History of Staffordshire, 4th ser., 19. Stafford and Keele: Staffordshire Record Society and The Centre for Local History, University of Keele, 1999.

Timmins, T. C. B., ed. *The Register of John Chandler, Dean of Salisbury, 1404-17*, Wiltshire Record Society Publications, 39. Devizes: Wiltshire Record Society, 1984.

Tuve, R. *Allegorical Imagery: Some Medieval Books and Their Posterity*. Princeton, NJ: Princeton University Press, 1966.

Venn, J., and J. A. Venn, *Alumni Cantabrigienses*, Part 1, 4 vols. Cambridge: Cambridge University Press, 1922-1927.

Watkin, A., ed. *Archdeaconry of Norwich: Inventory of Church Goods, Temp. Edward III*, 2 vols., Norfolk Record Society, 19. n.p.: Norfolk Record Society, 1947-1948.

Watson, A. G. *Medieval Libraries of Great Britain: A List of Surviving Books Edited by N. R. Ker. Supplement to the Second Edition*. Royal Historical Society Guides and Handbooks, 15. London: Royal Historical Society, 1987.

Wells, K. "Did Lydgate translate the 'Pèlerinage de vie humaine'?" *Notes and Queries* 222 (1977):

Wilson, R. H. "Malory and Caxton." In *A Manual of the Writings in Middle English, 1050-1500*, edited by A. E. Hartung, 3. New Haven, CT: Connecticut Academy of Arts and Sciences, 1972.

Wordsworth, C., ed. *The Tracts of Clement Maydeston, with the Remains of Caxton's Ordinal*, Henry Bradshaw Society, 7. London: Harrison and Sons, 1894.

Nota Bene: Brief Notes on Manuscripts and Early Printed Books

The Earliest English Wyclif Portraits?: Political Caricatures in Bodleian Library, Oxford, MS Laud Misc. 286[1]

MICHAEL P. KUCZYNSKI

To date, the earliest known English portrait of John Wyclif (d. 1384) has been the famous half-length woodcut in Bale's *Illustrium maioris Britanniae Scriptorum Summarium*, first printed in 1548, over a century and a half after Wyclif's death (figure 1). The margins of Bodleian Library, Oxford MS Laud Misc. 286, a fifteenth-century copy of Richard Rolle's *English Psalter*, contain what may be three much earlier Wyclif portraits, drawn probably by the book's two scribes, ca. 1430,[2] soon after Wyclif's posthumous burning on papal order following his condemnation by the Council of Constance (1415).[3] Three earlier Wyclif portraits, ca. 1410, appear in copies of his Latin works now in Prague; two of these are Evangelist-style depictions; the other is an unfinished, conventional portrait of a clerk wearing a skullcap, at his writing desk.[4] The Laudian caricatures, by contrast, may have been intended as part of Laud Misc. 286's anti-Lollard polemic, which begins with an anonymous metrical preface to Rolle's *Psalter* unique to this copy, and which may be reflected in certain revisions to some of Rolle's expositions to Psalms 1 through 17 in this copy of the *English Psalter* and in other of the book's marginalia.

None of the Laudian caricatures is very large: all are just under an inch long and are easily missed on an initial run-through of the manuscript, a hefty folio of 163 pages. Moreover, nowhere in the manuscript are the pictures explicitly identified as representations of Wyclif, unlike for instance the Bale woodcut, which has a clear caption: *Figura Ioannis Wicleui doctoris Angli*, or one of the Prague portraits, with its cropped caption.[5] But given the anti-Lollard bias of Laud Misc. 286 and the manuscript's date, close in time to Oldcastle's abortive 1414 coup and the burning of Wyclif's bones in 1428, it seems possible that the pictures were drawn as satirical portraits of the reformer himself, who was regarded by Lollardy's conservative opponents as the *fons et origo* of the heretical movement.

Each of the caricatures is keyed to a particular Latin psalm text or to one of Rolle's expositions, as a kind of visual gloss to the words. This relationship is clearest, however, in the case of the first and third caricatures. In

this survey I discuss the drawings sequentially, as they appear in the manuscript.

Caricature I (Figure 2)

The first caricature, drawn by the first scribe, is the most careful and
the least cartoonish. Stylistically it is indebted less to the tradition of the
marginal grotesque than to late-medieval panel portraiture, suggesting that
it may have had as its original a portrait of Wyclif drawn from life.[6] The scribe
develops it in the bottom margin of fol. 17[vb], from the descender of the letter
"g" in Latin *maligni*, in Psalm 9.36:

> *Contere brachium peccatoris et maligni:*
> *queretur peccatum illius et non invenietur.*
> [Break thou the arm of the sinner and of the malignant:
> His sin shall be sought, and shall not be found.][7]

Like the Bale woodcut, the Laudian caricature shows Wyclif in profile, with a long tapered beard and wearing the traditional doctoral *pileus* or
biretta, highlighted in the same red ink used throughout the manuscript to
rubricate psalm texts.[8] The attitude of the head is sober, like the "sad" or
philosophical visage of Theseus as Chaucer describes him at the close of the
Knight's Tale:

> Er any word cam fram hise wise brest,
> His eyen set he ther as was his lest.[9]

Here, however, the sobriety and wise aspect of the caricature ends. For the
scribe has also drawn Wyclif with a prominent bulbous nose, touched with
red like the eyes and mouth, perhaps to suggest drunkenness.

Next to nothing is known about Wyclif's actual appearance, the Bale
woodcut and all later portraits being based on painterly conventions and
vague traditions concerning Wyclif's character.[10] One of these traditions orig-
inates with Bale himself, or rather with his Latin translation of an English
copy of the *Examination of William Thorpe*, where Thorpe describes Wyclif as
having a slight frame, wasted by self-denial (*corpore macilentus, extenuatus, ac
viribus paene exhaustus*).[11] Wyclif was bothered enough by his reputation for
studied asceticism to state, in Chapter 12 of *De veritate sacra scripturae*, that in
fact his conscience was troubled by his having consumed too many of the
goods of the poor through excessive meat and drink.[12] So here the artist may
be combining suggestions of sobriety and drunkenness to imply hypocrisy.
Like the Son of Man and his harbinger, John the Baptist, Wyclif would have
been attacked by his enemies had he come eating and drinking or not.

As with the details of any good political cartoon, however, these features of the Laudian drawing have an extended moral significance. Chaucer's Parson observes, in describing the sin of gluttony, that drunkenness is "the horrible sepulture of mannes resoun."[13] More to the point, the anti-Lollard monastic chronicler, Henry Knighton, makes it a trope for that particular form of human irrationality known as heresy in his description of the Lollard John Purvey as "intoxicated with [Wyclif's] writings, having drunk deeply of them" (*maius de eius documentis debriatis, copiosius mente hauserat*).[14] Wyclif's own drunkenness in the Laudian portrait, in other words, might be intended as a manifestation not only of his personal hypocrisy but of the heretical nature of his opinions and influence.

Augustine, in his *enarratio* on Psalm 9, speaks of *maligni* in the plural in this psalm verse as representing all heretics, and explains in response to a question posed by David earlier in the psalm, "Why, O Lord, hast thou withdrawn so far off?" (*Ut quid domine recessisti longe?* Ps 9.22), that God allows heresy to flourish in the church for a time so that "by comparison with heretics the discovery of truth is more sweet" and Divine Providence thereby made manifest.[15] Elsewhere in the *Enarrationes in psalmos* (one of the chief patristic sources for Rolle's vernacular commentary, a text he knew piecemeal via Peter Lombard's twelfth-century psalm *catena* and, perhaps directly), Augustine amplifies David's own metaphor for this discovery of divine truth as "spiritual drunkenness" (e.g., in his remarks on Psalms 22.5 and 35.9).[16] He extols the soul's loss of sense when "it shall become Divine, and be satiated with the fulness of God's House."[17] Wyclif's drunkenness and the drunkenness of all heretics are of the opposite sort: the senselessness of wicked men who wilfully neglect God's law and lead others into sin.

Thus the Laudian scribe-artist draws a direct link, a visible line, between Wyclif in his singularity and the plurality of the malicious. His wickedness gave rise to theirs; theirs may be traced back to him. Moreover, the image implies a contrast, since it appears in a psalter, between the *maligni* and their ringleader, Wyclif *malignus*, and the *beati* and their prophet, King David or *Beatus vir* himself.[18] One of the leitmotifs of the Psalms is David's constant juxtaposition of the malice of his enemies and the blessedness of those who trust in God. And the anonymous anti-Lollard who wrote the metrical preface to this copy of Rolle's *English Psalter* describes Rolle himself three times as a "holy man" while caricaturing the Lollards as cartoon villains, who revised Rolle's commentary as a guise for their own heretical opinions in order to "vex" (*greue*) the ignorant.[19] The first Laudian portrait, in other words, may function not only as a local satiric gloss to the word *maligni* in Psalm 9.36 but potentially as a shrewd amplification of the anti-Lollard polemic of the metrical preface to this volume and an alignment of that polemic, its easy distinction between Rolleian orthodoxy and Lollard heresy, with David's own psalmic discourse, his poetic moral dichotomy between the malign and the blessed.

At the risk of interpreting this caricature too microscopically, it is also tempting to imagine that its artist was aware of and trying to counter by his cartoon a new development in early fifteenth-century Lollardy: regard for and references to Wyclif as *beatus*, a Lollard saint. Christina von Nolcken has shown how, in opposition to the cult of saints with its veneration of holy pictures and statues, the Lollards advanced via Wyclif's reputation a counterhagiography, a standard of sanctity based in respect for the *Doctor evangelicus*'s reformist teachings.[20] What could be more apt for resurgent English orthodoxy than to counter this counterhagiography by way of pictures of Wyclif himself which identify the reformer not as chief among God's saints but as an archetypal sinner?

Caricature II (Figure 3)

The second Laudian caricature, the first by the book's second scribe, makes a similar point in a more heavy-handed way by representing Wyclif with the traditional attributes of the Devil: a hooked nose, forked beard (highlighted with the same blue used for paraph signs in the psalm expositions), insidious grin, and a gesture toward a fuller figure in a blue line to the right, perhaps indicating a crookback.[21] This picture, in the bottom margin of fol. 21[ra], is keyed not to a Latin psalm verse but to Rolle's comment on a verse from the first of two *Dixit insipiens* psalms (Psalms 13 and 52) concerned with the figure of the Fool who says in his heart "God is not" (*Non est deus*). The portrait identifies Wyclif not with Lucifer's grandeur but with Satan's folly.

Like the first caricature, this one directly associates Wyclif in his devilish singularity with "mony men" who die spiritually because of their gluttony, a sin linked in the psalm exposition at hand with the moral error of "false spekers," who cause others to fall away from God's law. The Latin psalm verse in question is Psalm 13.5, *Sepulcrum pates est guttur eorum* ("Their throat is an open sepulchre"):

> Soþly, wiccod men [the same phrase is used of
> the *maligni* in the comment on Psalm 9] corrumpen hor
> neiȝburs, for hur þrote is like to a graue openynge
> þat sleþ men þurȝe euel eire, and swelleþ hom withinne.
> So fals spekers sleen hur herers, þat assenten to hom
> þurȝe hur wiccod error, bowing fro godes lawe in to
> vicious and delicate lifynge. For vche mon erreþ
> gretly þat takeþ or doþ any other biddyng þen cristus.
> For þur the leuyng of cristus biddyng, þei bene buried
> in obstinacion, þat is, þei ben endured to dwelle in hur
> synne all hur lif to hur end. Or by the openyng graue is

vndurstonden or bitokened glotonye, þat wastiþ boþe
bodily godes or gostly.

The association between gluttony and false speech is made even clearer in
Augustine's explanation of this psalm verse: "Either the voracity of the ever
open palate is signified; or, allegorically, those who slay, and as it were
devour those they have slain, into whom they instil the disorder of their conversation."[22]

In the expositions of Psalms 1-17 in Laud Misc. 286, the author
amplifies in subtle ways Rolle's original remarks in the direction of attacking
false teachers and provoking God's stern judgment upon them—for instance,
in commenting on Psalm 9.7 (the psalm illustrated by the first Wyclif portrait), *Inimici defecerunt framee in finem: et civitates eorum destruxisti* ("The swords of
the enemy fail in the end; and you have destroyed their cities"). Here is
Rolle's original:

> The swerdis of oure enmy ere the rebellions of the
> deuel, and sere |various| errours, in the whilk he slas
> wrecchid saules.[23]

The Laudian version is more pointed:

> The swerdes of our enemyes bene rebellious malice of þe
> fende and diuerse errors of wiccod men contrarious to
> godes lawe, with the whiche þe sle wrechid soules,
> ordenynge new rules and customes oþer þen þo perfite
> and holy and wise rule, þat Ihesu crist lifed aftur and
> taȝt. (fol. 14ᵛᵇ)

The contrast in this second passage between the elaborate artifices of the
institutional Church and the simple purity of Christ's own law was, oddly
enough, a commonplace of Lollard polemic and is likely not the Laudian
scribe's invention, but carried over from his exemplar, an *English Psalter* manuscript containing Wycliffite additions.[24] Even if it was not the scribe's, however, the copyist let the change stand, perhaps because he was unaware of
Rolle's original (having no sound copy against which to check his exemplar),
and possibly because it served, on some general rhetorical level, his own
moralistic instinct. In the heated atmosphere of late-fifteenth-century religious contention, even the coded terms of Wycliffite ecclesiological discourse
might be turned around, deflected back against the Lollards themselves, in
this case against their fondness for polemic and the kinds of sophistical argument that polemic often entails. The improvements to Rolle's phrasing in
this Laudian passage suggest that the rebelliousness of Satan himself is

reenacted by the contrariousness of wicked men's errors, and that these men are fiendlike in spreading moral confusion. Thus Wyclif gets presented as the archfiend in the botton margin of fol. 21ra, transformed by the ideologue scribe-artist into the Devil himself.

Caricature III (Figure 4)

The third Laudian caricature is the most crudely drawn but displays nevertheless as sophisticated a relationship between image and text as the first two pictures, and its topical satire may be sharp. In the top margin of fol. 115ra, Wyclif's head bobs puppetlike above the first line of Latin text like Father Conmee's above the pianola in Joyce's *Ulysses*. (Some trial balloon faces for this last portrait appear at the top of fols. 111r and 112r.) The scribe develops the cartoon from the elongated ascender of 'd' in Latin *manducabam* in the tenth verse of one of the penitential psalms, Psalm 101 (*Domini exaudi*):

> *Quia cinerem tanquam panem manducabam*
> *Et potum meum cum fletu miscebam.*
> |For I did eat ashes like bread,
> and mingled my drink with weeping.|

The expression in this cartoon is difficult to read. The portrait's eyes seem closed or may be wearing spectacles, one of the attributes of the devil-doctor in a French mystery play based on the Acts of the Apostles.[25] The mouth is turned down in a grimace, and the cheeks are streaked with what might be tears. The psalm verse itself describes the traditional "holy tears" of compunction, which were regarded in late antiquity and throughout the Middle Ages as a spontaneous outward sign of the soul's contrition.[26] Despite its penitential character, therefore, Augustine interprets the entire verse from Psalm 101 not bleakly at all, but hopefully, as indicative of Christ's promise of forgiveness and salvation to all who repent: "Eat ashes with bread and mingle thy drink with weeping; by means of this banquet thou shalt reach the table of God."[27] Wyclif himself, however, could hardly be held up as a model of compunction. He did not die at Lutterworth doing penance for his sins against the Truth but, as Anthony Kenny describes it, "until his death continued to expound his doctrines both in slender pamphlets and in bulky tracts," many of them notable for their "querulous tone."[28] If in this drawing the Laudian artist means to depict Wyclif in penance, he does so sarcastically.

His sarcasm may be deliberately cruel. Like the third volume of Thomas Netter's anti-Lollard *Doctrinale fidei catholicae* (a copy at Merton College, Oxford, has a picture of a jolly fellow with a face like Chaucer's Summoner, burning what are probably Wycliffite books[29]), Laud Misc. 286 was produced

shortly after an event of deep symbolic import for resurgent English orthodoxy: the exhumation and burning of Wyclif's bones at Lutterworth, the ecclesiastical living to which he retired from Oxford in 1381, only to die three years
later. Never prosecuted for heresy in his lifetime, Wyclif was condemned after
his death, in 1415 at the Council of Constance; by conciliar decree, his books
and bones were ordered to be burnt. This decree realized a request made to
the Pope four years earlier by Archbishop Arundel at the time of the 1411
burning of Wycliffite books in Oxford. The exhumation order came down from
Pope Martin V, to whom Netter had dedicated two of his volumes, and was
carried out by Bishop Fleming of Lincoln, who was regarded as an early but
now converted Wyclif disciple.

Margaret Aston has pointed out how the Pope's order improved on
the conciliar decree in two impressive particulars: Wyclif's bones were to be
burnt in public, and his ashes were to be disposed of completely (they were
dumped into a nearby river).[30] The act was not to be simply a response to
Wyclif as heretic, a formal and overdue judgment against an individual, but a
sign that orthodox forces intended to stamp out heresy in the realm entirely.
The year of Wyclif's exhumation also witnessed serious Lollard uprisings in
Norwich and a vigorous pursuit of heretics there by Archbishops Chichele
and Alnwick, as well as efforts by the convocation of Canterbury to improve
on legal procedures for prosecuting heretics. These activities, like Wyclif's
exhumation and burning, share an important rhetorical element with earlier
anti-Lollard efforts, such as the act De haeretico comburendo (1401), and anti-
Lollard polemics, such as Lydgate's strident poem, A Defence of Holy Church (ca.
1415): the urgent message that all heretics, all heresy, must be exterminated.

If the third Laudian caricature was intended as a Wyclif portrait, it
could be read in the context of these enterprises. The picture, keyed to a
Latin psalm verse referring to ashes and contrition, might allude to Wyclif's
posthumous burning and the triumph this represented for Lollardy's orthodox opponents. Thomas Fuller, in a striking metaphor from his Church-History
of Britaine (1655), describes how Wyclif's ashes were thrown into the River
Swift and thereby carried forth "into the main Ocean": "and thus the ashes of
Wickliff are the Emblem of his Doctrine, which now, is dispersed all the World
over." What we may have in Laud Misc. 286 is a different kind of emblem, of
triumph over the ridiculous, long-dead heretic, who is represented crying or
perhaps sweating as the fires stoked by righteous orthodoxy consume him.
Rolle's translation of the Latin psalm verse illustrated here is apt: "For aske
[ashes] i ete as brede and my drynke y mengyd wit gretyng [weeping]." It
might have recalled, for a sensitive medieval reader who knew the penitential
psalms, Rolle's exposition, following Peter Lombard, of an important verse
from Psalm 50, the chief penitential psalm: Docebo iniquous tuos; "I will teach
sinners your ways": "He that gret [wept]," Rolle writes, "now is he doctur

[teacher]."[31] The second Laudian scribe-artist, like the first, might have seen Wyclif as having reversed this Davidic paradigm of moral reform. Oxford's famed *Doctor evangelicus*, friend of powerful men like John of Gaunt, is now reduced to tears and to ashes. Unlike humble followers of the Psalmist, who learn from David's pride and penance, Wyclif fails to learn the lesson of the Psalms. He is not *Beatus vir*, one who delights in God's law, but *Malignus vir*, the man who sat down in the chair of pestilence.

I have been playing up the righteously indignant tone of this third Wyclif portrait because the same tone occurs in other parts of the book in which these pictures appear, the anti-Lollard metrical preface and revisions to Rolle's material in the expositions to Psalms 1-17. H. R. Bramley seems to have been unaware of changes to Rolle's material in the early part of Laud Misc. 286 when he used passages from it to fill gaps in the base text for his 1884 edition of the *English Psalter*, University College, Oxford MS 64.[32] Everett and (following her) Muir classify Laud Misc. 286 as an interpolated copy of Rolle's text, but one not necessarily Lollard in complexion. Moreover, Everett takes the metrical preface author's suggestion that a sound or faithful copy of Rolle follows as a mark of his own ignorance of the exact nature of his corrupt copy and of Rolle's original (he says it's chained to the author's tomb in Hampole), which had circulated quickly and widely beyond its immediate audience of one, the recluse Margaret Kirkeby.[33]

However, the caricatures in MS Laud Misc. 286 allow for another possibility. This copy of Rolle's commentary, its hellfire-and-brimstone tone in Psalms 1-17 aggravated considerably over the original, could have been deliberately passed off by a conservative copyist as Rolle's own work in order to counter the supposedly pernicious effects of Lollard copies.[34] In other words, the anonymous scribe of this version, perhaps the preface author himself, might have been guilty of some of the same kinds of editorial deception he criticizes in Rolle's Lollard interpolators, who used Rolle's orthodox reputation, in the words of Hope Emily Allen, as a "cloak" under which to advance their heretical views.[35] This view, like that of the preface author's innocent ignorance of the complex textual history of Rolle's text and of his own copy, cannot be proved. A partly erased ownership mark on the book's back flyleaf, in a hand similar to that of the metrical preface, reads "Richard Horis [?book]," and Emden records an early fifteenth-century Oxford scholar of that name who had contacts with the Roman curia.[36] Beyond such distant speculation, however, one cannot go. The fact remains that the text's tone in the early psalms is sterner than Rolle's and that this severity, like the caricatures I have been discussing, serves the book's polemical anti-Lollard bias.

Two additional examples of moralizing revision in Laud Misc. 286 deserve final mention, since the moral tone of each is amplified slightly in the book by a marginal gloss in the scribe's hand. Commenting on the fifth verse of the first psalm (*Beatus vir*), *Ideo non resurgunt impij in iudicio: neque peccatores in consilio iustorum* ("Therefore the wicked shall not rise again in judgment; nor sinners in the council of the just"), Rolle discusses, following Peter Lombard again, the four orders of men who will face divine judgment. Those who will receive the severest judgment, he explains, will be the last order, "fals cristen men, that has the trouth of ihesu crist withouten luf and goed werkes." Rolle continues:

> Thai sall greuoslyere be dampned than hethen men,
> for the vpbraidynge of crist, that thai wild noght luf
> him, that swa mykill goednes did til thaim, sall grefe
> thaim mare than any man may thynke.[37]

The Laudian version is sharper:

> Suche fals cristen men schul be dampned to harder peyne
> þenn hethen men, whi so for þey wytynli wrathed crist
> with hor euel lyuynge and wolde not luf hym kepynge his
> lawe, for alle be godenes þat he dud to hem. For þe
> wiche vnkyndenes be worme of consciens schal more bitturly
> and more sharpely byte hem þen any heþen men and peyne
> hem sarrer þenn any mon may þenke. (fol. 3ᵛᵇ)

All of this is signalled by the scribe, in the margin, with a gloss: *De Iudicio*, "Concerning Judgment." *Iudicio* here has a double reference: it echoes the psalm lemma, but perhaps more important, it anticipates the triumph of divine judgment over false Christians as described in the psalm exposition—the Last Judgment, when sinners will be damned to hell.

A like instance occurs in the Laudian version of Rolle's comment on the fourth verse of Psalm 2. The entire psalm entertains the question "Why do the heathen rage?", and depicts in its fourth verse God's derisive laughter at the expense of the vain (*Qui habitat in celis irridebat*; "He that dwelleth in heaven shall laugh at them"). Here is Rolle's comment, beginning with his translation of the Latin psalm verse:

> He that wonnys in heuens sall drif til hethynge thaim:
> and lord sal scorn thaim. Wele aghe we to brek thaire [these]
> bandis. of couatis & ill dred, that byndes men in synne:
> for god that wonnys in heuen. that is, in haly saules. and
> aungels, sall shew all tha worthi hethynge & scornynge
> that now ere dissayued thurght quayntis of the deuel and
> kitlynge of thaire flesch or heghnes of the world.[38]

The Laudian version seems to have been written by someone who identifies more deeply with God in his righteous laughter, especially at those who set their own intelligence above divine wisdom:

> "For he þat woneþ in heuen, schal dryue hem to scorken, and
> oure lord schal priuely scorn hem." // For þei setten hor
> wit byfore þe wysdam of god and holdun hor ordynaunce and
> rewle more perfyt þenn þe rewle and þe ordenaunce of god.
> As goddes lawe seyþe, god schal lawe in hor slawȝtre, þat is,
> whenn þey ben dampned to þe peyne of helle fro endeles lyf
> in ioy. (fol. 4rb-va)

To drive the message home, this Scriptural gloss by the scribe, circled in red, appears in the margin next to the revision: *Ego quoque in interitu vestro ridebo et substanabo cum vobis quod timebatis advenerit. Prouerbia.* The text is from Proverbs 1.26: "I also will laugh in your destruction, and will mock when that shall come to you which you feared."

The Lollards had good reason to fear God's wrath. If they were wrong about the church, its members and its doctrines, they stood to suffer not only persecution and death on earth, but endless torment in Hell. So there is something poignant about a possibly Lollard fragment of Rolle's *English Psalter* in a Yale manuscript, Beinecke Library MS 360, copied on the back flyleaf of a fifteenth-century English prayerbook.[39] This fragment conflates Rolle's comments on the two penitential psalms (Psalms 6 and 37) that begin with the plea, *Domine ne in furore tuo arguas* ("O Lord, rebuke me not in thy indignation"). The extract points up Rolle's main theme: that God's anger is not the mad or irrational anger of men, but righteous—the calm judgment of truth against falsehood. The extract ends with a Latin note derived from Peter Lombard, Rolle's source, which considers the theme of divine anger in another, non-penitential psalm, Psalm 105.38: *Iratus est furore dominus in populum suum* ("The Lord was furiously angry at his people"). Why, one might imagine a persecuted Lollard asking, is God so angry at his people? Because of the corruptions of the visible church? Or on account of dissent within its ranks? What is the true path, capitulation or resistance, obedience or rebellion?

The textual revisions to Psalms 1-17 in Laud Misc. 286, whether original with the Laudian scribe or carried over from his exemplar, are like the book's anonymous metrical preface and caricatures in promoting the self-righteousness of the orthodox and exploiting the fears of those who put their souls on the line by breaking with medieval orthodoxy. Aquinas assures the virtuous, in his *Summa theologiae*, that part of their joy in Heaven will consist in delight over the sufferings of the damned. And as any reader of Lollard copies of Rolle's *English Psalter* can testify, the Lollards themselves were liable to sometimes violent self-righteousness. But the ideological shadings of a manuscript like Laud Misc. 286 deserve more detailed study than they have hitherto received, for the book's words and pictures might point to hypocrisies among Lollardy's opponents that have yet to attract adequate literary historical notice. In his metrical preface to the volume, one vigorous anti-Lollard urges later copyists to transcribe the exemplar before them word for word:

> . . .wryte on warly lyne be lyne,
> And make no more then here is dygth.[40]
> [. . .copy the text carefully, line by line,
> and don't write anything more than is set down, here.]

A cautious scribe, following these instructions faithfully, might imbibe from his source covert verbal and visual messages that the modern scholar, flipping through the pages of MS Laud Misc. 286, can all too easily miss.[41]

Tulane University, New Orleans

NOTES

1. This essay is dedicated to the memory of Charles Till Davis, Department of History, Tulane University.

I am grateful to the Bodleian Library, Oxford, for permission to examine and quote from manuscripts in their care, and to the Keeper of Western manuscripts for permission to publish drawings from MS Laud Misc. 286.

2. For the shift in scribal hands at the end of Psalm 17 (*Diligam te domine*), on fol. 35^r, see Dorothy Everett, "The Middle English Prose Psalter of Richard Rolle of Hampole," *Modern Language Review* 17 (1922), p. 223. A third hand might be present in the manuscript, in Psalm 1 (*Beatus vir*), through fol. 5vb, although it bears a resemblance to the hand that takes over at the end of Psalm 17. In this essay, "the first scribe" refers to the dominant hand in Psalms 1-17, the scribe also responsible for the first Wyclif portrait.

The standard bibliography dates Laud Misc. 286 ca. 1400-50. See Laurence Muir, "Translations and Paraphrases of the Bible," in A *Manual of the Writings in Middle English*, 1050-1500, ed. J. Burke Severs, (Hamden, Conn.: Archon Books, 1970), vol. 2, p. 538. Secretary features of the two hands, however, suggest a date in the second quarter of the century, at least. For some analogues, see Andrew Watson, *Dated and Datable Manuscripts in Oxford Libraries, c. 435-1600* (Oxford: Clarendon Press, 1984), vol. 2, plates 330, 332, 333, 338, and 343; and *Dated and Datable Manuscripts, c. 700-1600, in the Department of Manuscripts, The British Library* (London: British Library Publications, 1979), vol. 2, plate 387. Both Laudian scribes write a good university book hand, although the second hand is a bit looser and less uniform than the first. .And both treat the

Latin in the text more formally than the English psalm translations and expositions, a feature of many *English Psalter* manuscripts. An Oxford provenance is possible for Laud Misc. 286, given the handwriting, but is by no means certain.

3. For a detailed discussion of post-medieval Wyclif portraits, see Margaret Aston, "John Wycliffe's Reformation Reputation," in *Lollards and Reformers: Images and Literacy in Late Medieval Religion* (London: Hambledon Press, 1984), pp. 243-71.

4. One of the Evangelist-style portraits appears in Prague Univ. Library MS VIII.C.3, fol. 2^r, at the beginning of *De veritate sacre scripture*. For reproductions, see the cover of the exhibition catalogue, *Wyclif and His Followers* (Oxford: Bodleian Library, 1984), and K. Stejskal and P. Voit, *Illuminované rukopisy doby husitské* (Prague: National Library, 1991), plate 24. The other Evangelist-style picture, and the portrait of Wyclif as clerk at his writing desk, appear in Prague Metropolitan Chapter Lib. MS C.38, fols. 17rb and 119vb, at the beginnings of *De mandatis* and Chapter 5 of *De veritate sacre scripture*, respectively. The *De mandatis* portrait has a sidenote, "venerabilis Johannes W[remainder erased]". I am grateful to Anne Hudson, Lady Margaret Hall, Oxford, for this information.

For an interesting modern portrait analogue of Wyclif wearing a clerical skullcap, see Ford Madox Brown's history painting, "Wyclif Reading His Translation of the New Testament to His Protector, John of Gaunt" (1847-48), reproduced in Kenneth Bendiner, *The Art of Ford Madox Brown* (University Park, PA: Penn State University Press, 1998), color plate 1.

5. For some instances of late-medieval caricatures meant to be identified as particular persons, without the help of a caption, see Hubert Hall, *The Antiquities and Curiosities of the Exchequer* (London: Elliot Stock, 1891), pp. 56-7.

6. On the international style in late-medieval panel portraiture, which valued the bust-length profile as the most definitive and stable rendering of human appearance, because least liable to distortion, see Jean Lipman, "The Florentine Profile Portrait in the Quattrocento," *Art Bulletin* 18 (1936), pp. 54-102.

7. Latin biblical quotations in this essay, unless otherwise indicated, are from MS Laud Misc. 286. English translations are from the Douai-Rheims version.

8. On doctoral caps at Oxford during Wyclif's time, see W. N. Hargreaves-Mawdsley, *A History of Academical Dress in Europe until the End of the Eighteenth Century* (Oxford: Clarendon Press, 1963), pp. 64-8. For additional information on medieval doctoral caps, see F. W. Fairholt, *Costume in England: A History of Dress to the End of the Eighteenth Century*, 3d ed. by H. A. Dillon (London: George Bell, 1885), vol. 1, pp. 198 and 266. On the wearing of scarlet by medieval doctors, at Oxford and elsewhere, see Hastings Rashdall, *The Universities of Europe in the Middle Ages*, ed. by F. M. Powicke (Oxford: Clarendon Press, 1936), vol. 3, pp. 390-93.

9. *The Riverside Chaucer*, 3d ed., ed. by Larry Benson (Boston: Houghton Mifflin, 1987), I(A)2985 and 2983-84, respectively. Quintilian describes the orator's lowering of his head before a speech as a visual shorthand for *humilitas*, although if this is the significance of the gesture in the first Laudian Wyclif portrait, it would have been intended

ironically. See *Institutionis Oratoriae*, ed. M. Winterbottom (Oxford: Clarendon Press, 1970), vol. 2, p. 667.

10. See *Dictionary of National Biography*, ed. by Leslie Stephen and Sidney Lee (Oxford: Oxford Univ. Press, 1917), vol. 21, p. 1133.

11. Bodleian Lib., Oxford MS e Mus. 86, fol. 100ra, as quoted in Walter Waddington Shirley, ed., *Fasciculi Zizaniorum Magistri Johannis Wyclif cum Tritico* (London: Longman, Brown, Green, Longmans, and Roberts, 1858), p. xlv, n. 3. These details do not appear in the surviving English text of Thorpe's *Examination*, from which Bale says he translated the Latin, leaving open the possibility that they might be Bale's pious invention. See Anne Hudson, ed., *Two Wycliffite Texts: The Sermon of William Taylor, 1406; The Testimony of William Thorpe, 1407* (Oxford: Oxford Univ. Press, 1993), p. 40. The details do appear, however, in Foxe's *Actes and Monuments* (1563), leading Shirley to wonder whether Bale's English original might have been Foxe's exemplar. On Bale as hagiographer, see L. P. Fairfield, "John Bale and the Development of Protestant Hagiography in England," *Journal of Ecclesiastical History* 24 (1973), pp. 145-60. Fairfield notes, for instance, Bale's fondness for ascetic details in his early hagiographic portraits of Carmelite saints (147). In his later efforts to sanctify Oldcastle, Fairfield observes, Bale denied the historicity of Oldcastle's 1414 coup attempt and invented an interview between Oldcastle and Henry V, emphasizing the protestant martyr's loyalty (153).

12. See Shirley, *Fasciculi Zizaniorum*, p. xlvi.

13. *Riverside Chaucer*, X(I)822.

14. *Knighton's Chronicle, 1337-1396*, ed. and trans. by G. H. Martin (Oxford: Clarendon Press, 1995), pp. 290-91.

15. *Patrologia Latina* 36, cols. 129 and 126, respectively: *sicut haereticorum comparatione jucundior est inventio veritatis.*

16. Ibid., cols. 182 and 351-52, respectively.

17. Ibid., col. 351: *et fit divina, et inebriatur ab ubertate domus Dei.*

18. To push the parallel a bit further, just as many medieval psalters (including a prominent Lollard copy of Rolle's *English Psalter* now in the Houghton Library, Harvard University, MS Richardson 36) begin with David portraits, icons of *Beatus vir*, this sequence of political caricatures in the Laudian manuscript begins with an elegant anti-Davidic icon, of *Malignus vir*. That is, the initial image may be read as setting an iconographic tone for any images (and texts) that follow it in this particular psalter.

19. H. R. Bramley, ed., *The Psalter or Psalms of David and Certain Canticles, with a Translation and Exposition in English by Richard Rolle of Hampole* (Oxford: Clarendon Press, 1884), p. 2.

20. "Another Kind of Saint: A Lollard Perception of John Wyclif," in *From Ockham to Wyclif*, Studies in Church History, *Subsidia* 5, ed. by Anne Hudson and Michael Wilks (Oxford: Basil Blackwell, 1987), pp. 429-43.

21. On medieval portraits of the Devil, see *L'umanesimo e 'l demoniaco nell'arte* (Rome: Centro internazionale di studi umanistici, 1952), and Luther Link, *The Devil: The Archfiend in Art from the Sixth to the Sixteenth Century* (New York: Harry N. Abrams, 1996). Hooked or crooked features suggest the Devil's deviation from the Truth or God, and

forked features symbolize his duplicity. Certain features, such as a sharp nose or forked beard, are related to animal imagery, for instance, representations of Satan with a bird's or goat's head. In his *enarratio* on Psalm 68 (*Salvum me fac deus*), verse 24 (*Obscurentur oculi eorum ne videant: et dorsum eorum semper incurva;* "Let their eyes be darkened that they see not: and their back bend thou down always"), Augustine explicitly associates the crookback with the Jews who crucified Christ, and by implication with all heretics. See *Patrologia Latina* 36, col. 860.

22. *Patrologia Latina* 36, cols. 111-12: *Aut voracitas significatur inhiantis gulae; aut in allegoria, qui occidunt et quasi devorant interfectos eos, quibus suorum morum perversitatem persuadent.*

23. Bramely, *Psalter,* p. 31.

24. Cf., for instance, the Lollard contrast between "new sects" ("mounkis, chanouns, and freris"), with the Pope as their head, and "Christ's sect," or the Lollard contrast between the visible church and the church of all believers (Anne Hudson, *Premature Reformation: Wycliffite Texts and Lollard History* [Oxford: Clarendon Press, 1988], pp. 347-51 and 314-27, respectively).

25. See A. N. Didron, *Christian Iconography; or, the History of Christian Art in the Middle Ages,* trans. by Margaret Stokes (London: George Bell, 1891), vol. 2, pp. 259-60. Unfortunately, the reference is to a sixteenth-century depiction.

26. See Sandra McEntire, *The Doctrine of Compunction in Medieval England: Holy Tears* (Lewiston, PA: Edwin Mellen Press, 1990).

27. *Patrologia Latina* 37, col. 1301: *Manduca cinerem velut panem, et fletum tuum, cum potu misce; per hoc convivium venies ad mensam Dei.*

28. *Wyclif* (Oxford: Oxford Univ. Press, 1985), pp. 96 and 99, respectively.

29. MS 319, fol. 41[r]. For a reproduction, see Anne Hudson, *Lollards and Their Books* (London: Hambledon Press, 1985), plate 5, p. 31.

30. See "William White's Lollard Followers," in Aston, *Lollards and Reformers,* p. 76.

31. Bramley, *Psalter,* p. 186.

32. See Bramley, *Psalter,* p. xvi, and his brief description of Laud Misc. 286, p. xxii. Bramley might have neglected some of the stridencies of the Laudian revisions because of his own religious opinions. He was not only fellow of Magdalene College, Oxford, but also Vicar of Horspath. Among his other publications are "Eternal Punishment: A Criticism of Dr. Farrar's 'Eternal Hope,'" a speech delivered to the Oxford Clerical Association, 1878, and "Unquenchable Fire, a Sermon," delivered in Oxford, 1873.

33. He "seems to have had no inkling of the fact" ("Prose Psalter of Richard Rolle," p. 223).

34. It should be noted that three other fifteenth-century copies of Rolle's *English Psalter* agree with Laud Misc. 286 in some of its interpolations to Psalms 1-17: MSS Merton College 94 (fragmentary), Bodley 877, and British Library Reg. 18.B.21. Even if the revisions to Psalms 1-17 did not originate with the Laudian scribe, however, their convergence with other polemical elements in this book (the anonymous metrical preface,

marginal caricatures, and certain marginal glosses, discussed below) is still ideologically significant.

35. *Writings Ascribed to Richard Rolle, Hermit of Hampole, and Materials for His Biography* (New York: D. C. Heath, 1927), p. 191.

36. A. B. Emden, A *Biographical Register of the University of Oxford to* A.D. 1500 (Oxford: Clarendon Press, 1958), vol. 2, p. 962.

37. Bramley, *Psalter,* p. 8.

38. Ibid., p. 9.

39. Michael P. Kuczynski, "An Extract from Richard Rolle's *English Psalter,*" *Yale Library Gazette* (October 1996), pp. 13-21.

40. Bramley, *Psalter,* p. 2.

41. For a recent analysis of the sophisticated interplay of text and (more elaborate) pictures in another vernacular manuscript of the same period, see Kathryn Kerby-Fulton and Denise L. Despres, *Iconography and the Professional Reader: The Politics of Book Production in the Douce "Piers Plowman"* (Minneapolis: Univ. of Minnesota Press, 1999). The literature on the interplay between marginal images and the texts they accompany has become large. For two examples, see the essays on medieval books in D. C. Greetham, *The Margins of the Text* (Ann Arbor: Univ. of Michigan Press, 1997) and Michael Camille, *Images on the Edge: The Margins of Medieval Art* (Cambridge, MA: Harvard Univ. Press, 1992).

Figure 1. John Wyclif. From John Bale's *Illustrium maioris Britanniae Scriptorum Summarium* (1548). By permission of the Houghton Library, Harvard University.

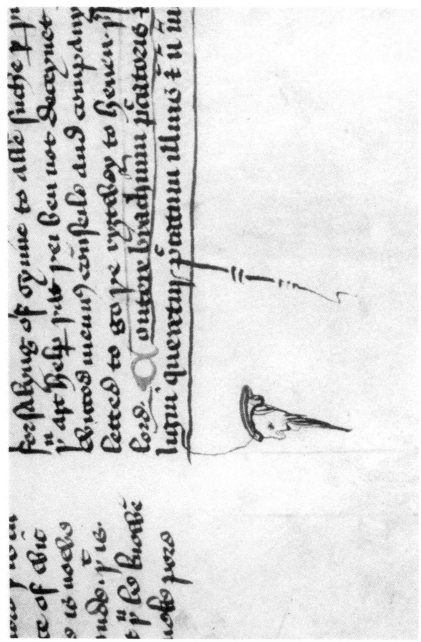

Figure 2. Caricature of a Doctor of Theology. Bodleian Library, Oxford MS Laud Misc. 286, fol. 17vb. 15th c. By permission of the Bodleian Library, Oxford.

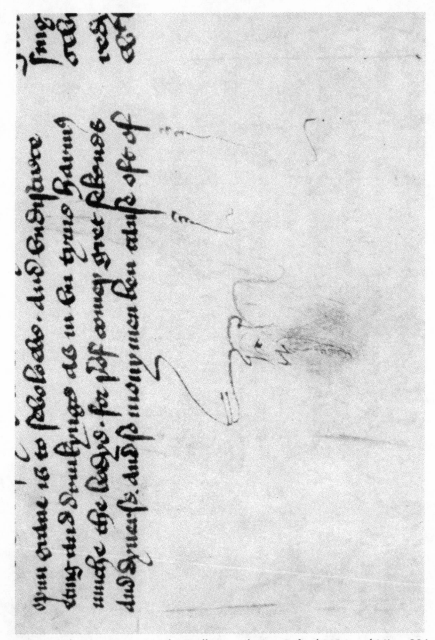

Figure 3. The Doctor as Devil. Bodleian Library, Oxford MS Laud Misc. 286, fol. 21ra. 15th c. By permission of the Bodleian Library, Oxford.

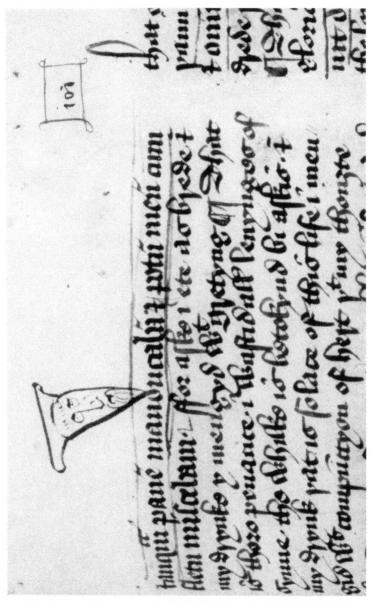

Figure 4. The Doctor Weeping. Bodleian Library, Oxford MS Laud Misc. 286, fol. 115ra. 15th c. By permission of the Bodleian Library, Oxford.

Family Ties:
the Use of the 'Shopping List' in
Manuscript Genealogy

CLAIRE JONES

In 1969, Henry Hargreaves wrote to the Librarian of St John's College, Cambridge, following his examination of MS 37 (B.15) in the College's collection. In his letter he included the following note on the manuscript:

> There is a close connection between your manuscript and Glasgow University Hunterian MS 117. Not only are some of the charms the same (note particularly the one on f. 23v, 'To helen a wounde wt a plate of led,' to which attention is called by the editor of the Glasgow catalogue), but the note found on your f.29 'her ben written al þe names al þe names [sic] of diuerse receytes for alle euelis but here faylen mani for þe defaute of þe samplarie' is found on f. 50 of the Hunterian manuscript. Despite the editor's wording, it clearly refers there to the preceding recipes rather than the following herbal, which is however the same is both manuscripts. Moreover, the recipe beginning 'Poudre of lif þat Frere Joh Bacheler mad & ʒaf it men drinkyn for þe feueres & for empostemes' in the collection beginning on f. 34v is also in Hunterian 117 and it is one I cannot remember anywhere else. But the fact that your manuscript begins imperfect makes it impossible for me to say if Hunterian 117 and the first part of your manuscript were once identical in all their contents. Nor have I enough evidence to indicate what the relationship between them is.

Nearly thirty years later, when I was starting to work on East Anglian medical manuscripts, this question had still not been resolved. Linda Voigts pointed out similarities in the St John's College manuscript, which I shall refer to as **SJC**, when I was working on an analysis of the texts in the Hunter manuscript (henceforth **Hu 117**). Closer analysis, and the benefits of dialectological work published long after Hargreaves was writing, show that these manuscripts are even more closely related than he had thought. The manuscripts share three texts which have been indexed in the *Manual of Writings in Middle English*, Vol 10, although they are not listed in two of the indexes[1]:

MWME 341a:	Uncorrupted Wounds of Christ Charm	**Hu 117:** ff. 33r-v; **SJC** 28r
MWME 345:	Charm of St William	**Hu 117**: f. 28r-v; **SJC** 23r-v
MWME 346:	Plate of Lead charm	**Hu 117**: ff. 28v-29r; **SJC** 23v

At present a thorough comparison of the texts in **Hu 117** and **SJC**, part 1, is yet to be completed in order to establish whether the contents of the manuscripts are identical, but a cursory examination suggests that this is the case.

    SJC is a composite manuscript, made up of three booklets, which may have been separate originally. The text of Booklet 3 has been indexed in a contemporary, though much less formal hand to the table of contents on ff. 8r-v. It is likely that this section was bound with the others at a late date, as a signature of 'M. Tomsun' dates from a later period, probably the sixteenth century, but is only found in this section of the book. The section which concerns us here is section 1: ff. 1r-47v. This section contains medical recipes and a herbal, together with a Latin copy of the *Antidotarium Nicholai*.

    Hu 117 is a medical recipe book written in one hand, which survives in its original binding. It is structured in five quires. Quires I-V were compiled at different times and from different sources than VI-VII (though copied by the same scribe).[2]

    Both manuscripts are written in a Norfolk dialect, and both are listed in LALME.[3] **SJC** has been localized to Norfolk, and much of the section which concerns us has been given a linguistic profile: LP 735, Grid 572 296. **Hu 117** has the linguistic profile LP 4622; Grid 637 304. On the map, these are not very close together. **SJC** is located in south-west Norfolk, whereas **Hu 117** is in the far east of the county. However, all these profiles can tell us is where the scribes learned to write, and so should not be taken as indicators of where the manuscripts were used or copied.

    So far the information, while providing further connections to those found by Hargreaves, does not provide any further insight into the relationship between the manuscripts. However, there is one piece of information of which Hargreaves was unaware, presumably because he had not seen the Glasgow manuscript. At the end of quire 5 in **Hu 117**, there is a leaf that was originally blank (f. 40r-v), but which now has a price list for salts, gums and other pharmaceutical ingredients added by the same scribe, but in different ink, and after the word 'Explicit' at the end of the main text. The rest of the leaf is blank, and the text restarts at the beginning of the next quire (f. 41r). The text on the following two quires is different in language and rubrication, with a much greater use of English, and different efficacy phrases.[4] It seems clear, then, that the 'shopping list' was added later, and that quires six and seven were bound up with this section later.

The same list is also found in **SJC**. However, in this manuscript, it immediately follows the herbal, is written and rubricated in the same way as the preceding text and as the next series of recipes, which immediately follow it (with no gap) on f. 34v. The conflation of the texts in **SJC** therefore suggests that it was copied after the booklets of **Hu 117** were combined, and, therefore, that **SJC**, if not a direct copy of **Hu 117**, is at least a descendant of it. In order to better establish the relationship, more work needs to be done in various areas: first, the texts in both manuscripts must be closely compared to see if they are identical. Secondly, the dialects of each should be thoroughly rechecked and compared with each other. Thirdly, the hands of each need to be examined. The scripts are similar, but at present I have not seen them side by side, so cannot say if they are in the same hands. Finally, the manuscripts containing the three connecting texts listed above should also be examined to see if similar patterns of texts can be found. The Charm of St William manuscripts seem to have strong East Anglian associations, as do the Plate of lead charm manuscripts. Further study of this kind will not only help to establish the relationships of the two manuscripts under discussion here, but will also help to further clarify patterns of textual dissemination in medieval East Anglia.

University of York

NOTES

1. G. Keiser, ed., *Manual of the Writings in Middle English: Volume 10, Works of Science and Information* (New Haven: Connecticut Academy of Arts and Sciences, 1998), pp. 3871-2. The manuscripts are not listed under 345 and 346.
2. M. C. Jones, *An Analysis of the Language and Style of a Late-Medieval Medical Recipe Book: Glasgow University Library MS Hunter 117* (Unpublished M.Phil. dissertation, University of Glasgow, 1997), p. 7.
3. A. McIntosh, *et al.*, *A Linguistic Atlas of Late Mediaeval English*, 4 vols. (Aberdeen: Aberdeen University Press, 1986).
4. See C. Jones, "Formula and formulation: efficacy phrases in medieval English medical manuscripts," *Neuphilologische Mitteilungen* 99 (1998), pp. 199-210.

"The Chronicles of Saints and Kings of England": Two Occurrences of the Middle English Prose *Brut's* "Peculiar Version" in MSS of the *Canterbury Tales*

DANIEL W. MOSSER

In *The Prose* Brut: *The Development of a Middle English Chronicle*, Lister M. Matheson's classification of "peculiar versions" includes a subcategory of "Texts Containing Brief King-Lists," comprising the versions found in MS Bodl. Digby 196 (two texts), Cambridge University Library MS Ff.1.6 (the "Findern Manuscript"), and Folger Shakespeare Library MS V.a.198.[1] The latter two refer to themselves as "The Chronicles of Saints and Kings of England."[2] As this title suggests, the text is primarily a listing of the kings of England (mythical and historical) and English saints. It begins with Brutus and the dating of the foundation of London "after the making of the world four thousand one hundred seventy-four years." In complete copies, of course, the date of the concluding entry may contribute significantly to the dating of the manuscript. Thus, for example, the Findern MS text ends with a reference to Henry VI and the date 1446, but, as the scribe left the number of years Henry reigned blank, the date becomes more elastic: 1446-1461. The Folger MS text concludes with the fifteenth regnal year of Edward IV, or 1475.

I propose adding two more examples to this listing, both occurring in manuscripts of the *Canterbury Tales*: University of Texas, HRC pre-1700 MS 143 (the "Cardigan Manuscript"); and British Library, Egerton MS 2864.[3] The contents of the Cardigan MS are *Canterbury Tales* (fols. 1r-244r); "Chronicles" (fols.

244r-245v); John Lydgate's *Siege of Thebes* (fols. 246r-304r); John Lydgate's *Churl and Bird* (fols. 304r-308v). The contents of the Egerton MS are *Canterbury Tales* (fols. 1r-292r); *Siege of Thebes* (fols. 292v-341r); "Chronicles" (damaged severely, fol. 341v). The Cardigan text of "Chronicles" is complete and ends with the "xxviij yere of kyng harry the sixte...M CCCC xlix." This entry has been used to date the MS to ca. 1450. As I have suggested previously, the current ordering of the contents of Cardigan may not reflect the sequence of copying, in which "Chronicles" was arguably the last item to be copied.[4]

The folio of the Egerton MS that contains the only part of "The Chronicles" to survive in the MS has lost from a third to a half of the left-hand side of the page (fol. 341v), taking with it substantial portions of text. This final gathering of the MS presently consists of only two folios (340 and 341), but may originally have been a gathering of at least four and may, therefore, once have contained a complete text of "The Chronicles...." The surviving fragment ends with a reference to Saint Thomas's translation in 1220, during the reign of Henry III, followed by an added line, in Latin (written by the scribe at the same time as the preceding text), at the foot of fol. 341v, fragmentary due to the damage described above: "...S[ancti] Gregorij Cant[uarie] A[nno] d[omini] M[l] lxxiij fundatus est." This, together with the association of its sister manuscript, British Library, MS Additional 5140, with Canterbury, might suggest that Egerton 2864 also had some connection with the Southeast, though the language of the scribe points to Suffolk.[5]

Manly and Rickert's descriptions fail to link the chronicle text in Cardigan to the one in Egerton 2864, referring to its occurrence in the Egerton MS as "[a] list, mainly of religious events, to 1349, f.341b."[6] In their description of Cardigan, "Chronicles" is characterized as "[a] chronological table to 1449, ff.244-45."[7]

My collations suggest that the Cardigan and Egerton texts of the Chronicle derive from a common exemplar and that the Findern and Folger texts also share an exemplar. The Digby text shares variants with each of the two subgroups. As Matheson notes, Richard Pynson's [?1518] "cronycle of all the kyngs names that haue ben in Englande: and how many yeres they reygned, and how many saynts & martyrs haue ben in this lande" (STC 9983.3) uses a text closely related to this group through the entry for Harold Godwinson (i.e., the last English king before the Conquest), but then continues with John Lydgate's "Kings of England" (IMEV 3632, with six added stanzas).[8]

Since the Cardigan and Egerton MSS have three texts in common, it is worth considering the nature of their relationship. The Cardigan exemplar of the *Canterbury Tales* was subsequently used by Rylands English MS 113 (the "Manchester Manuscript"). Although Egerton 2864 and Additional 5140 are textually related to Cardigan (and, more generally, to the *a-b* manuscript subgroups of the *Canterbury Tales*), they do not share an immediate common exemplar with Cardigan and Manchester.[9] Robert Earl Lovell's edition of the Cardigan text of *Siege of Thebes* argues for an affiliation with British Library, Additional MS 18,632. His stemma suggests that Egerton 2864-Additional 5140 inherited the exemplar subsequent to its use by the Cardigan scribe.[10]

For both of the Cardigan scribes, the dialect forms coalesce in Warwickshire, although Scribe A has some forms suggestive of a Herefordshire provenance. Cardigan Scribe B's spellings suggest at least a layering of East Anglian influence. This East Anglian layer may point to the layer of the stemma from which the Egerton and Cardigan exemplars were derived. The probable earliest owners of Cardigan, the Mantells, had holdings near "Daventry and Northampton, including Nether and Over Heyford,"[11] very near the Northamptonshire/Warwickshire border, though by the early sixteenth century the MS seems to have migrated to family holdings in Kent. As mentioned previously, the language of both the Egerton and Additional MSS is localized to Suffolk. The paper stocks in the Egerton MS are of the 1460s and 1470s,[12] thus dating the manuscript to a generation later than Cardigan and perhaps making intervening exemplars more probable. The Findern MS, which may be slightly earlier than Cardigan, was probably copied in south Derbyshire.[13] This location is proximate to the Mantell's holdings in Northamptonshire and even closer to the central Warwickshire localization indicated by dialect evidence in Cardigan. This raises the possibility that the Cardigan exemplar for "Chronicles" was derived from Findern or–perhaps more likely–its exemplar.

While the texts of "Chronicles" and the *Siege of Thebes* in Cardigan and Egerton 2864 are textually close (the damaged and fragmentary nature of "Chronicles" in Egerton does render the collation problematic), and the texts of the *Canterbury Tales* in both MSS derive from an *a* or *alpha* exemplar, exactly how these exemplars circulated and how closely they were associated remain open questions.

Virginia Tech

NOTES

1. Lister M. Matheson, *The Prose* Brut: *The Development of a Middle English Chronicle* (Tempe: Medieval & Renaissance Texts & Studies, vol. 180, 1998), xxi; 319-322.

2. Hereafter, "Chronicles." See Edward Donald Kennedy, "Chronicles and Other Historical Writing," A *Manual of the Writings in Middle English* 1050-1500, ed. Albert E. Hartung, vol. 8 (Hamden, CT: Archon Books for the Connecticut Academy of Arts and Sciences, 1989), 2637 ("Bodley Digby 196" and "The Cronekelys of Seyntys and Kyngys of Yngelond"); Patrick J. Horner, *The Index of Middle English Prose, Handlist III: A Handlist of Manuscripts containing Middle English Prose in the Digby Collection, Bodleian Library, Oxford*

(Cambridge, UK: D. S. Brewer, 1986), 59-61, Digby 196. The chronicle in the Findern MS is reproduced in facsimile, along with the rest of the MS in Richard Beadle and A. E. B. Owen, eds., *The Findern Manuscript, Cambridge University Library* MS. Ff.I.6 (London: Scolar Press, 1977), and the MS is examined in detail by Kate Harris in "The Origins and Make-up of Cambridge University Library MS Ff.1.6," *Transactions of the Cambridge Bibliographical Society* 8 (1983): 299-333, where the chronicle, however, receives little attention. A similarly brief notice appears in L. F. Casson, ed., *The Romance of Sir Degrevant* EETS o.s. 221 (London: Oxford University Press, 1949 [for 1944]), xii. Lister M. Matheson mentions the Findern, Digby, and Folger versions in his discussion of heavily abbreviated versions of the "Brut" ("Historical Prose," pp. 209-248 in A. S. G. Edwards, ed. *Middle English Prose: A Critical Guide to Major Authors and Genres* [New Brunswick: Rutgers University Press, 1984], 213).

3. For descriptions of the Cardigan and Egerton MSS, see John M. Manly and Edith Rickert, eds., *The Text of the Canterbury Tales: Studied on the Basis of All Known Manuscripts* (Chicago: University of Chicago Press, 1940), vol. 1, 71-78 and 143-147; Charles A. Owen, Jr., *The Manuscripts of the Canterbury Tales* (Cambridge, UK: D.S. Brewer, 1991), 15-22 and 90-92; Michael Seymour, *A Catalogue of Chaucer Manuscripts. Volume II, The Canterbury Tales* (Aldershot, UK and Brookfield, VT: Scolar Press, 1997), 39-43 and 111-116; and Daniel W. Mosser, "Witness Descriptions," *The General Prologue on CD-ROM*, ed. Elizabeth Solopova (Cambridge, UK: Cambridge University Press, 2000).

4. See, e.g., Daniel W. Mosser, "The Cardigan Chaucer: A Witness to the Manuscript and Textual History of the *Canterbury Tales*," *The Library Chronicle* n.s. 41 (1987): 82-111. Two pages from "Chronicles" are reproduced on pp. 98 (fol. 244v) and 101 (fol. 245v, the final page).

5. See Angus McIntosh, M. L. Samuels, and Michael Benskin, eds., *A Linguistic Atlas of Late Mediaeval English*, 4 vols. (Aberdeen, UK: Aberdeen University Press, 1986), LP 8301. Although Manly and Rickert as well as Michael Seymour (p. 116) count two hands, I believe it is a single scribe exhibiting variation, possibly due to a hiatus in the copying. Since the language of Egerton 2864 and the very closely related British Library MS Additional 5140 is virtually identical, it may represent the language of the exemplar, copied *literatim* by the scribes. It is most probable that these linguistic affiliations led Seymour to attribute—incorrectly—the Egerton and Additional MSS to the same scribe (p. 97).

6. Manly and Rickert, vol. 1, 143. Why they give the year "1349" as the date of the final entry is a mystery.

7. Manly and Rickert, vol. 1, 71.

8. Matheson 1998, 321.

9. See Peter M. W. Robinson, "A Stemmatic Analysis of the Fifteenth-Century Witnesses to *The Wife of Bath's Prologue*," in Norman Blake and Peter Robinson, eds. *The Canterbury Tales Project Occasional Papers* vol. 2 (Oxford: Office for Humanities Communication, 1997), 69-132; and Peter M. W. Robinson, "Analysis Workshop" and

"Stemmatic Commentary," *The General Prologue* on CD-ROM, ed. Elizabeth Solopova (Cambridge, UK: Cambridge University Press, 2000).

10. Robert Earl Lovell, "John Lydgate's *Siege of Thebes* and *Churl and Bird*: Edited from the Cardigan-Brudenell Manuscript," Ph.D. diss., University of Texas at Austin, 1969, lxxvii.

11. Manly and Rickert, vol. 1, 77.

12. Mosser, "Witness Descriptions," BL Egerton 2864: Watermarks.

13. Matheson 1998, 320; Harris, 303.

Imagined Histories:
An English Prophecy in a Welsh
Manuscript Context

JASON O'ROURKE

Middle English political prophecies are by their very nature imagined and imaginative histories, often strategic reworkings of material sourced from historical writings such as Geoffrey of Monmouth's *History of the Kings of Britain*. Political prophecies often include a handful of well-known historical facts from such sources in order to establish veracity. Assuming that the prophecy has already come true in parts, the audience is encouraged to accept the rest of its claims. The way in which these claims are made raises a number of issues: who collected these texts, and for what purpose? What does a reconstituted history tell us about the cultural milieu that it was produced in? These are particularly interesting questions to apply to the evidence provided by manuscripts from Wales and the English border country. In multilingual regions with histories of political turbulence and racial conflict such as these, connections between language, politics, and ethnicity are complex and problematic: if a political text is composed in English, for example, it does not necessarily follow that it rehearses nationalistic English sentiments.

In order to explore some of these issues, I will examine a short English prophecy, *When Rome Is Removed*, considering its manuscript context in two Welsh manuscripts: National Library of Wales MSS Peniarth 26 and Peniarth 50. Both of these manuscripts are collections of prophecies in Welsh, English, and Latin, and both can be dated to the middle of the fifteenth century.[1] Peniarth 26 was produced in Oswestry in west Shropshire, and Peniarth 50 in South Wales, probably in the Morgannwg area.[2] Peniarth 26 contains three examples of the prophecy: two are versions of the A text and one is a version of the C text. Of these, the first A text version is incomplete and runs to only six lines; the other A text is complete and contains eighty–five lines. The C text is a variant composed of thirteen single lines, some of which are culled from the A text and some of which are additions. Peniarth 50 has one version of the A text which is incomplete and contains ninety lines. Despite their presence in manuscripts that are predominantly in Welsh, the English prophecies in these two manuscripts are not derived from a Welsh-language tradition, but from various English-language sources. Of these, the Scottish tradition was very influential in the later Middle Ages, and in Scotland, conflict with the English often contributed to the composition of new political prophecies or the alteration and re-circulation of old ones. *When Rome Is Removed* was one of the most copied prophecies in the fifteenth century. Although it belongs to the Scottish tradition, the Peniarth versions that I am considering demonstrate a considerable amount of modification to suit Welsh agendas (in particular the C text in Peniarth 26).

The difference between versions of the prophecy is important when considering their socio-literary and political background, and it is worth comparing the English-biased version printed by Rossel Hope Robbins from Cambridge University MS Kk.1.5 with the Welsh versions.[3] In much the same way as the Peniarth versions manipulate the original Scottish text, the Cambridge version changes the symbolism to switch the bias towards the English.[4]

The prophecy can be broken down into a number of sections. In all versions of the text that I am considering, the opening lines (1-15) deal with predictions of ecclesiastical and social problems that will occur in Britain. The next section (16-50) is derived from Geoffrey of Monmouth and uses animal symbolism to make political vaticinations. This is the section of the text where most of the important variations occur. The main features of this passage in Cambridge Kk.1.5 are as follows. The lily will spawn in the winter: Cadwaladr shall return and, with Cynan's aid, will stir (or "worthe") up Wales; they will then go into Albany, where foreigners ("alienys") shall be harmed. King Albanactus will ally with the leopard (England).[5] The lion (Scotland) will bow before the leopard. The stepsons of the lion will be forced into subjection by the leopard, and an eagle from the east will strike down the stepsons of the lion. Lines 51 to 58 are concerned with ecclesiastical troubles and are a later addition. The next passage (lines 59-66) is also derived from Geoffrey of Monmouth, and uses alphabetical and numerical codes to predict the "dolorous" date on which the events will take place. The date is coded but could be 1382, in which case it may be a reference to the Peasants' Revolt, included as part of the prophecy's strategy for veracity.[6] The next section (lines 67-72) is again Galfridian and is devoted specifically to Berwick, predicting victory for the king in the Scottish wars. At this point (line 72)

Cambridge Kk.1.5 breaks off. The Peniarth A texts continue with another section, but only Peniarth 26 item 38b is complete. This section makes general predictions about social problems and wondrous events of nature that are related to the defeat of Scotland and France.

An interesting aspect of the Peniarth 26 and 50 texts is the way in which their variations reflect a particular political and linguistic context. The most important passage in this context is the second section (lines 16-50), with its political symbolism. A comparison of a few lines from this passage will illustrate the way in which the Peniarth text has been manipulated:

24   (Cambridge Kk.1.5) Tatcaldwers sall call on carioun the noyus
      (Peniarth 50)   Catwaladyr shall call on Kynon the nobyll
25   (C) and þan sall worthe vp wallys and wrethe oþir landis
      (P) And worth vp walys and worshipe her londes
26   (C) And erth on tyll Albany, if þai may wyne
      (P) y heryd in to albany at her own wyll
27   (C) Herme wnto Alienys, aneuer þai sall wakyne!
      (P) harmyng to alions anon shall wake
28   (C) þe brutis blude sall þame wakyne & bryttne wyth brandis of
            stell
      (P) when bruttus may braytyn with brondys of stele
29   (C) þer sall no bastarde blode abyde in þat lande
      (P) there may no bastarde bloode lyne in this lond.[7]

The first difference is important in that it demonstrates knowledge of Welsh prophetic traditions in the Peniarth texts and an ignorance of them in Cambridge Kk.1.5. In the Cambridge text the names "Cadwaladr" and "Cynan" are hopelessly misspelled ("Tatcaldwers," "Carioun"). In the Peniarth versions they are spelled correctly.[8] More important, the epithet attached to the name is different in the Peniarth texts: in Cambridge Kk.1.5 he is called "Carioun the noyus." In Peniarth 50 he is "Kynon the nobyll." Obviously, then, for the Welsh, Cynan is noble, and for the English, he is troublesome. In the next line the Peniarth texts are deferential to Wales, whereas the Cambridge text casts the Welsh in the role of aggravating other lands. In line 26, Cambridge Kk.1.5 displays doubt as to whether the Welsh may succeed in their mission in Albany, but the Peniarth texts are supremely confident. The reference to Albany may relate to the Welsh historical and literary traditions concerning the Old North, such as the *Gododdin*, which derive from the time of Anglo-Saxon expansion into the Welsh-speaking northern kingdoms. The idea of "inheriting" into Albany suggests that the Welsh are going to regain what was rightfully theirs: the lost northern kingdoms. Line 27 can be interpreted in different ways: for the English-biased text the term "Alienys," or "foreigners," may be applied either to the people of Albany or to the Welsh themselves. Likewise in the next line, the term "brutis" may be applied to the descendants of Brutus, the Anglo-Normans/English of Geoffrey of Monmouth's *Historia*, or to the British, the Brythonic inhabitants of the Island of Britain.[9] In the context of the rest of the passage, it is safe to assume that the Cambridge text considers the Welsh to be aliens and the "brutis blude" to belong to the English. From the Welsh viewpoint the situation is reversed, the aliens equating with the English and the "bruttus" equating with the Welsh. The last line of this passage indicates another difference of viewpoint: for the English, Albany is *that* land, distant and unfamiliar; for the Welsh it is *this* land, close and familiar, which may relate to the familiarity of the Old North from Welsh historical and literary traditions.[10] In the context of the wider passage, it can be seen in the Cambridge version that the original Scottish bias is reversed and victory given to the English, symbolised by the leopard. In both of the long Peniarth versions, the leopard is not even mentioned, and more attention is paid to the lily, which is traditionally associated with the kings of France in late medieval prophecies.[11] The lines concerning the lily in these texts may well hearken back to the support provided by the French to Owain Glyn Dwr during the rebellion, or to earlier instances. Alternatively, they may also express the hope for French assistance in any forthcoming conflict.

Perhaps the most significant variations of *When Rome Is Removed* occur in the C text from Peniarth 26. I present the text in full:

1	when rome ys remevyd yn to englon and ilke a preste
2	the pope ys powere yn hond bethwyx the sixte and
3	the iij how ys wyle vnderstond myckill wrath & woo schall
4	fale yn englonde. The iij – schall rekewyre and reckyn
5	of rulys that grevosly ar growyn mone longe days
6	ther schall tyde them astryffe by the water of hwmbyre
7	that a northrne flawe schall folwe them for euer
8	then walys wytte hyt well thatt wantys no
9	wyse to brynge vp hur brothyre with harde bryth brondes
10	her kynnys men of erlonde and yrllys of hawors
11	schall spende hure sperys with dyntys & dolorys to brynge
12	owte of brawe the keynde blode of brutus then[12]
13	the ryght schall to the lyne of gwladus [13]

A comparison with the A text will immediately identify a number of lines that have been lifted from the original and seemingly reassembled with little attention to the original context or meaning. One significant alteration to the A text is the change from "Britain" to "England" in line 4, which brings the war specifically to the English with no room for doubt or interpretation.[14]

Robbins states that the C text of *When Rome Is Removed* "shows how a short general prophecy can apply to almost any period."[15] This text has been altered to supply a border context, although it is not specific enough to be dateable. In political terms, the most important features of this text are the additional lines that do not originate with the A text. The first of these is line 5, which makes a general complaint about the law of the land. More significant are the lines that mention Wales. Line 8 sees the commencement of a short section which prophesizes a battle or war and the return of the crown to the Welsh.

In this prophecy the blood of Brutus refers to the Welsh, the descendants of the Britons. The most pointed reference is to "Gwladus." In all probability this is Gwladus Ddu, daughter of Llywelyn ab Iorwerth of the princely dynasty of Gwynedd.[16] It would seem that the author of the prophecy is predicting the accession of a Welsh king, although whether he is to sit on the English throne or become the ruler of a Welsh principality is not made clear. In the fifteenth century context, the likelihood is that the author is imagining the construction of a political entity along the lines of a new "Island of Britain" based on Welsh literary traditions.[17] Gwladus Ddu had an important and interesting genealogy: not only did her "line" descend from the dynasty of Gwynedd, but as a widow she married Ralph Mortimer. Her line back to the Welsh princes was exploited by the Mortimer family of Wigmore and their descendants in various political contexts throughout the fourteenth and fifteenth centuries.[18] For example, the Mortimer side of her genealogy is well illustrated in a fourteenth-century genealogy and chronicle of Wigmore Abbey (now University of Chicago MS 224).[19] The illustrator of this manuscript takes some pains to highlight Mortimer descent from Gwladus by giving her genealogy a large and intricately decorated capital.[20] The title leaves us in no doubt as to the connections between Llywelyn ab Iorwerth and the Mortimer family: "Hic incipit genealogia domine Gwladuse filie et heredis Lewelinn quondam principis gallie uxoris noblisuiri duc Radulphi de Mortuomar domine de Wyggemore."[21] Clearly Welsh royal blood was considered important to the author or patron(s) of the Wigmore genealogy. In fact it is probable that the Mortimer claims to Welsh royal descent were well known in households along the border. This is borne out by the Oswestry (west Shropshire) connections of Peniarth 26 and the Wigmore (west Herefordshire) connections of Chicago 224. The specificity of these lines indicates either that they were composed for this manuscript or that they were part of a border tradition. It is worth pointing out that the version of the C text printed by Robbins, from British Library MS Royal 7A.ix, does not mention Gwladus or the earls of Hawors, but adheres to the popular and traditional Galfridian character Brutus.[22]

Of course, Mortimer descent in the mid-fifteenth century was of no lesser importance than the foundation of the Yorkist claim to the throne of England itself. The C text of *When Rome Is Removed* can be read as a piece of political propaganda that draws out the connections between the Mortimers (and thus the York faction) and the Welsh princely dynasty of Gwynedd. It could be a useful tool for encouraging support for York, both in the Welsh and the English communities of Wales and the March. On the one hand, the Welsh could be enticed with the notion of a descendant of Llywelyn ab Iorwerth ruling over a newly constructed "Island of Britain." On the other hand, the English could perhaps be persuaded to accept a descendant of the powerful Marcher family that had previously held a legitimate claim to the throne in the person of Edmund Mortimer.

While this analysis provides a feasible political context for the prophecy, a number of questions still remain, particularly concerning the place of English-language texts such as *When Rome Is Removed* in two manuscript collections of prophecies with predominantly anti-English sympathies.

One of the most interesting features of Peniarth 26 and 50 is their linguistic makeup. The fact that they contain texts in Welsh, English, and Latin immediately suggests that their intended audiences were polyglot, although it is debatable whether they were aimed at individuals who could understand all three languages or at a community where all three were spoken. Most of the items in Peniarth 26 and 50 are Welsh verse prophecies that are polemically anti-English in their outlook, yet the English prose prophecies sit alongside them and are in many cases copied by the same scribes.

An explanation for the inclusion of English-language texts in an anti-English collection lies in the possible reasons for assembling such anthologies. This may not have been for political purposes at all but might, rather, stem from an interest in the genre itself. Manuscripts such as Peniarth 26 and Peniarth 50 could have been assembled at the behest of patrons who were simply collectors of prophecies and who may have had no quarrel with the English at all. On the other hand, some of the texts' references to contemporary politics could make the books dangerous to own in the wrong circumstances, and by commissioning them, the owners of these collections put their political sympathies on record—not necessarily the action of an antiquarian.

A more plausible reason for the inclusion of the English texts in these manuscripts concerns the connections between language and politics. There is no need to exclude the manuscripts from a pro-Welsh political culture simply because some of their texts are in the English language. Just because certain people in fifteenth-century Wales or the March speak English, it does not necessarily follow that they support English royal or governmental policy. Bilingual or monoglot-English children could be born to Welsh-speaking parents in Wales and the Marches and raised absorbing Welsh literary culture. Their political views could be influenced by their parents or spouses as well as by their own particular circumstances, experiences, and beliefs. In this way, an English-language speaker could easily be opposed to English policy and be content to listen to polemic anti-English prophecies. The Peniarth versions of *When Rome Is Removed* serve as a reminder to those who wish to link language and nationalism that nationalistic sympathies are not always expressed in the language one might expect, and that polemical texts are often composed in the language of the nation they are directed against.[23]

In its manuscript context, *When Rome Is Removed* belongs to two predominantly Welsh, trilingual, fifteenth-century collections of anti-English prophecies. Both books can be linked textually to the Yorkist faction in the Wars of the Roses, and in particular, the C text of *When Rome is Removed* demonstrates a strong interest in the Welsh descent of the Mortimers. In this context, it is reasonable to suggest that the manuscripts, although coming from different parts of Wales and the border, show a marked interest in the outcome of the Wars of the Roses. An obvious reason for such an interest is that a Yorkist victory would bring about what was, for many Welsh people, a longstanding political ambition: to see a descendant of the princely dynasties regain the crown of London for them.

Queen's University, Belfast

NOTES

1. The manuscripts are described in Evans, *Report*, vol. I, part ii; Peniarth 26 on pp. 351-354, and Peniarth 50 on pp. 389-399. See brief comments in Daniel Huws, *Medieval Welsh Manuscripts*, 17, 61, and n. 3 and 150. Peniarth 26 contains a note on p. 83, "This booke was penned in Anno ... 1456." Peniarth 50 is dated on four pages: 1425 (p. 62), 1445 (p. 82), 1451 (p. 221), and 1456 (p. 311). These dates occur in prophecies, so it is probable that the manuscript was compiled between ca. 1424 and ca. 1455, since there is little practical use for a dated prophecy after its events are supposed to have occurred.

2. For the provenance of Peniarth 26, see Marx, the *Index of Middle English Prose*, Handlist 14, 30. Welsh was spoken in Oswestry and other areas on the English side of the border well into the eighteenth century, See Llinos Beverley Smith, 17-19, and B. G. Charles pp. 85-110. There is a note on p. iv of Peniarth 50: "Y cwtta cyfarwydd o Vorganwg. y geilw rhai y llyfr hwnn o law Gwilym Tew. herwydd y dywyd pobl Gwlad Morgant." [The *Short Guide of Glamorganshire* some call this. in the hand of Gwilym Tew. According to the sayings of the people of the land of Morgant (Glamorgan)]. This inscription is in the hand of Robert Vaughan of Hengwrt. Evans believes the dates and the hand rule out Gwilym Tew as a scribe, especially when compared to his hand in Peniarth MS 51. One of the hands belongs to scribe A, "Dafydd" (his autograph is on p. 114), who, Evans believes, may have been a monk at Neath Abbey. *Report*, 389. The MS was reportedly owned by Sir Thomas Morgan of Ruperra, Glamorganshire. Evans,

Report, 399. Manon Jenkins (6) suggests a West Glamorgan provenance and identifies some material that is specific to Gower and Glamorgan (226 and n. 6).

3. Robbins, 118-120, and see 312-316. The C text is printed on p. 313.

4. Robbins, 314.

5. Albany is a region of northern England and the Scottish borders from north of the Humber to Caithness. Albanactus is the King of Albany.

6. The date is written "mccclxxxr." (Robbins, 119-120, ll. 61 - 64). The 'r' may have been mistaken for an original Arabic '2,' according to Lesley Coote, 148, n. 75.

7. Robbins 118, ll. 24 - 29; Peniarth 50, 4-5, ll. 24-29.

8. Peniarth 26 contains an error, spelling "Cynan" as "Caron." Most probably the scribe has followed his exemplar, possibly compounding a mistake already there. I do not believe this to be an indication that the scribe was unaware of Welsh literary or hagiographical traditions, especially considering that "Caron" is a saint's name.

9. The "Myth of Descent" from Brutus was manipulated by Geoffrey to legitimize the Norman invasion and occupation. Although originally applying to the Britons and therefore their descendants, the Welsh, Geoffrey also makes it apply to the Normans by having the Britons emigrate to Brittany, leaving the Anglo Saxons to rule all of Britain (except the barbarous areas such as Wales). The implication is then that the Bretons (descendants of the noble Britons) regained control of Britain with the aid of their Norman neighbors in the Conquest. This is discussed by Lewis Thorpe in his introduction to the *Historia*, see esp. 10.

10. It is worth mentioning that both of the long texts in Peniarth 26 and Peniarth 50 use "this" in the line.

11. Jansen and Jordan, 38; Taylor, 2-7.

12. The word "gwladus" has been written erroneously before "Brutus" in this line and struck through.

13. Peniarth 26, 122.

14. This is also the case in Robbins's text.

15. Robbins, 313.

16. See the *Dictionary of Welsh Biography*, 599-560 for Gwladus Ddu and Llywelyn ab Iorwerth.

17. An example of this notion can be found in the Peniarth 50 prophecy *Darogan yr Olew Bendigaid* [the Prophecy of the Blessed Oil] which is examined by Ceridwen Lloyd-Morgan, 24-26.

18. Gwladus' first marriage was to Reginald de Braose (d. 1228). For the de Braose family, see the *Dictionary of Welsh Biography*, 48-50.

19. University of Chicago MS 224. For a description of this MS, see Mary E. Giffin, 316-325).

20. University of Chicago MS 224, fol. 51v.

21. "Here begins the genealogy of the lady Gwladus, daughter and heiress of Llywelyn formerly prince of Wales, noble wife of Duke Ralph de Mortimer lord of Wigmore."

22. Printed in Robbins, 313-314.

WORKS CITED

PRIMARY SOURCES

Aberystwyth

National Library of Wales, Peniarth MS 26.

National Library of Wales, Peniarth MS 50 [Y Cwtta Cyfarwydd, "The Short Guide"].

Chicago

University of Chicago MS 224.

SECONDARY SOURCES

Charles, B. G. "The Welsh, Their Language and Place-names in Archenfield and Oswestry." *Angles and Britons.* Cardiff: University of Wales Press, 1963. 85 - 110.

Coote, Lesley A. *Prophecy and Public Affairs in Later Medieval England.* York: York Medieval Press, 2000.

The Dictionary of Welsh Biography. London: Honourable Society of Cymmrodorion, 1959.

Evans, J. Gwenogvryn. *A Report on Manuscripts in the Welsh Language.* 2 vols. London: HMSO, 1902.

Geoffrey of Monmouth. *Historia Regum Britanniae.* [The History of the Kings of Britain]. Translated by Lewis Thorpe. Penguin Classics series. Harmondsworth: Penguin, 1966.

Giffin, Mary E. "A Wigmore Manuscript at the University of Chicago." *National Library of Wales Journal* 7 (1951-52): 316-325.

Huws, Daniel. *Medieval Welsh Manuscripts.* Cardiff: University of Wales Press, 2000.

Jansen, Sharon L., and Kathleen H. Jordan. *The Welles Anthology (MS Rawlinson C. 813): A Critical Edition.* Medieval and Renaissance Texts and Studies Series. New York: Centre for Medieval and Renaissance Studies, 1991.

Jenkins, Manon B. "Aspects of the Welsh Prophetic Verse Tradition in the Middle Ages." PhD. thesis. Cambridge University, 1990.

Lloyd-Morgan, Ceridwen. "Prophecy and Welsh Nationhood in the Fifteenth Century." *Transactions of the Honourable Society of Cymmrodorion* (1985): 9-26.

Marx, William, ed. *The Index of Middle English Prose: Manuscripts in the National Library of Wales (Llyfrgell Genedlaethol Cymru), Aberystwyth.* Handlist 14. Woodbridge: Brewer, 1999.

Robbins, Rossel Hope, ed. *Historical Poems of the XIVth and XVth Centuries.* Edited by New York: Columbia University Press, 1959.

Smith, Llinos Beverley. "The Welsh Language Before 1536." *The Welsh Language Before the Industrial Revolution*. Edited by Geraint H. Jenkins, *Social History of the Welsh Language series*. Cardiff: University of Wales Press, 1997.

Taylor, Rupert. *The Political Prophecy in England*. New York: AMS Press, 1967.

A New Manuscript by the Hengwrt / Ellesmere Scribe? Aberystwyth, National Library of Wales, MS. Peniarth 393D

ESTELLE STUBBS

Aberystwyth, National Library of Wales, MS. Peniarth 393D (formerly Hengwrt 328, hereafter "Hn"), is a copy of *Boece*, Chaucer's translation of Boethius's *Consolation of Philosophy*.[1] It came to the National Library in 1909 as part of the Hengwrt collection, along with a copy of Chaucer's *Canterbury Tales*, MS. Peniarth 392 (hereafter the Hengwrt *Canterbury Tales* or "Hg"). It is an intriguing possibility that the two Chaucer manuscripts found their way into a much earlier collection from the same ultimate source. Such a hypothesis could be supported by the fact that "Hn" and "Hg" show striking similarities in both script and decorative features and could be either the work of a single scribe, or of two scribes of very similar training working in close co-operation.[2] The scribe of the Hengwrt *Canterbury Tales* also copied San Marino, Huntington Library MS. El. 26 C 9 (hereafter the Ellesmere Chaucer or "El"). Even if the "Hg"/"El" scribe was not the copyist of the Hengwrt *Boece*, there is evidence to suggest that he was involved in its making.

Apart from the Hengwrt and Ellesmere *Canterbury Tales*, the only other known examples of this scribe at work have been identified by Doyle and Parkes. He copied the second stint in the Trinity Gower, for which Doyle and Parkes label him "Scribe B," and two single-leaf fragments of Chaucer's *Troilus and Criseyde*.[3] A leaf from the "Prioress's Prologue and Tale" may be in his hand.[4] Therefore, there are three, possibly four, Chaucer copyings and one Gower. The discovery of yet another work by Chaucer which may be associated with this scribe would establish him still more as a Chaucer scribe, much as Scribe "D" of the Trinity Gower specialized in copying the *Confessio Amantis*.[5] An assessment of the relationship between the similar hand and the identical decorative features of "Hg" and "Hn" will increase our understanding of the scribes responsible for the early dissemination of Chaucer's work. The brief description of "Hn" which follows is intended to stimulate further debate.

Like the Hengwrt *Canterbury Tales*, the *Boece* manuscript is incomplete, 27 parchment leaves surviving from a probable 64. The four gatherings which remain were originally quires of eight leaves, though as they now survive, one leaf is missing at the head of the volume, two after folio 15, one after folio 19 and one after 27. Four more quires of eight leaves would probably have contained the remainder of the text. The folios measure 292 mm x 194 mm, with a written space measuring 225 mm x 113 mm. The text is in single columns with an average of 39 lines per page. The frame, ruled in brown crayon, comprises a rectangle with two single vertical lines crossed by two sets of horizontal lines top and bottom which are carried into the margins. Pricks to guide the ruling are visible on almost every folio where not obscured by mold. The horizontals enclose the text at the head and foot of each folio. The hand is an *Anglicana Formata* script dated to the first quarter of the fifteenth century.

The illumination is comparable to that in the Hengwrt / Ellesmere *Canterbury Tales* and may have been carried out in the same workshop. Two- to three-line illuminated capitals introduce the books on folios 8r and 17v. They are executed in gold on a background of blue and rose pink and highlighted with white. The black stems of flourished sprays, with trefoil leaves and buds decorated with gold, extend into the margin from top and bottom of the illuminated letter. Each prose and meter begins with a 2-line blue initial set in a frame of intricate red penwork and infilled with the same. The red serrated penwork extends into the margin above and below the letter, along the side of the text, with elongated tendrils ending in curls or knots. The paraphs are alternately blue and red.

The wording of *incipits*, *explicits*, catchwords and Latin *lemmata* is picked out in red ink and contained within box-like features, also drawn in red. Distinctive red penwork decoration, the 'tremolo or knot' described at length by Doyle in the Ellesmere Essays, may both precede and follow the bracket-like ends of the box feature.[6] (See Fig. 1). This same tremolo stroke with knot, also in red ink, is attached to the exaggerated ascenders of top lines of folios and occasionally to ascenders contained within the boxed headings. Red ink is also used to define interlinear glosses, *virgulae* and the words 'Boece' and 'Philosophye' within the text.

Punctuation is marked by *punctus*, *punctus elevatus* and *virgula* or double *virgula*, the latter executed sometimes in the pale brown ink of the text, sometimes in rubric, and occasionally in brown and red ink. Though difficult to distinguish because of fading of the ink, I believe there may be a few examples of the wedge-shaped *paragraphus*, like an inverted triangle,[7] found also in the prose sections of "Hg" and "El " and in the *Equatorie of the Planetis*.[8] Insertions are by caret mark, deletions, in red ink.

In features of illumination, intricate red penwork infill, idiosyncratic punctuation and the distinctive execution and placement of tremolo marks, "Hn" would seem to be closely connected with the illuminators, flourishers and the scribe of "Hg" and "El." The most notable similarity is in the use of the tremolo and knotted tremolo. These are not abbreviations for the "nota" but decorative features whose configuration is entirely consistent in all three manuscripts. The distinctive placement of such a feature against exaggerated ascenders, and after boxed headings, links together the making of these manuscripts. However, there is one significant difference that should be noted. In "Hg" and "El" the tremolo strokes, with and without knot, are executed in the ink of the text by the "Hg"/"El" scribe himself and are a part of his scribal repertoire. In "Hn" they are in red ink applied as a separate operation after the manuscript was copied. If the scribe of *Boece* is the "Hg"/"El" scribe, then he corrected and adorned his own work after copying. If the hand is that of a scribe of very similar training, then the "Hg" scribe was acting in the role of corrector and 'finisher.'

The hand of the Hengwrt/Ellesmere scribe has been described in detail by Doyle and Parkes.[9] The *Anglicana Formata* and the Bastard *Anglicana* scripts are thought to be of late fourteenth-century type, which apparently were not common in vernacular books, occurring more frequently in documents of the period.[10] The text of the *Boece* is copied by a single scribe in an *Anglicana* script very similar to the hand of "Hg" and "El," though more rounded and squat than in any other examples of his writing. On closer examination, it appears to have the "distinctive combination of the same forms and features . . . performed in the same manner and with the same mannerisms."[11] Yet the hand appears to me to be less fluent, and despite a more rounded appearance, bears more resemblance to the "neater, squatter" aspect of the Cambridge Kk fragment about which Doyle expresses some doubt.[12] The combination of common elements, however, make it worthy of consideration as a manuscript either in the hand of Scribe "B" or a scribe of the same school. The individual letter forms for *g*, 8-shaped *s*, tilted *y* with lowered fork and I with extended headstroke, all features contributing to the identification of the hand by Doyle and Parkes, are found in abundance in "Hn." Two of the three types of A as distinguished in "Hg" and "El" can be found though as yet I have not been able to locate the third form with an open angular lower compartment. The upper lobe of the two-compartment lower case *a* almost invariably stands above the surrounding letters. Single-compartment lower case secretary *a* occurs occasionally (see fol. 21, line 19, "amenusith").

Variations in lower case *b*, *h*, and *l*, with both angular and rounded base and head of stem, and stems completed with either closed loops or angular open hooks, are all represented in "Hn." As in "Hg" and "El," the hook-like heads are mainly reserved for the exaggerated ascenders where there is space to accommodate the stroke. These are usually decorated with red ink, frequently with attached knot feature.

Round *e* is found throughout, usually though not exclusively in final position (see fol. 15r line 28, "blyssefulnesses"). The *e* with extended tongue is used not only in the Latin *lemmata* but occasionally in final position.

The scribe's *g*, set slightly at an angle, with projecting tag on the right side of lower and sometimes upper lobes is distinctive, though there are several examples of secretary *g* also represented (see fol. 17v, line 22, "mariages"). The letter l with upright stem is sometimes curtailed but more often has head and foot strokes looped to the left, with greater or lesser extensions depending on space. Occasionally the left-angled stroke at the foot of l is set almost at right angles to the main shaft. Some shafts sport the shortened cross strokes on the left side; some are defined by punctus marks as occurs frequently in "Hg" and "El" (see fol. 13v, line 11, "I trowe", and on last line "I clepe").

Three *r*'s are distinguishable, with long *r* joined to the following letter, 2-shaped *r* used after *o* (fol. 13v, line 3, "forthy") and occasionally *p* (fol. 13v, last line, "precious"). Short *r* can be found in names in the text (see fol. 23v, line 4, "Arestotle") and in headings, as in "Hg."

The 8-shaped *s*, standing slightly proud of preceding letters, is found in final positions throughout the manuscript. Sigma *s* is more usual in initial positions, though long *s*, always used within a word, is occasionally used initially also (see fol. 17v, line 12, "sterre" and line 19, "stryven").

Both forms of *v* conform to the "Hg" description but the *w*'s are rounder though still within the pattern of variation described in the "Introduction" to the Ruggiers facsimile. The letter *y* is sometimes dotted, sometimes not, with no distinguishing pattern, but the fork of the two limbs joins in a position which is usually lower than the base of the surrounding letters.

Thorn is used occasionally, not only with a superscript *t* for the abbreviated version of "that," but also with the extended version (see fol. 17v, line 13). The Tyronian note is used occasionally in the body of the text and the "etc" sign sometimes follows the Latin *lemmata*. Macrons for abbreviation, where present, are almost always curved strokes as in "Hg" and "El" (see fol. 16v, line 11, "reson").

All of these letter forms replicate those found in the established work of the "Hg"/"El" scribe. While the rounded aspect of the script here is not found in any manuscripts attributed to him, it might still be within the repertory of styles which this scribe could write, or did write within his career as copyist. Even if attribution to him is doubted, the coincidence of so many letter forms and particularly the addition of the decorative tremolo, signals an association with the "Hg"/"El" scribe. The scribe of "Hn" may have been attempting to imitate the same style; he may have been trained in the same school or he was supervised by the "Hg" scribe himself.

Mold has stained the vellum of "Hn" and there are circular black marks on all folios, with holes in some. At the top right-hand side of the first folio is the name "William Morris" and the date "1740." The initials "E. I." are lower down in the right margin of the same folio. In the bottom margin of folio 27, the last extant leaf, is the following : "This Fragment of an Old English Mss was given me William Morris of Holyhead—by Mr Edwd Iones of Caernarvon ; about the Year of Our Lord MDCCXXXVII." How the manuscript arrived in Wales is not known. Its history after Morris's ownership is not clear, but it may have been in the collection of John Lloyd of Hafodunus (1749-1815). It came to the National Library of Wales with the rest of the Hengwrt collection and is listed as Hengwrt MS. 328 in the catalogues compiled in the nineteenth century by Aneurin Owen and by W. W. E. Wynne.

The manuscript was unbound in 1896 when M. H. Liddell examined it for his edition in the *Globe Chaucer*. His description accompanies the manuscript (folio v), and he suggests that the text "has very few mistakes." He continues, "If the manuscript were complete I should say it was the best of the texts that have come down to us." According to Ralph Hanna and John Lawlor, who provided the explanatory notes for *Boece* in the *Riverside Chaucer*, "Hn" is "one of the three manuscripts most faithful to O^1 "(i.e., the ancestor of all surviving manuscripts).[13] Brian Donaghey's personal transcription of all the *Boece* manuscripts also confirms this opinion, and he suggests that there is evidence that "Hn" was supervised and corrected at the time of writing. It would appear, then, that just as with the Hengwrt texts of the *Canterbury Tales*, the scribe or supervisor of this manuscript had access to an authoritative text of Chaucer's *Boece*. It is equally important that, like "Hg," "Hn" shows evidence of supervision and correction. Since *Boece* was a completed work which "must have achieved some degree of circulation by around 1387,"[14] the scribe or supervisor of "Hn" may have had access to an authorial copy text from which to "correct" his work. Alternatively, as I have suggested may have been the case with the Hengwrt Chaucer, he may have had contact with, or direction from, the author himself.[15] This may accord him special status as a Chaucer copyist.

University of Sheffield

NOTES

1. My thanks are due to the National Library of Wales for giving me access to a draft description of the manuscript prepared by Daniel Huws, to Linne Mooney for accompanying me to Wales and encouraging me to pursue my examination of Peniarth 393D, and to Brian Donaghey for sharing with me his ongoing research of all the Boethius manuscripts.

2. Endorsement for an identification of the hand comes from Donaghey and Mooney. Donaghey believes that "There is a good case for proposing that the scribe is either identical with one of the copyists of the Hengwrt *Canterbury Tales*, or trained in the same script very closely, possibly working in the same workshop." |Quotation from supporting notes supplied by Donaghey for a paper given by me at the Early Book Society Conference in Cork, 2001. Donaghey has also identified another manuscript containing the B-text of *Piers Plowman*, Trinity College Cambridge MS. B.15.17, which he believes was also copied in the same period in a very similar hand|. Linne Mooney believes that the hand of "Hn" is sufficiently similar to have been written by the Hengwrt / Ellesmere scribe.

3. Trinity College, Cambridge, MS R.3.2, described by Doyle and Parkes in: Doyle, A. I., and M. B. Parkes. "The Production of Copies of the *Canterbury Tales* and the *Confessio Amantis* in the Early Fifteenth Century." In *Medieval Scribes, Manuscripts, and Libraries: Essays Presented to* N. R. *Ker.* Ed. M. B. Parkes and A. G. Watson. London: Scolar Press, 1978. 163-210, (hereafter referred to as Doyle and Parkes, Production of Copies). The *Troilus and Criseyde* is a Hatfield House Fragment, (Cecil Papers, Box S/1) described by Doyle in: Doyle, A.I. "The Copyist of the Ellesmere *Canterbury Tales*." In *The Ellesmere Chaucer: Essays in Interpretation.* Ed. Martin Stevens and Daniel Woodward. San Marino, CA & Tokyo: Huntington Library & Yushodo Co., Ltd., 1995. 58-59, (hereafter referred to as Doyle, Ellesmere Essays).

4. Cambridge University Library MS. Kk.1.3/20. For images and a description of these fragments see: Doyle, Ellesmere Essays, 60-62.

5. See Doyle and Parkes, Production of Copies, 174-177, for a summary and description of manuscripts copied by the "D" Scribe.

6. Doyle, A. I. and M. B. Parkes. "Paleographical Introduction." In *The Canterbury Tales: A Facsimile and Transcription of the Hengwrt Manuscript, with Variations from the Ellesmere Manuscript.* Ed. Paul Ruggiers. Norman, OK: University of Oklahoma Press, 1979, xxxiii (hereafter referred to as Doyle and Parkes, Intro.). And see also Doyle's extended description of the display features of this scribe in Doyle, Ellesmere Essays, 52.

7. See fol.7, lines 21 and 23.

8. See the reference to the manuscript of D.J. Price, *The Equatorie of the Planetis*, (Camb: Univ. of Camb Press, 1955), esp. p. 145. Peterhous MS. 75, and the suggestion that it could be an autograph manuscript of Chaucer: Doyle and Parkes, Intro. xxxviii. Also, Pamela Robinson, *Catalogue of Dated and Datable manuscripts*, C. 737-1600 *in Cambridge Libraries* (Camb: 1988), 1.83; and J.D. North, *Chaucer's Universe* (Oxf. UP, 1988), 157-81.

9. See all three descriptions in Doyle and Parkes, Production of Copies, 163-210, Doyle and Parkes, Intro. xix-xlix, and Doyle, Ellesmere Essays, 49-67.

10. Doyle, Ellesmere Essays, 50.

11. Ibid.

12. Doyle, Ellesmere Essays, 60. The general aspect of the hand in Kk is the main feature which causes Doyle to hesitate about a Scribe "B" attribution.

13. Benson, Larry D., ed. *The Riverside Chaucer*. 3rd ed. Boston: Houghton Mifflin, 1987, 1151.

14. Ibid. 1003.

15. Stubbs, Estelle, ed. *The Hengwrt Chaucer, Digital Facsimile*, Scholarly Digital Editions, 2000. See "Observations" section.

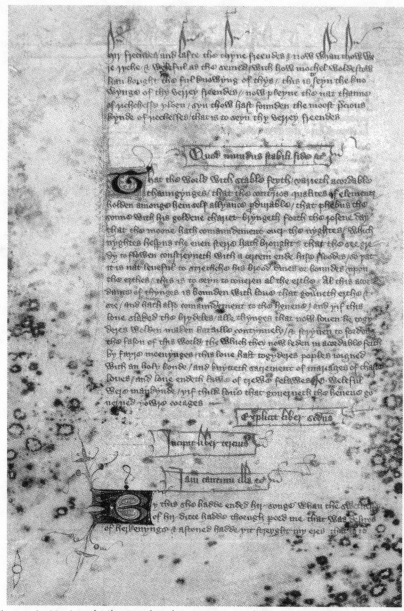

Figure. 1. National Library of Wales, MS Peniarth 393D, folio 17v, showing letter forms, tremolos and knotted tremolos attached to top line ascenders and to the boxing features around *incipits*, *explicits* and Latin *lemmata*. Reproduced by permission of the National Library of Wales. Smaller than actual size and cropped.

Assessing Book Use by Women in Late Medieval England

SATOKO TOKUNAGA

Recent studies of ownership and readership have examined important aspects of the interest that medieval women held in learning and reading, but it remains uncertain whether books known to have been owned by medieval women were actually read or used by their owners. One means of establishing how such books were used is to construct an argument from evidence obtainable directly from them; it is widely believed that additional writings such as marginalia and calendar entries provide significant indications of use. However, such evidence does not necessarily mean that a book was used by its owner herself, and hence such evidence must be interpreted with an awareness of its complexity.

Textual evidence such as *ex-libris* inscriptions can provide the clearest indications of provenance and ownership of manuscripts, as several examples demonstrate. In London, the British Library MS Cotton App. xiv—an approximately hand-sized manuscript with ample margins and several beautifully illuminated and decorated pages—an *ex-libris* inscription written by a scribe (fol. 56ᵛ) states that "for whos [Elizabeth's] vse thy boke was made" at the commission of John and Margaret Edward; Elizabeth was a daughter of John and Margaret who became a nun of Syon. Bodleian Library MS Douce 322, a manuscript consisting of English devotional materials, also has an engrossed contemporary inscription at the front indicating that the volume was a gift from William Baron, Esquire, intended "to remayne for euyr to the place and nonrye of Detforde, and specially to the vse of dame Pernelle Wrattisley, sister of the same place," who was a "nece" or a granddaughter of the donor.[1]

These inscriptions clearly indicate that these manuscripts were produced for the "vse" of these particular women.

It must be noted, however, that such evidence cannot always be taken at face value. It is often difficult to determine if the person for whom an *ex-libris* inscription indicates a manuscript was made actually possessed that manuscript, or if she made use of it if she did possess it. That is, although a small, gorgeous manuscript may purport to have been made "for vse" by Elizabeth, this does not prove that Elizabeth actually made use of it. It is not always the case that information about book use can be deduced from *ex-libris* indications of either possession or use.

The difficulty of assessing such evidence of book use is further complicated when a book contains more than a single woman owner's name; when a manuscript contains multiple inscriptions, it is not always possible to know when it came into the possession of each owner. However, the position or repetition of inscriptions sometimes affords insight into the use particular owners made of a book.[2] The British Library MS Harley 1706 is inscribed with at least three women's names—Elizabeth Beumont, Elisabeth Oxford, and Margaret Oswall[?]—which appear more than once in the volume. The first two names belong to the same person, for Elizabeth married first Beaumont and then Vere, Count of Oxford.[3] Yet Elizabeth's writing style presents interesting variations: the inscription "Elysabeth Beumont" on fol. 216[r] is seemingly written in a clumsy hand, whereas the one on fol. 11[r] is more elegant. Elizabeth may have mastered the practice of writing during the period in which she owned the book, or she may have had the later inscription written for her, perhaps by a professional scribe in her household. Although both explanations are plausible and the inscriptions offer valuable evidence of a woman's book ownership, the actual use women made of books is still uncertain, because not all women had the ability or freedom to write, nor did all have access to trained scribes.[4]

Here, the issue of medieval women's literacy warrants consideration, for the assessment of evidence for book use is further complicated by the nature of reading and writing in the Middle Ages, which differed from that of today. Medieval manuscripts frequently contain additional writings such as marginalia or calendars, some of which are quite relevant to the contents of the manuscripts in which they are found, but it is often difficult to determine when or by whom these additional writings were added. In particular, if the handwriting of additional writings is different from that of the inscription, even if it appears to be quite contemporary, it is open to question whether the writer of the inscription made the addition or another owner did so.

Moreover, it must be considered probable that a person other than the owner was responsible for the writings in a given manuscript. Those who lack what Julia Boffey calls "orthographic capabilities" were not necessarily

precluded from making use of books, and this point must be noted in arguments concerning book use based on additional writings.[5] Insofar as the skills
of writing and reading did not necessarily accompany one another, the notion
of medieval writing differed from the modern one; "writing" in the Middle
Ages was not always synonymous with "composing," and even those who
were able to write in the narrow sense frequently employed other people to
write for them.

That is, the physical act of writing in the Middle Ages was quite distinct from the process of composition. In consequence, for instance, at least
three nuns are known to have composed or translated saints' lives from
French during the Middle Ages,[6] yet it is not known whether they wrote down
their compositions themselves, or if someone else served as scribe. In the
case of anonymous manuscripts, it is particularly difficult to identify female
involvement in copying or writing, and almost impossible to determine
whether woman authors were responsible for composition.

Moreover, it was uncommon for medieval women to acquire ortho-
graphic capabilities, as reflected in The Book of the Knight of the Tower, wherein the
author specifically forbids his daughters from the act of writing, though he
allows them to read books for their edification.[7] Thus it may be true that the
writing attributed to Julian of Norwich shows that she acquired comprehensive skills as a reader, listener, and thinker, but it is nonetheless doubtful that
Julian achieved "orthographic capabilities." Although David Bell has raised
the possibility of scribal activities among the medieval nuns of Barking,
Ickleton, and Chester, whose ownership inscriptions are preserved in each
manuscript, he also admits that none of these cases comprises incontrovert-
ible proof that nuns actually wrote these manuscripts; Bell thus acknowl-
edges the difficulty entailed in assessing evidence for women's involvement
in book production.[8]

In regard specifically to women's writing ability, particular difficulty
arises from the general impossibility of deducing the gender of a scribe from
the appearance of a hand. For instance, let us consider the twelfth-century
manuscript produced at St. Mary's Abbey, Winchester, known as Nunnaminster,
now Bodleian Library MS Bodley 451 (S.C. 2401), which contains a copy of
Smaragdus of Saint Mihiel's Diadema monachorum, a collection in Latin of mis-
cellaneous sermons, and an anonymous moral treatise.[9] The colophon of this
manuscript indicates that it was written by an anonymous scriptrix. In her
analysis of this manuscript, P. R. Robinson argues that woman scribes were
more widespread in the twelfth century than has been assumed,[10] and it is
likely that other women were also able to write texts. However, the plausibil-
ity of the evidence supporting this contention is still uncertain: the handwriting of the scribe of this manuscript displays no difference in duct from that of

contemporary male scribes, and thus it is impossible to determine this scribe's gender definitively from the script alone.[11]

This point applies in general to female scribal activities in English, examples of which can be found in the surviving manuscripts of medieval nunneries. Lambeth Palace Library MS 546, which is a collection of devotional materials in a number of late fifteenth-or sixteenth-century hands, includes a unique text labelled the Lambeth Devotion by Hope Emily Allen and bearing the name of "Sister EW" (fol. 56r); a woman scribe has recently been identified as having written this manuscript, but the supporting evidence is not the hand but rather the scribe's reference to herself in the colophon as a "wreched syster."[12] It has been suggested that Cambridge University Library MS Hh. 1.11 belonged to a convent of nuns, possibly the Franciscans at Bruisyard, and this manuscript has been presumed to have been written by these nuns;[13] but this is mere supposition. The British Library MS Harley 494 contains a prayer to the Sacrament written in the late fifteenth-or early sixteenth-century in an ill-formed and shaky hand; although it has been suggested that this was an autograph prayer not only inscribed but also written by Anne Bulkeley,[14] it is now doubted whether the hand is indeed that of Anne Bulkeley herself, and there is no way to determine this definitively.[15]

Such uncertainties raise several questions. If one cannot claim with confidence that scribal activities recorded in a book were performed by the women indicated, how can one establish the actual use of books by their medieval woman owners? Is there no way to interpret evidence for book use by woman owners from additional writings without clear evidence of scribal activities by women? Is it possible to argue for, or even make suppositions about, the use of books by women without such evidence? In approaching these questions, it is important to consider how the practice of reading in the Middle Ages, like that of writing, differed from the modern practice, for an understanding of the variety of ways that reading was practiced in the Middle Ages reveals that books were not used exclusively by those who had acquired "orthographic capabilities."

Specifically, an important distinction that applies to the practice of reading in the Middle Ages is that which existed between "phonetic literacy" and "comprehension literacy."[16] This distinction is particularly apparent in the manner in which Latin texts were read; most women did not read liturgical texts in the same way that we read in our modern sense, except in the now narrower context of modern religious observances. Although some were able to decipher the meaning of the texts they read, others may have been able to read only phonetically, or simply to follow by rote while listening to another reader, repeating orally when required without understanding. The differentiation of these levels of reading ability is especially significant in considering reading performed in private by the owner of a book, which in the medieval period contrasted with the predominant modern practice of reading silently to oneself. In the Middle Ages, reading could be oral/silent or public/private not only in Latin and French but in English as well. For example, Margery Kempe was apparently lacking in "orthographic capabilities"s as well as the ability to read texts in the modern sense; nonetheless, Margery's autobiographical text, though this was recorded by male scribe, reveals that she was familiar with such texts as the *Revelations* of St. Bridget of Sweden, Hilton's book, Bonaventura's *Stimulus Amoris* (*The Prick of Love*), and *Incendium Amoris* (that is, Richard Rolle's *The Fire of Love*, often attributed to Bonaventura), all of which she reports were read aloud to her by her priest.[17] Margery would be described today as illiterate, but in the Middle Ages the practice of experiencing books by hearing them read aloud was common even in literary milieus. Cecily, Duchess of York (1415–1495), also reports that she heard works read aloud, remembered them, and passed them on to her companions. In Felicity Riddy's words, this amounts to "a textuality of the spoken as well as the written word"; textuality begins in the book, usually with it being read aloud by clerics, but is transmitted among women orally.[18]

This communal notion of reading is significant to arguments concerning book use; indeed, some surviving volumes owned by medieval nuns actually bear traces of such communal use. First, two manuscripts from a priory at Campsey (Cambridge University Library MS Additional 7220 and the British Library MS Additional 40675) have press-marks—O.E.94 and d.d.141—which suggest that nuns catalogued books belonging to the nunnery.[19] In addition, both books contain the same description, "Cest liuere est a covent de Campisse"; this appears in both manuscripts on different folios from those containing the press-marks. Another manuscript from Campsey, British Library MS Additional 70513, which contains a collection of saints' lives, indicates that the book was used at meal times ("Ce liure deviseie a la priorie de Kampseie de lire a mengier").[20] Thus these books apparently were not personal possessions but rather belonged to the convent. Among the surviving volumes owned by nuns, only one other manuscript—one that comes from Barking—bears a press-mark. Though their number is small, these volumes support the fascinating possibility that a system may have existed to facilitate their constant use by nuns. The Benedictine order had an annual distribution of books to promote private reading by nuns, and its *Ordinale* records that there was a book-cupboard and a female librarian at the abbey.[21] Considering all the evidence, it seems probable that these volumes were kept at the nunneries as communal property. Of course, the actual way in which these books were used is again difficult to determine; they may have remained on bookshelves untouched and covered with dust.

Another important factor complicating the analysis of women's use of spiritual texts is the role men played as readers, writers, and owners of texts. As mentioned above, Margery Kempe reports that she went to her chaplain to hear books read aloud. Similarly, clerics must have acted as chaplains or confessors to convents of nuns as they did to noblewomen in secular households; to consider the case of one such person, two manuscripts preserved in the Essex Record Office contain copies of the will and probate inventory of William Pownsett of Eastcheap, who was a steward of the estates of Barking just before its dissolution. The inventory includes a list of books that are described as "Pownsett's books left in the abbey of Barking at his death." It has been argued that some of these books may have belonged to the nunnery, but that more likely they belonged to the steward, since most of them are in Latin.[22] Yet the role such a chaplain would have played in reading texts for women, particularly Latin texts, probably had great significance for nuns. Without such a reader, most women—including nuns—would not have been able to comprehend such texts, given contemporary levels of literacy, and there is no clear explanation of why there is a significant number of Latin volumes (23 percent) among the surviving books owned by medieval nuns.

Therefore it must be concluded that using books was not always private; it was at times a communal activity among medieval women and at times an activity shared between women and their chaplains. Moreover, it must be concluded that those who frequently heard texts read aloud were thereby significantly involved in book culture; this conclusion offers evidence to be used in assessing women's use of books, but it also makes this task more difficult. Even if an annotation in a book was made by a cleric, the annotation may well reflect the use of the book by the woman or women who owned it.

The assessment of evidence of book use by women is always complicated by methodological difficulties. The different practices of reading and writing in the Middle Ages make it difficult to determine actual book use. Moreover, it is difficult to establish who is responsible for additions to books owned by women—that is, whether it was the owner of a manuscript herself or her chaplain who penned any additional writings. It is furthermore difficult to determine whether evidence demonstrates personal or communal use of a given book. In short, that medieval women made additions to books, handled

I would like to express my sincere gratitude to Dr. Valerie Edden, who supervised me as I pursued this issue in the course of completing my thesis at the University of Birmingham. I would also like to thank Dr. Maureen Bell and Dr. Julia Boffey, who read an early version of this paper and offered invaluable comments. I am deeply grateful to Mrs Doreen Simons and Mr Michael Keezing, who helped to polish the English of this paper. Part of this study is supported by the grant awarded me by the Japan Society for the Promotion of Science.

books themselves, or otherwise made use of books cannot always be argued with confidence, yet the cautious assessment of evidence, informed by an awareness of the complications outlined in this paper, nonetheless affords new possibilities for exploring aspects of book use by medieval women.[23]

Keio University, Tokyo

NOTES

1. David N. Bell, *What Nuns Read: Books and Libraries in Medieval English Nunneries*, Cistercian Studies Series, CLVIII (Kalamazoo, MI and Spencer, MA: Cistercian, 1995), 133; A. I. Doyle, "Books Connected with the Vere Family and Barking Abbey," *Transactions of the Essex Archaeological Society*, n.s. 25 (1955–1960): 222–243 (228–229).

2. I owe this idea first to Mary C. Erler's argument concerning "shared reading" between Joan Regent, her daughter Agnes, and her friend Katherine Pole (a granddaughter of Cecil Neville, Duchess of York); see her "Devotional Literature," in *The Cambridge History of the Book in Britain*, 7 vols (Cambridge: Cambridge University Press, 1999–), III: 1400–1557 (1999), ed. by Lotte Hellinga and J. B. Trapp, 495–525 (522–523).

3. For this manuscript, see Doyle's article in note 1.

4. For the problems to be considered in dealing with the ownership issue and for limitations inherent in the use of documents such as wills as evidence, see Carol M. Meale's argument, "'. . . alle the bokes that I haue of latyn, englisch, and frensch': Laywomen and Their Books in Late Medieval England," in *Women and Literature in Britain*, 1150–1500, ed. Carol M. Meale, Cambridge Studies in Medieval Literature, XVII, 2nd ed. (Cambridge: Cambridge University Press, 1996), 128–158 (esp. 130–136); Anne M. Dutton, "Passing the Book: Testamentary Transmission of Religious Literature to and by Women in England 1350–1500," in *Women, the Book and the Godly: Selected Proceedings of the St Hilda's Conference*, 1993, ed. Lesley Smith and Jane H. M. Taylor (Cambridge: Brewer, 1995), 41–54 (43–44).

5. Julia Boffey, "Women Authors and Women's Literacy in Fourteenth- and Fifteenth-Century England," in *Women and Literature in Britain*, 1150–1500, ed. Carol M. Meale, Cambridge Studies in Medieval Literature, XVII, 2nd ed. (Cambridge: Cambridge University Press, 1996), 159–182 (162).

6. Clemence of Barking "wrote" a *Life of St. Catherine of Alexandria*. Another nun from Barking translated the *Life of St. Edmund the Confessor*. A nun named Marie seems to have translated Thomas of Ely's Latin *Life of St. Etheldreda of Ely*. See Bell, 69.

7. *The Book of the Knight of the Tower*, EETS s.s. 2, trans. William Caxton, ed. M. Y. Offord (London: Oxford University Press, 1971), 122.

8. Bell, 66–67.

9. Bell, 216.

10. P. R. Robinson, "A Twelfth-Century *Scriptrix* from Nunnaminster," in *Of the Making of Books: Medieval Manuscripts, their Scribes and Readers: Essays Presented to M. B. Parkes*, ed. P. R. Robinson and Rivkah Zim (Aldershot: Scholar Press, 1997), 73–93.

11. Robinson, 79.

12. Veronica O'Mara, "A Middle English Text Written by a Female Scribe," N & Q 235 (1990): 396–398 (397).

13. Alexandra Barratt, "Books for Nuns, Cambridge University Library MS Additional 3242," N & Q 44 (1997): 310–319.

14. Josephine Koster Tarvers, "'Thys ys my mystrys boke': English Women as Readers and Writers in Late Medieval England," in The Uses of Manuscripts in Literary Studies: Essays in Memory of Judson Boyce Allen, ed. Charlotte C. Morse, Penelope B. Doob, and Marjorie C. Woods, Studies in Medieval Culture, XXXI (Kalamazoo, MI: Medieval Institute Publications, Western Michigan University, 1992), 305–327 (317).

15. Veronica O'Mara, "Female Scribal Ability and Scribal Activity in Late Medieval England: The Evidence?" Leeds Studies in English, n.s. 27 (1996): 87–130 (101–102).

16. Paul Saenger, "Books of Hours and the Reading Habits of the Later Middle Ages," in The Culture of Print: Power and the Uses of Print in Early Modern Europe, ed. Roger Chartier, trans. Lydia G. Cochrane (Cambridge: Polity, 1989), 141–173 (143). See also M. B. Parkes, "The Literacy of Laity," in Literature and Western Civilization: The Medieval World, ed. David Daiches and Anthony Thorlby (London: Aldus, 1973), 555–577.

17. The Book of Margery Kempe, ed. Barry Windeatt (Harlow: Longman, 2000), 280.

18. Felicity Riddy, "'Women Talking about the Things of God': A Late Medieval Sub-Culture," Women and Literature in Britain, 1150–1500, ed. Carol M. Meale, Cambridge Studies in Medieval Literature, XVII, 2nd ed. (Cambridge: Cambridge University Press, 1996), 104–127 (111).

19. Bell, 40–43; 123–124.

20. Bell, 124–125.

21. P. Gambier, "Lending Books in a Medieval Nunnery," Bodleian Quarterly Record 5 (1927): 188–190.

22. Bell, 116–120.

23. With attention to the concerns raised in this paper, I plan to present particular instances of book use by women in a forthcoming issue of this journal.

William Worcester Reads Chaucer's *Boece*

DANIEL WAKELIN

Compared to many Middle English translations, quite a lot is known about the prose version of Boethius's *De Consolatione Philosophiae*. There is little doubt that the extant translation is that which Chaucer claims in other works to have completed, and there calls *Boece*. Several of the work's earliest readers are also known, from references to the work in wills and from extant manuscripts. However, only three of the ten manuscripts record or imply Chaucer's authorship of the translation.[1] In Cambridge, University Library MS Ii. III. 21, *Boece* incorporates two lyrics which are ascribed to Chaucer (fols 52v-54r), and in London, British Library, MS Additional 16165 prologuic verses by John Shirley praise Chaucer's translation (fols 1r-1v). On the first leaf of the third such manuscript, copied in the first half of the fifteenth century, a later hand has written "Istud opus est translatum per Chawcers armigerum Ricardi 2di" (Cambridge, Pembroke College, MS 215, fol. 1r; on deposit in Cambridge University Library). So late a note can add no confirmation to an already secure attribution; however this hitherto unidentified annotator gains in interest when we recognize his jagged hand as that of William Worcester (1415-c.1483). Worcester's use of this manuscript enlarges our growing understanding of *Boece's* reception history.

Worcester was an assiduous antiquary, a keen amateur classical scholar and, in his day job, secretary to the famous war veteran Sir John Fastolf of Caister (c.1380-1459).[2] From some twenty-one other manuscripts which contain Worcester's detailed notes, marginalia, corrections or *ex libris*, we can trace Worcester's intellectual interests fairly closely and can read the annotations to Pembroke College MS 215 in the light of these known interests. Some characteristic William Worcester graphs found in this copy of *Boece* include: the large and unwieldy two-compartment *a*; the *w* made with four very simple strokes; the final tiny ticks to the right on the tail of *g* or the last minim of *m*; or *p* where the ends of the bowl cross the down-stroke pronouncedly. This hand's spiky and erratic aspect is unmistakable.[3] Moreover, such an observation on *Boece*'s authorship recalls similar fleeting references to literary and scholarly history throughout Worcester's marginalia and notebooks: for example, he provides a brief biography of the renowned scholar John Free at the front of a manuscript acquired from him (Oxford, Balliol College, MS 124, fol. 1r).

What does Worcester's inky presence reveal about this manuscript's hitherto shadowy provenance? Manuscript 215 had still not reached Pembroke College as late as the end of the seventeenth century, and an unidentified blazon drawn in ink on the end flyleaf offers the only other clue to its earlier peregrinations.[4] Unfortunately, we cannot state categorically that Worcester owned this manuscript during the mid or late fifteenth century: it does not contain his *ex libris*, although the last couple of quires are lost, and he sometimes marked his ownership or the date of his reading after the colophon (for example in Cambridge, University Library, MS Additional 7870, fol. 30v). Moreover, Worcester's extant notes also name over eighty individuals or institutions from whom he acquired books or gained access to them as visitor or borrower. Pembroke College MS 215 may never have been his.

However, there is one possible trail for the manuscript's movements before Worcester read it. In summer 1449, Worcester's acquaintance John Crop, who was carrying out genealogical research on behalf of Sir John Fastolf in the west of England, wrote to Worcester and, after business news, announced that one Master Ralph Hoby had "*graunte*" him "the copy of walens de vita *et* doctrina philosoforum also the queier*e* of oved de vetula de remedio amoris, de Arte amande *and* of the verse vp on Boicius."[5] Ralph Hoby was a Franciscan friar in Oxford until at least 1442, and so probably lived there while Worcester himself attended the university between 1432 and 1438. Worcester verified some astronomical tables with Hoby in the late 1430s.[6] Besides Boethius, the works granted are John of Wales's *Breuiloquium de uirtutibus*, Ovid's *Ars amatoria* and *Remedia amoris* and the pseudo-Ovidian *De Vetula*, all of which Worcester later went on to cite in his notebooks and more polished writings; in fact Worcester dated his marginalia to a copy of John of Wales's *Breuiloquium* only a year later in July 1450. However his copy of John of Wales was the French translation (Cambridge, University Library, MS Additional 7870, fols 6r-30v).[7] Could Crop, therefore, also refer to a translation when he mentions not Boethius *per se* but "the verse vp on Boicius"? Perhaps, but "the verse" sounds more like Walton's verse translation of 1410 than Chaucer's earlier rendering into prose. Whether Pembroke College MS 215 was ever the property of Hoby or Worcester remains uncertain.

However, this manuscript can illustrate some of the uses which Chaucer's *Boece* served in the fifteenth century, if we briefly compare Worcester's notes here with his other writings. Firstly, a notebook largely compiled in the 1470s, now known as his *Itineraries* (Cambridge, Corpus Christi College, MS 210), reveals that, with customary persistence, Worcester also took notes from a copy of Boethius in Latin (interestingly, beneath notes from Ovid). Whether Hoby's copy was English or Latin, Worcester must also have once had access to a manuscript of this author in the other language. However, in his *Itineraries* Worcester copied from the Latin only some passages from book IV, metre 3 and prose 3 which he highlighted with two of his eight marginal notes on this Middle English *Boece* (fols 66r-66v).[8] There are no other extant Latin notes by Worcester from Boethius's *De Consolatione Philosophiae*. Secondly, in Pembroke College MS 215, Worcester annotated *Boece* book I, prose 4, with four notes and a pointing finger, which witness his interest in Boethius's account of himself as a public servant to the commonweal (what Worcester calls his "officium rei publice", fols 6r-9r). This portrait of Boethius as civic hero reappears in Worcester's political treatise *The Boke of Noblesse* in terms which loosely echo Chaucer's vocabulary in *Boece*: "The said juge Boecius loved rightwisnesse to be kept, and the pore comyns of Rome in that susteyned and maynteyned that he spared nothir lord ne none astate" and so on.[9] A gloss elsewhere in *The Boke of Noblesse* on the "proude beestis clepid Centaurus, that be of halfe men and halfe best" may also recall Chaucer's expansion of Boethius as glossed by Trevet: "the proude Centauris (half hors, half man)".[10] Worcester's reading of *Boece* appears to have facilitated his wider intellectual enquiries into Latin literature and political thought.

In summary, we can be certain only that this manuscript of *Boece* must have at some point passed under Worcester's eyes before his death in *c*.1483. However, William Worcester and Ralph Hoby are possible fifteenth-century owners; their associates like Fastolf and the Pastons may include the bearer of the heraldic blazon doodled on the back flyleaf. More intriguingly, Worcester's use of *Boece* develops our emergent picture of Chaucer's useful contribution not just to poetry but to fifteenth-century scholarship, a contribution which Worcester recognized but literary criticism today sometimes forgets.

Trinity Hall, Cambridge

NOTES

1. All quotations and line references follow *The Riverside Chaucer*, gen. ed. Larry D. Benson, 3rd edn (Boston: Houghton Mifflin Company, 1987; Oxford: Oxford University Press, 1988). For details of *Boece*'s circulation, see pp. 1003-04, pp. 1151-52 and M. C. Seymour, *A Catalogue of Chaucer Manuscripts*, 2 vols (Aldershot: Scolar, 1995-97), I, pp. 43-53, compiled in collaboration with Ralph Hanna.

2. K. B. McFarlane, "William Worcester: A Preliminary Survey," printed in his *England in the Fifteenth Century: Collected Essays*, ed. G. L. Harriss (London: Hambledon, 1981), pp. 199-224, first published in 1957, offers the fullest biography to date. Professor Linne Mooney and Dr Richard Beadle kindly shared their unpublished lists of manuscripts containing Worcester's hand. Further discussion of Worcester's notebooks will appear in my forthcoming thesis on "Vernacular humanism in fifteenth-century England" for the Faculty of English in the University of Cambridge.

3. Jean F. Preston and Laetitia Yeandle, *English Handwriting 1400-1650: An Introductory Manual* (Binghampton, NY: Center for Medieval and Renaissance Studies, 1992), pp. 18-21 (no. 7) offer a clear facsimile and abstracted alphabet of Worcester's hand.

4. Seymour, *A Catalogue of Chaucer Manuscripts*, I, pp. 52-53.

5. Oxford, Magdalen College, Archives, MS Additional 99 (Lovell Papers), fol. 21r. P. S. Lewis, "Sir John Fastolf's Lawsuit over Titchwell," *Historical Journal*, 1 (1958), 1-20 (pp. 12-16) describes this letter and Crop's research.

6. A. B. Emden, *A Biographical Register of the University of Oxford to A.D. 1500*, 3 vols (Oxford: Clarendon Press, 1957), II, 939.

7. Jenny Swanson, *John of Wales: A Study of the Works and Ideas of a Thirteenth-Century Friar* (Cambridge; Cambridge University Press, 1989) does not mention this manuscript of the translation, which otherwise apparently appears only in Oxford, Bodleian Library, MS Laud. misc. 570. Although that manuscript also contains the date 1450 (fol. 93r) and the motto of Worcester's employer, Fastolf, textual differences suggest that it was not copied from Cambridge, University Library, MS Additional 7870, nor vice versa.

8. William Worcestre, *Itineraries*, ed. John H. Harvey (Oxford: Clarendon Press, 1969), p. 391.

9. [William Worcester], *The Boke of Noblesse*, ed. John Gough Nichols (London: Roxburghe Club, 1860), pp. 52-53.

10. [Worcester], *The Boke of Noblesse*, pp. 20-21; *Boece*, IV. m. 7, lines 29-30. Cambridge, Pembroke College, MS 215 has lost all leaves after *Boece*, IV. pr. 5 so we cannot know whether Worcester also annotated this passage. The other references to Boethius in [Worcester], *The Boke of Noblesse*, p. 3, p. 50 could have come from any copy.

Descriptive Reviews

MARY-JO ARN, ED.
Charles d'Orléans in England (1415-1440).
Woodbridge, D.S. Brewer, 2000. X + 231pp.
9 plates, 1 col., 8 b&w.

This groundbreaking volume comprises twelve papers on various aspects of the life and literary production of Charles d'Orléans during his captivity in England. The theme is illustrated by the frontispiece, a full-color reproduction of fol. 73 of BL MS Royal 16 F. ii, depicting Charles in the Tower of London (the illustrations in this manuscript are discussed in this volume by Janet Backhouse). Michael K. Jones investigates the political dimension to the duke's protracted captivity, with special attention to the circumstances surrounding the siege of Orléans. William Askins establishes that there was a great deal of interaction between Duke Charles, his brother Jean d'Angoulême and their English keepers, a conclusion borne out by Gilbert Ouy's survey of the manuscripts copied by (or for) the two brothers during their captivity. The status of Charles's English poetry comes under particular scrutiny. Mary-Jo Arn compares the layout of Paris, BN MS fr.25458, a copy commissioned by Charles in the late 1430s of his French poetry written before and during his captivity, and BL MS Harley 682, copied nearer the time of his release and gathering his English poetry. Six plates support Arn's argument that both manuscripts were supervised by the duke himself, and that divergences in layout are due to differing purposes: the French collection was open-ended, but Charles did not intend to add any English poems to his *oeuvre* after returning to France. Claudio Galderisi analyzes Charles's relationship with his mother tongue during his twenty-five years of captivity, while John Fox elucidates in his "Glanures" four specific textual riddles which reveal Charles's linguistic versatility and playfulness. Rouben C. Cholakian stresses the abstract nature of the world depicted in Charles's poems, both during and after his captivity. The theme of captivity itself, however, is not always treated in such a symbolical manner. Jean-Claude Mühlethaler's analysis of *La Chasse d'Amours* and *Le Départ d'Amours* (1509, published by Antoine Vérard), thus shows that several key ballads of Charles were omitted from the anthology or edited because of their explicit biographical dimension. The duke's poetry is considered alongside that of contemporary works in English by A. C. Spearing, who compares and contrasts the device of dreams in *The Kingis Quair* and Charles's English book, and Derek Pearsall, whose work on the authorship of the Fairfax sequence suggests that Charles had a greater influence on other English writers than has tended to be acknowledged. A.E.B.

Coldiron concludes with the question as to why Charles d'Orléans has not found his place in the English literary canon, pointing towards nationalistic distrust of a French aristocrat, and aesthetic sensitivities unsympathetic to his favored medium of expression. However, the bibliographical supplement at the end of the book indicates an upsurge in scholarly interest over the past decade, which bodes well for the future reception of Charles's *oeuvre*.

Françoise Le Saux, University of Reading

PETER BEAL AND MARGARET J.M. EZELL, EDS.
Writings by Early Modern Women, English Manuscript Studies 1100-1700, 9 (1999). vi + 309 pp. ISBN 0-7123-4674-0.

In his life of John Hoskyns, lawyer, wit, poet and defender of free speech, John Aubrey tells us of the "booke of Poemes, neatly written by one of [Hoskyns'] Clerkes, bigger then Dr Donne's Poemes, which his sonn Benet lent to he knowes not who, about 1653, and could never heare of it since."[1] Donne himself, we should remember, experienced some difficulty when in 1614, he attempted to gather in some manuscript copies of poems he had circulated among friends for a putative printed collection: "I am," he complained, "made a Rhapsoder of mine own rags, and that cost me more diligence, to seek them, then it did to make them."[2] Manuscripts, even when neatly-written and of considerable bulk, have their fates, as early modern writers never tire of reminding themselves and their readers. A useful source of reusable paper, any spare inch was likely to be filled with material more or less connected with the other contents of a page; while of course many manuscripts, like printed pages, could look forward only to the ignominy of lining a pie-tin, lighting a pipe or wrapping a peck of pepper. Other manuscripts, though, went on to higher things, and the number that are preserved today in our libraries is remarkable, hinting surely at the quantity that has been lost. In recent years the fate of the manuscript in early modern studies has been a tale of rising to great place. No longer the concern primarily of textual editors on the look-out for variants as they pursue the source of the stemma, the culture of the manuscript and of what has come to be known as 'scribal publication' has become the focus of mainstream literary criticism. This is thanks largely to the pioneering work of scholars such as Harold Love, Peter Beal and Arthur Marotti.[3]

Especially welcome has been the productive interaction between this renewed concentration on manuscripts and the study of early-modern women's writing. Taking the concept of scribal publication seriously means that we have to revise our notions of authorship, and of the categories of public and private writing. In contrast to the relatively small number of women who made their way into print, in manuscript we find a thriving culture of women's writing. And we find women using the manuscript page with resourcefulness, creativity and policy.[4] *English Manuscript Studies* 1100-1700 has played a vital part in the rejuvenation that I have described, and this issue devoted to early modern women's writing is, as might be expected, an invaluable volume. The range of essays is wide, yet the issue retains an impressive sense of coherence, partly through small linked sub-groups of essays (there are two essays each on the renowned calligrapher Esther Inglis and on Elizabeth Ashburnham Richardson, as well as other connections I will highlight below). And the volume is, as we have come to expect, beautifully and thoroughly illustrated with excellent reproductions of the manuscripts discussed.

One of the great advantages of a collection such as this over a perhaps more heavily policed volume is that it addresses the multiplicity and complexity of questions that can be raised about women's writing in manuscript. Here we have essays announcing new discoveries, performing sophisticated analyses of the *mise-en-page* of manuscripts, highlighting the active nature of reading and re-writing that takes place in their pages, and describing the sometimes shifty ways in which manuscripts were framed by their compilers or subsequent editors. Between them they add more features, both geological and architectural, as it were, to our picture of the landscape of literary production in early modern England and continental Europe. The new discoveries are themselves varied, and put to varied critical use. Steven W. May has found two previously unknown letters from Mary Sidney Herbert, Countess of Pembroke, at Longleat House. They offer a fascinating and teasing glimpse into the Countess's activities as a patron, and May suggests that the later letter (dated 1 June 1596) may be evidence of her employment of a scrivener. David Norbrook marshals a formidable array of evidence to support his very convincing attribution of the poem 'Order and Disorder' to Lucy Hutchinson and his essay is an extremely useful companion to the edition of the poem he has recently published.[5] It also offers a suggestive picture of the vibrant manuscript culture in which Hutchinson was involved during the later years of her life—an area that demands further study. A brilliant essay by Victoria Burke not only announces the discovery of two new manuscripts of Elizabeth Ashburnham Richardson (in the Folger Shakespeare Library and Sussex County Records Office) but also deftly uses this new material to reconsider the nature and importance of Richardson's writings. Burke shows that in manuscript Richardson deliberately places her texts in the tradition of maternal advice-writing: her writings in this genre spanned forty years, and, an inveterate reviser, she never considered them finished. Richardson's writing may have been addressed to her daughters but they cannot be dismissed as belonging purely to the private sphere: rather she is a figure who shows how fluid the boundaries of public and private, print and manuscript were in this period, as she modifies the pages of her printed book for presentation to members of her family.

No less important than these discoveries are essays like those of Frances Teague and Georgina Ziegler, which show how meaning is made by the layout of a manuscript, and how we might go about recovering it. Teague's study of Princess Elizabeth's *Glass of the Sinful Soul* suggests that this manuscript, usually considered interesting by its association with the queen-to-be, can if read as an artefact in its own right be interpreted as a synec-dochic equivalent of Elizabeth herself, to be used in marriage negotiations. The book advertises Elizabeth's well-trained hand, her relationship with Katherine Parr, and her embroidery skills. Here, as throughout the volume, we see a book being used as a kind of transaction, without losing sight of the fact that it is a text as well as an object.

The manuscript page is a place where one can observe the processes of reading, writing and revision, and Margaret Hannay's essay about Elizabeth Ashburnham Richardson's meditation on the Countess of Pembroke's *Discourse of Life and Death* (nicely linking with May and Burke) shows just how active and appropriative early-modern engagements with a text could be. Here the Countess's translation and appropriation of Mornay's *Excellent discours* (1576) is in turn transformed in Richardson's meditation, which accentuates gendered concerns and replaces the Stoicism of its source with Christian emphases and Biblical references. Comparing this manuscript (Hannay provides a full transcription) with its sources allows us to see a text being made personal in an act of reading which is at the same time an act of writing.

The transformations that texts can undergo in their passage between different kinds of readers are also highlighted in essays by Sylvia Brown and Elizabeth Clarke. Brown describes the way in which Thomas Goud's activities as posthumous editor of Elizabeth Jocelin's works make his female author a figure 'safe' for his purposes. Her aspirations and actions as teacher and preacher are minimized by Goud, worried as he is by the notion of a woman with a 'calling.' Clarke finds a woman's writing again being manipulated for others' ends, showing that the apparently autograph manuscript of Elizabeth Jekyll's *Spiritual Diary* is in fact scribal and arguing that we might see it as a political exploitation of the dead woman and her reputation by her husband.

There is very little to criticize in this excellent volume, and much more to celebrate than I have space for here (Heather Wolfe's first class article on *Lady Falkland: Her Life* and Jane Stevenson's useful survey essay deserve mention). Above all, the collection makes one wish to see the case studies here expanded, and the archival and the interpretive integrated still further. The understanding of the individuals and communities who made books in early modern England that is advanced here does not just change the landscape of early modern literary culture as we see it, but also offers us new maps for finding our way around it.

David Colclough, Queen Mary, University of London

NOTES

1. Oliver Lawson Dick (ed.), *Aubrey's Brief Lives* (Harmondsworth: Penguin, 1962), p. 247.

2. John Donne, *Letters to Severall Persons of Honour* (London, 1651), p. 197.

3. Harold Love, *Scribal Publication in Seventeenth-Century England* (Oxford: Clarendon Press, 1993), repr. as *The Culture and Commerce of Texts: Scribal Publication in Seventeenth-Century England* (Amherst: University of Massachusetts Press, 1998); Peter Beal, *In Praise of Scribes: Manuscripts and their Makers in Seventeenth-Century England* (Oxford: Clarendon Press, 1998); Arthur F. Marotti, *Manuscript, Print and the English Renaissance Lyric Manuscript* (Ithaca: Cornell University Press, 1995).

4. Nottingham Trent University's Perdita Project has been instrumental in demonstrating the extent and variety of women's writing in manuscript.

5. Lucy Hutchinson, *Order and Disorder*, edited by David Norbrook (Oxford: Blackwell, 2001).

T. WEBBER AND A. G. WATSON, ED.
The Libraries of the Augustinian Canons.
Corpus of British Medieval Library Catalogues 6.
British Library in Association with the British Academy, 1998.
xxvii, 572 pp.

JAMES P. CARLEY, ED.
The Libraries of King Henry VIII.
Corpus of British Medieval Library Catalogues 7.
British Library in Association with the British Academy, 2000.
xcii, 407 pp.

The format of the series of the Corpus of British Medieval Library Catalogues is now sufficiently established for one to approach each volume with a degree of confident expectation as to the nature of the materials included and their presentation. These two volumes, the latest in the series, focus some of the problems of dealing with the materials subsumed under the term 'British Medieval Library Catalogues' for the purpose of this series.

The question insistently raised by both these volumes is the extent to which they can legitimately be termed 'medieval library catalogues.' *The Libraries of the Augustinian Canons* brings together forty-one catalogues or related documents that shed light on the institutional holdings of these bodies. These materials range from the late twelfth to the sixteenth centuries. But the majority are very late; twenty-four are derived from Leland (A2, 3, 5-9, 11-14, 18-19, 21, 23-24, 26, 28, 30-32,34, 37, 39) and seven others (A10, 15, 22, 25, 33-4, 40) from the Lincolnshire list, *c.* 1530. Of the remaining ten documents (some of which are by no means securely linked to the houses with which they are here associated), only three, for Lanthony Secunda (A16),

Leicester (A20), Selborne (A29) and Waltham (A38), are attempts at either systematic catalogues or inventories. And of these Leicester dominates the volume, amounting to nearly three hundred pages (pp. 104-401) out of about four hundred and fifty.

This situation, it must be said, can be partly replicated in other volumes in this series. For example, eighteen out of twenty Cistercian catalogues are Leland or Leland-related. And Leland (together with Bale) provides most of the exiguous information about Dominican libraries. One may have some reservations about an undertaking that contains so few actual medieval catalogues and lacks wider contexts for the surviving holdings from libraries. More might have been done to fill out the picture of surviving books by more extensive cross-referencing to Ker's *Medieval Libraries of Great Britain*.

But there is, for the Augustinian canons, at least some medieval material. *The Libraries of King Henry* VIII is the first volume of the Corpus to deal with a secular library. It is also the first to deal with catalogues that are wholly post-medieval. Although Henry's library included a number of volumes collected by Edward IV and Henry VII, it is clear that his was the main role in the creation of a substantial royal library in the early sixteenth century. It, like the Watson/Webber volume, depends centrally on a single volume, in this case the Inventory of the Royal Library made in 1542 and updated after Henry's death, which comprises about two hundred pages (pp. 30-236) of the nearly three hundred of Carley's main text.

It is clear that this volume has no proper claim to be a medieval library catalogue. Apart from the volumes he inherited, Henry seems to have had only limited interest in medieval works or in manuscripts. Some manuscripts of importance were added to the library, like BL Harley 2278 (290), the presentation copy to Henry VI of Lydgate's *Lives of* SS *Edmund & Fremund*, one of the most sumptuously illustrated Middle English manuscripts of the fifteenth century, which must have actually been restored to royal possession in Henry's reign. But of the roughly twelve hundred items listed in the main inventory, about half are identified certainly or probably with printed books.

I make these points about both catalogues not, in any sense to disparage their achievements, but to stress the limits on the useful conclusions that it is possible to draw from such materials. It should be stressed that both volumes do a magnificent job of editing their materials and tracing items from the surviving catalogues or lists. In the case of Carley's volume, there is the further achievement of establishing the various contemporary channels by which manuscripts entered the Royal library: Henry's wives, Leland, Cromwell, New Year's Presentations and Henry's own acquisitions. It is hard to overpraise the patient, sustained scholarship that has gone into this reconstruction. It is a definitive achievement.

But such opportunities are atypical of the series as a whole. A number of the catalogues in other volumes have already appeared in print, and there is limited scope for enlarging the range of identifications or correcting transcriptional errors. It is not clear (at least to me) quite how much this *corpus* is going to significantly change our understanding of the *corpus* of medieval English libraries. One might wonder, for instance, why there is no scope for the inclusion of records of the libraries of individuals.

One point that can be made about both volumes is the inadequacy of the General Indices. For example, in both volumes there are interesting references to Chaucer (Watson and Webber, p. 106), Carley, p. xli). In neither instance are these references retrievable through the index. A more expansive sense of material to be included would have been helpful.

A. S. G. Edwards, University of Victoria

RUTH J. DEAN, ED.
WITH THE COLLABORATION OF MAUREEN B. M. BOULTON.
Anglo-Norman Literature: A Guide to Texts and Manuscripts.
Anglo-Norman Text Society Occasional Publication Series no. 3.
Anglo-Norman Text Society: London, 1999.

The appearance of this volume is a mark of the changing nature of medieval studies, and our growing interest in multi-lingual, code-switching environments. When Johann Vising published *Anglo-Norman Language and Literature* (Oxford, 1923), he could get the entire bibliography for the field on three pages (pp. 101-103). It was not until 1963 that the annual MLA bibliography included Anglo-Norman as a separate heading within 'French Medieval Literature.' That year there were four entries (PMLA 78 [1963]: 205, nos. 6750-6753). Go into Google today and type 'Anglo-Norman,' and you will retrieve over 16,000 entries. A search for 'Anglo-Norman Literature' brings you down to 4,120. Refine the search to entries with "manuscript" as a key word, and you still get 1230 items. One of the most useful starting-places, www.anglo-norman.net, lists all 58 volumes, thirteen occasional publications, and four-teen Plain Texts published by the Anglo-Norman Text Society since it began in 1939. *Anglo-Norman Literature* is clearly a volume which has been badly needed and will be widely used.

It is also a remarkable personal achievement on the part of Professor Ruth Dean, who celebrated her hundredth birthday on March 10. Johann Vising's is a volume of 111 pages, listing 419 manuscripts. *Anglo-Norman Literature: A Guide to Texts and Manuscripts* contains 553 pages describing 986 texts, most extant in multiple copies. Vising's was a volume primarily useful to those working on French texts composed in England, and is strongest on the holdings of British libraries. Vising, for instance, includes only two manuscripts from the Vatican; Dean has eleven. Vising includes one manuscript from an American collection; Dean includes items from Ann Arbor, Baltimore, Berkeley, Boston, the American Cambridge, and on through the alphabet to San Marino. There are new discoveries even in familiar collections, such as the fragment of a Benedictine Rule in St. John's College Cambridge MS E. 10 (113), which M.R. James missed (no. 711).

Ruth Dean has personally examined almost every item. The descriptions, dates, and analyses of variant versions of texts reflect her careful eye and wealth of knowledge. The clarity of the layout of the present volume is a tribute to the computer and design skills of Maureen Boulton and Ian Short. Numbers are in bold; entry titles are in italic block capitals, and titles of works are in italics. White space sets off *incipits*, manuscript shelfmarks and bibliographical information. There is even room in the top and bottom margin for one's own notes. Its utility is further enhanced by a series of indices, which include a concordance of Vising's numbers with ANL items, and separate indices of manuscripts, *incipits*, titles, authors, patrons and sources. And all the cross-references from the indices work. In short, the volume is a delight to use.

Anglo-Norman Literature provides a careful identification of texts and manuscripts, with clear bibliographical information. Vising is one of those exasperating treasure-troves compiled for an audience unfazed by the need to expand such references as Knust, Gesch. d.h. Katharina von Alex. u.d. h. Maria Aeg. (1890), or Walberg, Ro. xliv, 407. The references here are mercifully complete, reflecting a scholarly world in which students who as yet know little about Anglo-Norman and less about any other foreign language can still use the volume with profit. Information includes full citations for the most recent edition of all or part of a text; earlier editions if they provide information not in their successors; critical studies of text and manuscript problems; and translations of a work into modern English. Facsimiles and individual plates are mentioned, so the reader tracing a particular scribe or style knows whether or not an edition includes a photograph of the manuscript. The plates have been examined critically—that in R. C. Johnston's 1976 article is better than the one in his 1981 edition of Jordan Fantosme's Chronicle (no. 55). Unedited texts are clearly marked "No edition" near the end of the entry. If the work is a translation or adaptation of an earlier work in French or Latin, the source is indicated, and its most recent edition noted. Editions available only in foreign or U.S. dissertations are included. The notes also identify which manuscript (or manuscripts) an editor has used. The number of lines and verse form of poetic texts is indicated.

The tendency is to include rather than exclude. No. 500, a verse version of the *Gospel of Nicodemus* by an otherwise unknown Chréstien, survives in two manuscripts, both English, one from Nuneaton (Cambridge, Fitzwilliam

Museum Maclean 123), and the other now in Florence, Biblioteca Laurentiana Conventi soppressi 99. Vising thought it was not linguistically Anglo-Norman; Paul Meyer, however, thought it might have been composed in England. According to the introduction to *Anglo-Norman Literature*, cultural evidence counts, so the Gospel is included. The ANL also includes works circulating in substantial numbers of Anglo-Norman manuscripts, such as the histories of the Norman *Wace*, and works whose sole surviving copy is Anglo-Norman though the language looks continental, such as the *Pèlerinage de Charlemagne*. (no. 80). Manuscripts are dated as precisely as possible. Chronicles can often be given a *terminus a quo* by the last child of a king included in a genealogy, or a specific event (e.g. "after 1307" for a work ending with the death of Edward I). Some are identified within a quarter of a century (e.g. XV 1/4), some only as first or second half (e.g. XIII2). Superscript "in," "ex" and "m" refer to the beginning, end, or middle of a century. For the most part, these dates reflect Ruth Dean's personal examination of the manuscripts. If there is any question, evidence for the date is supplied.

This volume is also a tribute to the community of scholarship which flourished in the Bodleian Library under Richard Hunt and Tilly De la Mare, who believed that people working on medieval manuscripts should know and talk to each other. Questions got answered and references traded in Duke Humphrey, on the Bodley stairs, and in the King's Arms across the street. And so in *Anglo-Norman Literature*, other scholars of several generations are cited in many entries, often from personal communications. Open the volume to pp. 362-63, and you will find references to manuscripts of Confessions identified and reported to Dr. Dean by Frank Mantello, by Isabel Aspin, and a note of a forthcoming publication by Tony Hunt. A number of members of EBS will find themselves in its references: Pamela Robinson at 832; Linda Voigts at 436 and 437; James Carley at 552. *Anglo-Norman Literature* will be a fertile hunting-ground for dissertations and articles. About a quarter of the items described (27 out of 104) in the first section, historiographical works, are either incompletely edited, or not edited at all. The same is true of scientific and medical texts. Many are variant versions of works which have been edited, but it is precisely those variations which give us the individual voice, frequently placed and dated. Scholars wishing to trace female authors or patrons, or lay authors, or noble patrons, will find the indices an excellent starting place.

What will readers of JEBS find in *Anglo-Norman Literature*? Nearly a thousand texts, edited and unedited, to explore. The field is especially rich for those interested in the thirteenth and fourteenth centuries. Short texts such as prayers and lyrics continue to be composed in Anglo-Norman in the late fourteenth and fifteenth centuries, as do grammars and glosses. This leads one to conclude that the language was alive and well, being read and taught. But in the hagiographical section, for instance, (nos. 504-586), no texts and only a handful of manuscripts from the fifteenth century appear, and most of these are Continental. They include one English and four Continental copies of the life of the German St. Alban included in *Mandeville's Travels* (no. 506.1); a Continental copy of *La Vie du Pape Saint Gregoire* (no. 514); a "late Continental copy" of *St. Patrick's Purgatory* (no. 550); and a copy of *Le Tournoiement Anticrist* of Huon de Mery dated XIV/XV (no. 586). There are occasional Anglo-Norman copies of earlier chronicles in fifteenth-century hands, but original composition of chronicles in French seems to disappear after the reign of Richard II. *Anglo-Norman Literature* is a book which might never have appeared without computer technology. But, at the same time, it is not a book a computer could have generated. Entry after entry shows that the texts have been, not just catalogued, but read carefully, with an attention to detail which rarely appears in reference volumes. Sometimes a scribe's information seems simply wrong; what led the scribe of Dublin, Christ Church Cathedral Black Book to remark that Clement of Llanthony succeeded Becket as Archbishop of Canterbury (no. 483)? The note on No. 58, *The Walling of New Ross*, tells us that the women of that Irish town helped carry and place the stones on Sundays when the walls went up in 1265; why, one wonders, only then? Sometimes one can trace the growth of a legend; does King John die of a sudden illness (nos. 42 and 45) or of poison (no. 46) or specifically of venom from a toad given him by a monk at Swineshead (no. 44)? John died in 1216; can one trust a toad first mentioned in 1307?

Anglo-Norman Literature is not a book to be read cover to cover, but one can't open it without learning something, or close it without those unanswered questions which are the lifeblood of scholarship. The *incipits* are frequently full enough to give the flavor of the text. Adam was born in the first lunation; this makes it a good time to teach children their letters, or to begin any new undertaking (no. 367). If Christmas comes on Sunday, it will be a good but windy winter (no. 370). But if the first night of Christmas is too windy, kings and bishops will perish in the coming year (371). The instructions for making Greek Fire by several different methods in Cambridge, Emmanuel College MS 69 are, alas, still unprinted (no. 388), as is the treatise on Spatulomancy—a word for divination by shoulder-blades of an animal which I discovered first appears in English in 1652. Perhaps the practice was earlier confined to French-speaking circles? And does anyone know why are lapidaries more popular in England than France?

In the spirit of precision, I learned from checking references for Professor Dean, perhaps I should point out that current dating puts the manuscript of the French version of the *Charter of St. Patrick* (no. 552) possibly earlier than the thirteenth-century addition to William of Malmesbury's Latin chronicle; this raises the interesting possibility of translation from French into Latin. And, in the spirit of keeping a reference book current, one might add to no. 287 and related entries Andres M. Kristol, "L'Intellectuel 'anglo-normand' face à la pluralité des langues: le témoinage implicite du MS Oxford, Magdalen Lat. 188," in *Multilingualism in Later Medieval Britain* (ed. D.A. Trotter, Woodbridge: D. S. Brewer, 2000, 37-52), which includes partial editions of some texts, and plates of details from fols. 12v and 31v. For anyone working with manuscripts and texts written in England in the later Middle Ages, *Anglo-Norman Literature* is an indispensable and irresistible guide.

Jeanne Krochalis, Penn State University, New Kensington

D. THOMAS HANKS, JR., ED.
The Social and Literary Context of Malory's Morte Darthur.
Arthurian Studies 42.
Cambridge: Brewer, 2000. 157pp. ISBN 0261–9814

This volume, the forty-second in the Arthurian Studies series, opens with a discursive and lively essay by Terence McCarthy on the reception of the Caxton Malory in the Tudor period, "Old Worlds, New Worlds: King Arthur in England," and continues with a series of essays on the ideology and practice, real ("Malory and the Battle of Towton," P. J. C. Field) and virtual ("The Symbolic Importance of Processions in Malory's *Morte Darthur* and in Fifteenth-Century England," Ann Elaine Bliss). Essays about warfare include: "'Thou woll never have done': Ideology, Context and Excess in Malory's War," by Andrew Lynch; "Malory's Anti-Knights: Balin and Breunys," by D. Thomas Hanks, Jr.; and "Malory's Argument against War with France: the Political Geography of France and the Anglo-French Alliance in the *Morte Darthur*," by Robert L. Kelly.

The two essays of apparently most obvious interest to JEBS readers are those by Karen Cherewatuk on "Sir Thomas Malory's 'Grete Booke'" and Kevin Grimm on "Wynkyn de Worde and the Creation of Malory's *Morte Darthur*." The former begins as an essay on the circulation of chivalric texts in courtly and aristocratic circles at the time of the *Morte Darthur*. A competent restatement of current research on the content and context of Sir John Paston's 'Grete Booke' and related manuscripts appears, however, to serve only as an introduction to Cherewatuk's thesis that these books offered the model to Malory for the *Morte Darthur*, a similarly "cumulative and syncretic vision of knighthood," a thesis which she argues through more or less illuminating comparisons between the various chivalric texts of these books and the discrete tales of the *Morte Darthur*.

Kevin Grimm's essay is a more straightforward piece of work, which supports the current trend to rehabilitate Wynkyn de Worde as a competent editor in his own right. Grimm's argument is that de Worde played a significant role in audience reception of the *Morte Darthur* by an "aggressive packaging of the text." The term 'aggressive' is perhaps over-loaded, but Grimm's argument that the integration of text and woodcut is carefully designed with the needs of the reader in mind is sufficiently subtantiated, together with much interesting information on the role of cutter and printer, by his close examination of layout and design in Caxton's and de Worde's prints.

Sue Powell, University of Salford

DEREK PEARSALL, ED.
New Directions in Later Medieval Manuscript Studies.
York: York Medieval Press, 2000.
vx + 213 pp. £50/$90. ISBN 1-903153-01-8.

This volume comprises the proceedings of a conference held at Harvard in 1998 which focused on new directions in medieval manuscript studies. In the introductory chapter, Ian Doyle casts a retrospective look over recent directions in manuscript studies which provides a comprehensive account of scholarship concerned with many aspects of manuscript culture in Northern Europe during the Middle Ages. As well as providing a comprehensive summary of previous approaches, Doyle also anticipates many of the new directions discussed in the later chapters. Doyle's final consideration concerns the importance of digitization and hypertext for manuscript study in which he initiates a discussion which permeates the entire volume. While acknowledging the potential importance of such developments for the provision of manuscript catalogues and facsimiles, Doyle's assessment sounds a note of caution, warning that electronic media must not be allowed to replace print versions but rather to exist alongside more traditional formats for texts. David Benson's paper, "Another Fine Manuscript Mess: Authors, Editors and Readers of *Piers Plowman*," surveys the editorial tradition of *Piers Plowman*, demonstrating how many of our conceptions of the text are based upon editorial assumptions rather than manuscript evidence. Benson's task is not to provide solutions to these textual uncertainties but rather to demonstrate how much textual and codicological information has been suppressed by modern editors of the poem. N.F. Blake then discusses the work of the *Canterbury Tales* Project which aims to address many of the problems highlighted by Benson by providing readers and editors of Chaucer's work with access to transcriptions and digital images of all the witnesses of the poem.

These resources are to be made available on CD-ROM. Blake describes the software used by the Project for collating the electronic transcripts which highlights relationships across the manuscript tradition in its entirety, thereby enabling scholars to identify later manuscripts which are important for reconstructing Chaucer's text. Julia Boffey's contribution suggests some of the archives which may still retain Middle English texts as yet undiscovered. Boffey considers mainly public record offices, although her discussion is also relevant to family archives, the libraries of cathedrals, schools and other specialized institutions. Martha Driver assesses the importance of electronic media for the future of both teaching and research into medieval manuscripts. She guides the reader through a wealth of on-line materials, commenting particularly on their usefulness for teaching medieval studies. One problem with an analysis of this kind is the constantly changing nature of the Internet. Driver notes that a search of the Internet for the term "medieval manuscripts'" using the Alta Vista search engine finds 2316 Web pages. The same search performed at the time of writing this review found 1,165,448 web pages. This is evidently an expanding field and one which can be rather overwhelming for the uninitiated. As such, Martha Driver's essay is an important aid for identifying useful resources and potential pitfalls in exploiting the Internet for both teacher and researcher. A.S.G. Edwards provides an historical overview of methods of representing the Middle English manuscript, charting the rise of facsimiles and critical editions. Edwards shows how modern conceptions of both kinds of edition are influenced by the work of nineteenth-century editors, such as Skeat and Madden, and he signals the potential for improvement in the provision of such editions provided by computers, stressing that what is needed is not simply a representation of the manuscript in its entirety but a presentation which "offers the opportunity to study in a variety of ways pertinent formal aspects of the manuscript." Editions of this kind are becoming available although these frequently display the continued influence of nineteenth-century practices. Ralph Hanna's contribution presents a reconsideration of the Auchinleck manuscript; part of a wider study which examines the literature of fourteenth-century London as that of a provincial locale. By comparison with other book production in the capital, particularly by the community of legal scribes, Hanna argues that the Auchinleck manuscript is not as unusual as is commonly assumed but has a number of analogues in the extensive legal volumes produced in the capital. Connections between literary and legal books are also drawn by Kathryn Kerby-Fulton in her investigation into "Professional Readers of Langland," which examines the political associations revealed by the manuscripts of *Piers Plowman*, particularly among civil servants, legal scribes, colonial administrators and politicians. Drawing upon the evidence of chancery script, bureaucratic annotation and redaction, and sketching practices and illustrations common in the Exchequer, Kerby-Fulton suggests ways in which the poem was transmitted and received among reformist political thinkers. Linne Mooney's contribution moves the focus from professional readers to professional scribes, and specifically those scribes active in more than one medieval manuscript. Mooney discusses a number of such scribes including John Shirley, the Hammond Scribe, the 'hooked-g' scribe, and Doyle and Parkes' scribes B and D. Mooney helpfully suggests a number of characteristics which allow us to identify a professional scribe: the presence of the hand in more than one manuscript, the ability to write in a variety of styles while maintaining a consistent standard of duct and aspect, the adoption of certain details of layout, and collaboration with other scribes or artists. Mooney closes by proposing the production of a digital archive of samples of the work of such scribes with characteristic features highlighted to enable future identifications by other scholars. The high quality of these and other contributions not discussed here make this book an important and authoritative series of statements on the current progress of manuscript studies and new directions for its future.

Simon Horobin, University of Glasgow

PAUL SAENGER, AND KIMBERLY VAN KAMPEN, EDS.
The Bible as Book: The First Printed Editions.
London and New Castle, DE: The British Library and Oak Knoll
in Association with The Scriptorium: Center for
Christian Antiquities, 1999.

This handsome volume is the second to result from the symposium on pre-1520 Bibles as books sponsored by the Scriptorium: Center for Christian Antiquities in cooperation with the Van Kampen Foundation and conducted at Hampton Court, Herefordshire in May 1996. Unlike the first volume, reviewed by Susan Powell in JEBS 2, that included essays covering the manuscript period of Bible production, this volume focuses on incunable Bibles from "a span of approximately sixty years—roughly from Gutenberg to Erasmus" (xi). Nonetheless, the essays in the volume range across the languages, ancient and vernacular, in which the Bible was first transmitted in print and examines how this transmission has contributed to the idea(s) of the Bible, and of books in general. These "Bible Stories" admirably achieve the editors' stated aim of contributing to "a multi-faceted portrait of a text about which, all too often, errant generalizations are made" (xi) by collecting essays that concentrate on individual texts produced in specific places with ones that range across texts and time. It contains an even, and perhaps suspiciously numerological, dozen essays, many that are illuminated by the forty-four, black-and-white plates that are tipped in between pages 116 and 117. A concern for examining how individual acts of printing, based on varying knowledge of and access to manuscript sources, shaped the practices of printing Bibles binds the collection together. Arthur Kinney's introduction to the volume situates the essays in relation to one another, and he also situates the volume in our time when he observes that the tags and daggers in the early printed editions of *Glossa Ordinaria* were intended to be hypertext links between different *corpora* (4).

The first Bible Stories following the introduction fittingly discuss the adaptation of *Glossa Ordinaria* to print. J.P. Gumbert's essay, "The Layout of the Bible Gloss in Manuscript and Early Print," creates a continuity with the earlier volume of *The Bible as Book* while sounding a theme that echoes through this volume: the often amazing ways in which early printers adapted manuscript practices and sources to their new purposes. The next essay in the collection, by Karlfried Froehlich, celebrates "An Extraordinary Achievement: the *Glossa Ordinaria* in Print" by showing what a daunting technical problem this act of adaptation was and how gamely early printers met the challenge. In "Biblical Blockbooks," Nigel F. Palmer informs or reminds us that neither the whole Bible nor movable type tells the whole story of the Biblical text in the incunable period. Paul Saenger's contribution, "The Impact of the Early Printed Page on the Reading of the Bible," made its impression on this reader by the way it builds upon the kind of work reported in the first three essays. While the first three essays primarily show what printers did with the Bible, how they did it, and what their efforts put into the hands of readers, Saenger's essay also tries to understand what readers made of these Bibles and how the Bibles, in turn, were affected by them.

The next several essays return productively to the strategy of a more limited focus, while surveying the printing of the Bible in various languages. For instance, Paul Needham's "The Changing Shape of the Vulgate Bible in Fifteenth-Century Printing Shops" shows how later printers built upon the heritage of Gutenberg and his imitators, and diversified the formats for the Vulgate in the process. One of his working assumptions, that printers' manipulation of texts can often be understood as the activity of businessmen who perceive the demand for a particular product and are willing to supply it, helps to make sense of the metamorphoses discussed in this essay. "Hebrew Printing of the Bible in the XVth Century" is the subject of Adrian K. Offenberg's essay that intends to correct previous explanations of the relative lateness of Hebrew Bibles in print. Offenberg suggests that what has often been considered an ideological phenomenon may in fact have been a technical one. Like the essay that precedes it, Kimberly Van Kampen's "Biblical Books and the Circulation of the Psalms in Late-Medieval England" not only focuses on a single book in a single place, but also purposes to understand the paradox of the Wycliffite Bible alongside the lateness of the first English Bibles in print. Guy Bedouelle's essay "The Bible, Printing and the Educational Goals of Humanists," which was translated by Barbara Beaumont, resembles Saenger's by placing the technical developments within the context of the history of thought and reading.

Standing alone in the collection, as in the history of the book, is "The Printing Press at Alcalá de Henares: the Complutensian Poltyglot Bible" by Julían Martín Abad, translated by Timothy Graham. Abad's historical overview of the press at Alcalá de Henares aims to show how such an oddly ambitious and expensive project as the Polyglot Bible arose and was completed. The results of this project can be seen in Figure 36, among the illustrations that interpose after the end of Abad's essay. Following the illustrations, Michael Welte's "The Problem of the Manuscript Basis for the Earliest Printed Editions of the Greek New Testament" acts as a corrective to earlier notions of the sources for these Bibles, and in this respect is reminiscent of the contribution on Hebrew Bibles mentioned above. William Sherman's penultimate contribution "'The Book Put in Every Vulgar Hand': Impressions of Readers in Early English Printed Bibles," adds the interesting aspect of reader reception to this repertoire of "Bible Stories" as he surveys the kinds of traces left by early readers in their Bibles. This essay shows how times changed even during the relatively short period covered in this volume by showing how the margins had become a contested space where readers and printers debated with traditional glosses. The collection ends as fittingly as it began with "The Re-Evaluation of the Patristic Exegetical Tradition in the Sixteenth Century" by David Steinmetz. This contribution notes that there appears to have been far less consensus among reformers and Catholics respectively outside the most contested passages than we might expect. Once again, we are reminded that the remains of past cultures stubbornly refuse to conform to our generalizations about them.

As with the earlier volume, this one may be of interest to scholars of the history of Biblical transmission, although it may not offer anything terribly new to their thinking. Nonetheless, it is full of interesting texts and interesting ways of looking at texts, and provides a useful introduction to the field for novices. Therefore, it may be a welcome addition to many college libraries.

Bryan P. Davis, Georgia Southwestern State University

BONNIE WHEELER, ROBERT L. KINDRICK AND
MICHAEL N. SALDA, EDS.
The Malory Debate: Essays on the Texts of Le Morte Darthur.
Cambridge: Brewer, 2000. 420pp. ISBN 0-85991-583-2

Although the editors of this volume claim it, justifiably, as necessary reading for those interested in the text of Malory's *Le Morte Darthur*, the scope of these essays and the range of evidence utilized to further the debate make it an illuminating volume for any scholar with an interest in textual issues. At the heart of the volume is the disputed status of the printed text published by Caxton vis-á-vis the Winchester manuscript as the best witness to the original text. The late William Matthews, a renowned Arthurian scholar, whose essays appear here, posited the view that Caxton's text was 'a much better text than that presented in W,' and his essays, forming Section A of the volume, provide the background for a re-airing of the debate which, while not solving the problem of the relationship between the two texts, offers stimulating observations.

Section B lays out differing arguments for Winchester or Caxton. The essays here are by the late Charles Moorman (an unrevised reprint), Shunichi Noguchi, P.J.C. Field, Yuji Nakao (all revised from their first appearance), and new essays by Edward Kennedy and N.F. Blake. Section C, described by the editors as a group of essays "which considers the next steps in the ongoing edition of Malory's *Le Morte Darthur*," includes new essays by Helen Cooper, D.Thomas Hanks, Jr., Shunichi Noguchi, Meg Roland, Sue Ellen Holbrook, and one written before his death by Paul Yeats-Edwards, formerly librarian at Winchester College. The essays in this section generally raise interesting questions about the future editing of a Malory text, though two in particular are worth noting. Helen Cooper, in "Opening Up the Malory Manuscript," offers an informed and fascinating tour of numerous scribal features of the

Winchester manuscript, features excised in Vinaver's influential editorial work, but used by Cooper to question the widespread assumption that Vinaver's editions reflect the Winchester manuscript. And Sue Ellen Holbrook, in her essay "On the Attractions of the Malory Incunable and the Malory Manuscript," gives a detailed and stimulating account of the possible production process of the printed text in Caxton's workshop, and offers an intriguing theory concerning the relationship between the Winchester and the Caxton texts.

Carole Weinberg, University of Manchester

SUSAN POWELL AND JEREMY J. SMITH, EDS.
New Perspectives on Middle English Texts: A Festschrift for R. A. Waldron.
Cambridge: Brewer, 2000.
pp. xi+190. £45/$75. ISBN 0-85991-590-5.

This volume is a collection of 13 essays in honor of Ronald Waldron whose contents reflect the wide scholarly interests of the recipient. The volume is divided into two parts: the first part deals with the interpretation of Middle English alliterative verse, while the second has a more general focus on Middle English texts. Malcolm Andrew opens the first section with a study of the setting and context of the works of the *Gawain*-poet, highlighting the subtle and sophisticated use of the setting of a particular event for understanding its significance for the narrative as a whole. Rosamund Allen investigates the structure of *The Alliterative Morte Arthure*, which has implications for the controversial question of the poem's genre. Many scholars have used their analysis of genre and meaning to inform their understanding of its structure. Allen begins with the premise that the poem was designed to be recited aloud and analyzes its 'performative' structure, the way in which the text was divided for oral performance. Allen argues that the text has a seven-part structure with the conquest of the Roman Emperor forming the climactic fourth section. In using this structure the poem echoes the cyclical structure of tragedy, and the dominant motif of Fortune's wheel. George Kane's discussion draws upon his recent experience in producing a glossary of *Piers Plowman*. He offers a number of new interpretations of specific readings, while also providing useful models for subsequent editors faced with similar cruces such as "the letter-group *lo+two minims+e*" (p. 45) which is represented by eighteen headwords in the *Middle English Dictionary*, including 'lof,' 'lone,' 'loue,' 'louen,' 'love' and 'loven.' Susan Powell offers a study of Gawain's pentangle, focusing on its vernacular title 'the endless knot.' Powell examines the various senses of ME 'knotte' which as well as a 'knot' can also refer to an intellectual problem or mystery, or an agreement or bond between two persons. She contrasts the endless knot which cannot be untied with the knotted girdle which can be easily loosened: a contrast which evidently has important moral implications. The significance of the knot is further eluci- dated with reference to heraldic evidence and the common appearance of knots on heraldic badges, such as the knot of Solomon associated with the fourteenth-century Italian *Compagnia del Nodo*. This is an extremely rich and persuasive line of enquiry which suggests many more avenues for future research. In his contribution, "Semantics and Metrical Form in *Sir Gawain and the Green Knight*," Jeremy Smith unites Ronald Waldron's interests in allitera- tive poetry and semantics. Smith demonstrates the link between alliterative patterning and phonaesthesia, or sound symbolism. By demonstrating that the *Gawain*-poet only alliterates the sl- cluster with itself, Smith argues that this sound had a particular salience for the poet and his audience. The phonaesthetic associations of words such as 'slide,' 'sleep,' and 'sly' with morally-dubious concepts such as evil, carelessness, sloth would therefore have had significant implications for a contemporary understanding of the poem. This approach has many implications for a more scientific, linguistic assessment of such connotations within the Middle English lexicon more generally.

The first part is in many ways the more focused portion of the book, given its greater thematic coherence, while the second part appears superfi- cially to be more fragmentary. However there are a number of important indi- vidual studies in this section. Norman Blake discusses the links in the *Canterbury Tales*, considering the possibility that these links survive in different authorial versions. While textual critics have accepted that individual tales were revised by Chaucer, different versions of linking passages are generally considered to be scribal. Blake considers the "Man of Law's Endlink," the "Nun's Priests' Prologue and Endlink" and the "Canon's Yeoman's Prologue," arguing that the existence of variant versions of these links, combined with their absence from some manuscripts, is the result of authorial revision rather than scribal error or difficulties in obtaining copy. Blake suggests that this theory may explain the two versions of the Merchant-Squire-Franklin links in the Hengwrt and Ellesmere manuscripts: both sets could be author- ial indicating that Chaucer experimented with different orders for these tales and altered the links to fit these arrangements. Elton D. Higgs traces the themes of temporal and spiritual indebtedness in the *Canterbury Tales*, demon- strating their pervasive influence and the persistent tensions between human debts and those owed to God. He focuses on the thematic importance of indebtedness in the tales of the Wife of Bath, Pardoner, Shipman and Franklin, producing a rather disappointingly superficial commentary on contracts, debts, obligations and agreements in these complex tales. Derek Pearsall's study of Henryson's *Testament of Cresseid* offers an important reading of the poem dealing principally with themes of responsibility and punishment, and the place of Chaucer's *Troilus* within Henryson's poem. While there is no explicit discussion of what the new perspectives offered in this volume are, the book provides a *compilatio* of stimulating studies from which many new perspectives emerge. The first part makes a particularly important contribution to the study of ME alliterative poetry and a fitting tribute to one of its finest critics.

Simon Horobin, University of Glasgow

Notes on Libraries and Collections

Ripon Cathedral Library
on deposit in The Brotherton Library,
University of Leeds,
Leeds LS2 9JT, UK
Telephone: (0)113 3435518
E-mail: special-collections@library.leeds.ac.uk
For access, see
http://www.leeds.ac.uk/library/spcoll/rshome2.htm

      We owe the older part of Ripon Cathedral Library to the collecting activities of Anthony Higgin, who was Dean of the then Collegiate Church from 1608 until his death in 1624, and who decreed in his will that his books should eventually pass "to the church of Ripon for a liberarie," which at that time it appeared to lack. Excluding manuscripts, over 1,100 books still in the cathedral library date from before 1625. The incunabula include a copy of Chaucer's *Boethius*, printed by Caxton before 1479, and formerly included the unique 'Ripon Caxton,' the *Epitome Margaritae Eloquentiae* of Laurentius Gulielmus de Saona (1480; ISTC it00427770), which was discovered in the library in 1952.[1] This book was sold in 1960 to raise money for a choir school and was bought by the Brotherton Collection of Leeds University Library, where the remainder of the Cathedral Library has been on deposit since 1986 (the printed books, which in total number over 2,700 volumes, are all listed in the University Library's main catalogue).

      Dean Higgin, whose personal contacts included other Yorkshire collectors such as William Crashaw and Henry Savile of Banke, acquired books over many years and from a wide variety of sources.[2] As one might expect, his collections were strongest in theology, including a large number of works on controversial subjects. The former extent of his theological holdings can be seen from his surviving autograph catalogue of this portion of his library (now MS 35), which lists 758 volumes, of which some 250 have since disappeared. Medieval manuscripts and printed books are listed side by side in this catalogue, the former usually distinguished by the note "in pergam." or similar. Most of the eight medieval manuscript codices that still survive (all of which are listed by N.R. Ker and A.J. Piper in *Medieval Manuscripts in British Libraries*, IV, 1992) can be matched with entries in Higgin's catalogue. However, none of them has come through from the library that must have existed at Ripon in the Middle Ages, although MS 8, the Ripon Psalter, presented to the Cathedral by the Marquess of Ripon in 1874, is distinguished by special offices for the feast of St Wilfred and was presumably made for use in the fifteenth-century monastic church. Higgin himself evidently acquired books formerly belonging to other northern religious houses. Thus MS 2, Anselm, belonged to the preaching friars at Newcastle upon Tyne, MSS 3-4, twelfth-century commentaries on the Apocalypse, to Bridlington Priory, and MS 6, the *Meditationes Vitae Christi*, to Mount Grace Priory, these last two both in north Yorkshire. Two of the incunabula once belonged to Fountains Abbey.

Eight is a disappointingly small number of manuscript codices, but a mass of other medieval manuscript material exists in the form of binding fragments, of which sixty numbered examples have been removed from the (mainly, sixteenth-century) printed books concerned, but most of which remain *in situ*. (A small number are listed in Neil Ker's *Fragments of Medieval Manuscripts Used as Pastedowns in Oxford Bindings*, 1954.) While many of the fragments are from theological or liturgical manuscripts, there are some striking secular examples, including leaves from a French prose romance, from a commentary on Ovid's *Metamorphoses*, and from Walter Burley's commentary on Aristotle's *Physics*, not to mention a bifolium—still in place as the wrapper around two otherwise unbound printed pamphlets of 1573—containing part of a Middle English prose *Mandeville's Travels*.[3] A very large amount of work remains to be done by way of cataloguing and identifying the Ripon Cathedral binding fragments, with potentially important results for our knowledge of the provenance of Higgin's books, of sixteenth-century binding practices, and of the post-medieval availability of medieval manuscript material.

There is further scope for research in the separate Dean and Chapter Archives, which were deposited in the Brotherton Library in 1980. This large body of documents covers the history of the Cathedral from the Middle Ages to the twentieth century; a detailed listing of its contents is available from the Library. Notable medieval material includes Chapter act books (largely printed by the Surtees Society in the nineteenth century), fabric and property records, account rolls, and Canon Fee Court books.

The Special Collections department of the Brotherton Library welcomes enquiries from researchers about the Ripon Cathedral material in its care.

Oliver Pickering, Leeds University Library

NOTES

1. Ronald H. Martin, "The *Epitome Margaritae Eloquentiae* of Laurentius Gulielmus de Saona," *Proceedings of the Leeds Philosophical and Literary Society, Literary and Historical Section*, 14: 4 (1971), 99-187.

2. See Jean E. Mortimer, "The Library Catalogue of Anthony Higgin, Dean of Ripon (1608-1624)," *Proceedings of the Leeds Philosophical and Literary Society, Literary and Historical Section,* 10: 1 (1962), 1-75.
3. A. C. Cawley, "A Ripon Fragment of 'Mandeville's Travels'," *English Studies,* 38 (1957), 1-3.

Robbins Collection
School of Law, Boalt Hall
University of California
Berkeley, CA 94720
Lucia Diamond, Librarian
e-mail: robbins@law.berkeley.edu
Phone: (510) 643-1211
Fax: (510) 643-8770
Hours: M-F 9-6

The Music Library
240 Morrison Hall
University of California
Berkeley, CA 94720
John Roberts, Librarian
e-mail: mweber@library.berkeley.edu
Phone: (510) 642-2623
Fax: (510) 642-8237
Hours: M-Th, 9-10; F 9-5; Sat, 1-5; Sun, 1-10

The Bancroft Library
University of California
Berkeley, CA 94720
Tony Bliss, Curator, Rare Books and Literary Manuscripts
e-mail: bancref@library.berkeley.edu
Phone: (510) 642-6481
Fax: (510) 642-7589
Hours: M-F 9-5; Sat 1-5

Just a mile or so up the hill from where Berkeley's fog and wisteria-draped landscape finally dissolves into San Francisco Bay, a remarkably large and diverse selection of medieval manuscripts and early-print books finds refuge in three special collections libraries on the Berkeley campus of the University of California. The Robbins Collection is housed on the campus's heights within the confines of fabled Boalt Hall. This immense collection focuses on civil and religious law, and includes 200 medieval items—books, documents, and fragments—along with almost as many incunables and another 2000 titles printed before 1600. Among medieval manuscripts, the Robbins Collection is especially strong in decretals and penitential manuals; of particular interest in this period is a copy of the *Sententiarum libri* IV of Peter Lombard from Paris, produced about 1250. The Collection's recently remodeled reading room is both comfortably appointed and well-equipped with CD ROM research tools such as CETEDOC and MGH on its computers and an excellent selection of hard-copy reference works on its shelves. The catalogue of incunables is online (at http://www.law.berkeley.edu/library/robbins/), and a descriptive catalogue of the medieval manuscript collection is forthcoming at the same site. The Boalt Hall complex also recently added Café Zeb, whose sunny courtyard makes an inviting spot for lunch or an espresso break. While you're there, ask the locals about Uncle Zeb.

Downhill from Boalt, in the Music Department's Morrison Hall, UC Berkeley's Music Library houses a surprisingly multi-faceted collection. Jewels from the medieval period include the eleventh-century Wolffheim Antiphonal, a fourteenth-century treatise on musical theory, and numerous twelfth-century noted liturgical fragments. A comprehensive guide to these holdings is John A. Emerson's Catalog of Pre-1900 Vocal Manuscripts in the Music Library, University of California at Berkeley. For scholars of the early-print period, the music collection of Florentine publisher Aldo Olschski—most of which the library acquired in 1955—includes a wealth of sixteenth-century editions. The Music Library is also very strong in reference works; among these, a particularly massive aid to medievalists and historians of music alike is the *Analecta Hymnica*, a 55-volume compendium of medieval hymns. Facilities for consulting manuscripts and early books at the Music Library are humble yet cozy: there is room for one researcher at a time to occupy the small writing table reserved for this purpose behind the reference and circulation desk. For this reason, advance notice of a visit is advisable; find contact information at the library's web-site: (http://www.lib.berkeley.edu/MUSI/).

Located across Faculty Glade and Strawberry Creek from the Music Library and in the shadow of the Berkeley campus's icon, the Campanile, the Bancroft Library is the primary special collections library on the Berkeley campus. The library's holdings from the medieval period include 140-some codices and hundreds of documents and manuscript fragments. Favorites from this wide-ranging collection include a fifteenth-century list of books held in the Bibilothèque des Célestins in Paris, which was found in the binding of one of the Bancroft Library's eighteenth-century books; a thirteenth-century Italian schoolbook preserving notes on Ovid's *Heroides* and Virgil's *Aeneid*; and a copy of Domenico Cavalca's translation of Jerome's *Vitas patrum* with 30 historiated initials executed by fifteenth-century Italian artist Cola Rapicano. A recent acquisition of special interest to students of medieval

book production is an unfinished Book of Hours. The book's surviving decoration, which was abandoned at different stages across the book, provides a
kind of step-by-step record of the process of medieval manuscript illumination. From the early-print period, the Bancroft Library houses over 400
incunabula and has a noteworthy collection of classical texts, representing
editions from the fifteenth through the eighteenth centuries, including many
from the Aldine Press. The library is also strong in works of English literature,
including all four Shakespeare folios as well as early editions of works by Ben
Jonson, Chaucer, Spenser, and Milton. A still largely uncharted territory in the
Bancroft's vault is the Fernán-Nuñéz Collection. Acquired by the library in
1985, this 225-volume of manuscript books from the archives of the Dukes of
Fernán-Nuñéz in southern Spain—dating from around 1490 to 1800—comprises a substantial repository of literary, diplomatic, and historical texts. A
preliminary guide to the collection is kept at the Reference Desk in the
Bancroft's reading room. Scholars wishing to make use of materials in the
Bancroft Library will need to present two pieces of identification at the regis-
tration desk. A short jaunt downhill from the Bancroft to the newly-opened
Free Speech Café annexed to Moffitt Undergraduate Library means you will
never need to leave your books for long.

   A searchable database of descriptions of the medieval items held in
all three of these libraries, together with at least one image of each, is available online in the Digital Scriptorium (at http://sunsite.berkeley.edu/scripto-
rium/). For a look at the unfinished Book of Hours mentioned above, search
on UCB 167.

   Martha Rust, New York University

About the Authors

David Colclough is Lecturer in English at Queen Mary, University of London. He has published articles on the manuscript transmission of John Hoskyns's poetry and on Renaissance rhetoric and is completing a book on freedom of speech in early Stuart England. He is editing Francis Bacon's *New Atlantis* for the new Oxford *Francis Bacon*.

Robert Costomiris is an Assistant Professor in the Department of Literature and Philosophy at Georgia Southern University. He has published a number of essays on the volumes of Chaucer's works edited by William Thynne. Currently, he is investigating the literary endeavors of other members of Henry VIII's household.

Bryan P. Davis currently teaches at Georgia Southwestern State University where he is an Assistant Professor of English and the lone medievalist in his department. Most of his publications to date have dealt with the manuscript culture of late Middle English, especially the manuscripts of *Piers Plowman*, although he has also written about the early English printers John Day and William Seres for the *Dictionary of Literary Biography*. He has recently begun to investigate the fate of Middle English literary texts in the early modern period, especially *Piers Plowman* and Chaucer's *Troilus and Criseyde*.

Martha Driver is Professor of English at Pace University in New York. A co-founder of the Early Book Society for the study of manuscripts and printing history, she writes and lectures about illustration from MS to print, book production, and the early history of publishing. In addition to publishing a number of articles, she has edited eight journals in five years, including *Film & History: Medieval Period in Film*, and with Deborah McGrady, a special issue of *Literary & Linguistic Computing*, "Teaching the Middle Ages with Technology" (1999). She is now at work on a book about fifteenth-century English text and illustration for British Library Publications.

A.S.G. Edwards is Professor of English at the University of Victoria.

Kristen M. Figg is Professor of English and Coordinator of the Honors Program at Kent State University-Salem. She recently published *Jean Froissart: An Anthology of Narrative and Lyric Poetry* (Routledge, 2001), which presents a new edition and the first English translations of many of Froissart's major poems. She is also co-editor, with John B. Friedman, of *Trade, Travel, and Exploration in the Middle Ages: An Encyclopedia* (Garland Publications, 2000).

Simon Horobin is a Lecturer in English Language at the University of Glasgow. He has research and teaching interests in Old and Middle English language and literature, manuscript studies, and humanities computing. He is the author of articles on Middle English and on Chaucer's language and text. His book, *The Language of the Chaucer Tradition*, is forthcoming with Boydell and Brewer. He is also reviews editor for the journal *Literary and Linguistic Computing*.

Erik Inglis is Assistant Professor of Art at Oberlin College, where he teaches medieval and Northern Renaissance art. His research interests are in secular manuscript illumination of the Late Middle Ages.

Claire Jones completed her doctorate on "Vernacular literacy in late-medieval England: the example of East Anglian medical manuscripts" at the University of Glasgow in 2000. She is currently a Research Fellow at the Centre for Medieval Studies, University of York, working on an AHRB-funded project, 'Privately-owned English Urban Manuscripts, 1300-1476: A Database.'

Jeanne Krochalis is Associate Professor of English and comparative literature at Penn State New Kensington, as well as palaeography consultant for the Walters catalogue. Her current scholarly interests include manuscripts on rolls and texts associated with pilgrimage.

Michael P. Kuczynski is Associate Professor of English and Medieval Studies at Tulane University, New Orleans, and chair of the Tulane English Department. He has published a book on the Psalms in late medieval England (*Prophetic Song: The Psalms as Moral Discourse in Late Medieval England*; Univ. of Pennsylvania Press, 1995), several essays on late medieval religious manuscripts, and is currently finishing an edition of a Lollard commentary on the Psalms in MS Bodley 554.

F. H. M. Le Saux is Senior Lecturer at the University of Reading (UK) and Director of the Graduate Centre for Medieval Studies (U. of Reading). She is also editor of *Reading Medieval Studies*. Formerly of the Universities of Lausanne (Switzerland), and Freiburg-im-Breisgau (Germany), she has published extensively on the medieval translations of Geoffrey of Monmouth's *Historia Regum Britanniae*.

Linne Mooney is Professor of English at the University of Maine (USA); for the calendar year 2002 she is Leverhulme Visiting Professor at the Centre for Medieval Studies, University of York, England. She works on Middle English verse (revising the IMEV for electronic publication) and on late medieval English manuscripts and the scribes who wrote them.

Daniel W. Mosser is Professor of English and Director of the Center for Applied Technologies in the Humanities at Virginia Tech. He is co-editor of *Puzzles in Paper: Concepts in Historical Watermarks*, author of "Witness Descriptions" of the manuscripts and pre-1500 editions of the *Canterbury Tales* on the *Canterbury Tales* Project's CD-ROM editions, co-editor of *The Thomas L. Gravell Watermark Archive* (www.gravell.org).

Jason O'Rourke is a member of the 'Traditions of the Book' research group at Queen's University, Belfast. His research interests include patronage and book production in Wales and the Marches, and the activities of book owners and collectors both in Wales and further afield. He is especially interested in multilingual manuscripts (in English Welsh, French and Latin) and their socio-literary context.

Oliver Pickering is Deputy Head of Special Collections in Leeds University Library and Associate Lecturer in English. He has published widely in the field of medieval English, and has recently compiled (with Veronica O'Mara) the *Index of Middle English Prose* volume for Lambeth Palace Library (1999). He is also the editor of *The Library: The Transactions of the Bibliographical Society* [of London].

Susan Powell is a Senior Lecturer in English Language and Literature at the University of Salford, where she teaches the history of the English language, Chaucer and medieval Arthurian literature. Her research interests are in manuscripts and early printed books, with particular relation to late medieval and Tudor preaching and devotional texts.

Martha Rust is Assistant Professor of English at New York University and has recently completed her PhD in English at UC Berkeley. She is currently working on a book manuscript, "Odd Texts and Marginal Subjects: Sightings from Late Medieval English Books."

Estelle Stubbs joined the Humanities Research Institute at the University of Sheffield in 1994 as Transcriber and Research Associate on the *Canterbury Tales* Project. In 2000 Estelle edited 'The Hengwrt Digital Facsimile.' As well as digital images of the Hengwrt manuscript, the CD contains the transcriptions of Hengwrt and Ellesmere, both copied by the same scribe, as well as observations made during the course of her work on the early manuscripts. In March 2001, Estelle began work for the Research Group of the House of Commons, developing an electronic version of the early *Journals of the House*.

R.N. Swanson is Professor of Medieval Ecclesiastical History at the University of Birmingham, UK. His books include *Religion and Devotion in Europe, c.1215-c.1515* (Cambridge University Press, 1995), and *The Twelfth-Century Renaissance* (Manchester University Press, 1999). A major current interest is the history of indulgences, which includes examination of relevant early printed ephemera.

Satoko Tokunanga is a doctoral student at Keio University, Tokyo, working on the early printing of Chaucer. She is a research fellow of the Japan Society for the Promotion of Science. Her research has been published in *The Library* and in a recent catalogue of manuscripts and early printed materials at Keio University.

Daniel Wakelin is finishing his doctoral dissertation on 'Vernacular Humanism in Fifteenth-Century England' at the University of Cambridge, where he is in the third year of a post-graduate studentship from the Arts and Humanities Research Board (AHRB) in Britain. He has published or has at press articles on a medieval lyric in MS Sloane 2593 and on vernacular humanism in fifteenth-century England.

Carole Weinberg is a Senior Lecturer in the Department of English and American Studies at the University of Manchester where she teaches medieval literature. Her present area of research is medieval Arthurian literature, and among her publications she has co-edited a parallel text/translation of the complete text of Layamon's *Brut*.

QUÆRENDO

A Quarterly Journal from the Low Countries Devoted to Manuscripts and Printed Books

EDITED BY A.R.A. CROISET VAN UCHELEN
(AMSTERDAM, THE NETHERLANDS) ET AL

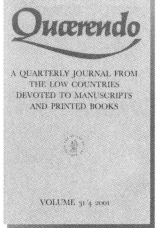

Quærendo is a leading journal in the world of manuscripts and books. It contains a selection of scholarly articles connected with the Low Countries. Particular emphasis is given to codicology and palaeography, printing from around 1500 until present times, humanism, book publishers and libraries, typography, bibliophily and book binding.

Since 1971 *Quærendo* has been establishing itself as a forum for contributions from the Low Countries concerning the history of books. Its appearance in the great libraries of the world as well as on the book shelves of individual professors and scholars, shows it to be an invaluable reference work for their research.

Each volume contains, besides a selection of high-quality original papers, special sections on "Varia Bibliographica", "Book Reviews" and "Notes and News". These sections give particular attention to recent discoveries, publications and current events.

VOLUME 32
(2002, 4 ISSUES PER YEAR)
ISSN 0014-9527
INSTITUTIONS
EUR 146.- / US$ 169.-
INDIVIDUALS
EUR 89.- / US$ 99.-
PRICE INCLUDES
ONLINE SUBSCRIPTION

Academic Publishers

 BRILL

P.O. BOX 9000
2300 PA LEIDEN
THE NETHERLANDS

TEL +31 (0)71 53 53 566
FAX +31 (0)71 53 17 532
E-MAIL cs@brill.nl

112 WATER STREET, SUITE 400
BOSTON, MA 02109
USA

TEL 1 800 962 4406 (TOLL-FREE)
FAX (617) 263 2324
E-MAIL cs@brillusa.com

www.brill.nl